Women on the Renaissance stage

MANCHESTER
UNIVERSITY PRESS

To my mother, Eileen McManus,
and in memory of my father, Bernard McManus

Women on the Renaissance stage

Anna of Denmark
and female masquing
in the Stuart court
(1590–1619)

Clare McManus

Manchester University Press
Manchester and New York

distributed exclusively in the USA by Palgrave

Published by Manchester University Press, Oxford Road, Manchester M13 9NR, UK *and* Room 400, 175 Fifth Avenue, New York, MY 10010, USA
www.manchesteruniversitypress.co.uk

Distributed exclusively in the USA by Palgrave, 175 Fifth Avenue, New York, NY 10010, USA

Distributed exclusively in Canada by UBC Press, University of British Columbia, 2029 West Mall, Vancouver, BC, Canada V6T 1Z2

British Library Cataloguing-in-Publication Data
A catalogue record for this book is available from the British Library

Library of Congress Cataloging-in-Publication Data applied for

ISBN 0 7190 6092 3 *hardback*
0 7190 6250 0 *paperback*

First published 2002

10 09 08 07 06 05 04 03 02   10 9 8 7 6 5 4 3 2 1

Typeset in Bembo
by Carnegie Publishing Ltd
Printed in Great Britain
by Biddles Ltd, Guildford and King's Lynn

Contents

Figures

Acknowledgements

This book is burdened with long years of debts, most of which can't be repaid in full. Heartfelt thanks goes to Kate Chedgzoy and Peter Davidson, for their constant support and inspiration as supervisors at the University of Warwick, and in particular to Kate for being as exemplary a role model as any woman in academia could ever wish for or need. Stephen Orgel's kindness and generosity helped this project through its earliest stages, and James Knowles's encouragement, friendship and support were unstinting at all times. I would also like to thank J. R. Mulryne and Margaret Shewring of the Centre for the Study of the Renaissance at the University of Warwick, where, as a doctoral student, I carried out the research for this book, and Bernard Capp and Lois Potter for their advice and assistance as examiners.

Many people have been generous with their time and advice beyond the call of duty, among them Fran Brearton, Mark Burnett, Alison Cressey, Ewan Fernie, Julie Sanders, Ceri Sullivan, Sue Wiseman and Ramona Wray. Thanks also go to Kiernan Ryan for suggestions for the title and to Nigel Harkness for polishing my French translations. Julie Sanders and Sue Wiseman commented on the introduction in another form, and A. A. MacDonald, Sally Mapstone and Luuk Houwen did likewise with portions of chapter 2. The greatest debt, though, is owed to Eileen and Elizabeth McManus.

The work for this book was carried out with a British Academy studentship. I am also grateful for the financial assistance received from the Queen's University Belfast Publications Fund. Materials in the introduction are reproduced from C. McManus, 'Defacing the Carcass: Anne of Denmark and Jonson's *Masque of Blackness*', in Julie Sanders, with Kate Chedgzoy and Susan Wiseman (eds), *Refashioning Ben Jonson: Gender, Politics and the Jonsonian Canon*, 1998, by permission of Palgrave Publishers. A version of chapter 2 was earlier published as C. McManus, 'Marriage and the Performance of the Romance Quest: Anne of Denmark and the Sterling baptismal celebrations for Prince Henry', in L. A. J. R. Houwen, A. A. MacDonald and S. L. Mapstone (eds), *A Palace in the Wild: Essays* on *Humanism and Vernacular Culture in Renaissance Scotland*, 2000, by permission of Peeters Publishers. I thank all the editors for their permission to reuse these materials.

Select table of court masques (1604–19)

Date	Poet, designer (where known); title	Venue
1604	Samuel Daniel; *The Vision of the Twelve Goddesses*	Hampton Court Great Hall
1605	Ben Jonson, Inigo Jones; *The Masque of Blackness*	Whitehall Banqueting House 1
1606	Jonson, Jones; *Hymenaei*	WHBH 1
1607	Thomas Campion, possibly Jones; *Lord Hay's Masque*	Hall of Whitehall Palace
1608	Jonson, Jones; *Haddington Masque*	WHBH 1
	Jonson; *The Masque of Beauty*	WHBH 2
1609	Jonson, Jones; *The Masque of Queens*	WHBH 2
1610	Jonson, Jones; *Prince Henry's Barriers*	WHBH 2
	Daniel, Jones; *Tethys' Festival*	WHBH 2
1611	Jonson, Jones; *Oberon*	WHBH 2
	Jonson, Jones; *Love Freed From Ignorance and Folly*	WHBH 2
1612	Jonson; *Love Restored*	WHBH 2
1613	Campion, Jones; *The Lords' Masque*	WHBH 2
	George Chapman, Jones; *The Memorable Masque*	The Hall at Whitehall
	Frances Beaumont; *The Masque of the Inner Temple and Gray's Inn*	WHBH 2
	Campion, de Servi; *The Somerset Masque*	WHBH 2
	Jonson; *A Challenge at Tilt*	WHBH 2
1613 ⎫ 1614 ⎭	Jonson; *The Irish Masque at Court*	WHBH 2
1615	Jonson, Jones; *The Golden Age Restored*	WHBH 2
1616	Jonson, Jones; *Mercury Vindicated*	WHBH 2
1617	Robert White; *Cupid's Banishment*	Greenwich Palace Disguising Theatre
1618	Jonson, Jones; *Pleasure Reconciled to Virtue*	WHBH 2
	Jonson, Jones; *For the Honour of Wales*	WHBH 2

An early modern female stage

In 1605 Queen Anna of Denmark (wife of James VI and I) commissioned *The Masque of Blackness* from Ben Jonson. Danced by the Queen and eleven of her women in the Banqueting House at Whitehall, this masque formed part of the court's Twelfth Night entertainment. Sir Dudley Carleton's emotive eye-witness account of the night's masquing at the Jacobean court leaves little doubt as to the impact of Anna's performance and proves an apt way to begin this book:

> At night we had the Queen's Maske in the Banquetting House, or rather her Pagent ... Their Apparell was rich but too light and Curtizan-like for such great ones. Instead of Vizzards, their Faces, and Arms, up to the Elbows, were painted black, which was Disguise sufficient, for they were hard to be known; *but it became them nothing so well as their red and white, and you cannot imagine a more ugly sight than a Troop of lean-cheek'd Moors.*[1]

Carleton's outburst is one of the most-used sources for criticism of the court masque in the last decade, figuring prominently in investigations of the discourses of race and empire staged so powerfully in the blackened faces of these Jacobean noblewomen.[2] As far as a study of Jacobean female performance itself is concerned, however, such remarks also offer a means of considering that phenomenon in its own right. These courtly criticisms of the performance of *Blackness* are concerned with the transgressive representation of the female masquers; importantly, Carleton found fault with their appearance, not with their presence on stage. This strongly suggests that the act of female performance was not at issue here. Women were, rather, necessary and desirable participants within the court masque and it is from this starting point that I will discuss the practice of female masquing in the courts of early modern Scotland and England.

Centring upon the cultural production of Anna of Denmark (she used the name 'Anna', not 'Anne'), this book investigates her masque performances and cultural agency in terms of the political and cultural status of the elite female courtier and the nature of a queen's court. Within the more or less chronological framework of Anna's careers in the Danish,

Scottish and English courts of the late sixteenth and early seventeenth centuries, this book traces her agency and the dynamics of the performances in which she was involved. Suggesting some reasons for Jacobean women's masquing and considering the impact of female performance upon the court masque, the book also sites these instances within an emerging wider tradition of female performance which would eventually culminate in the appearance of the professional female actor after the Restoration.

While the court masque has been the subject of many studies and women's masquing has also received growing attention, the performance dynamics and conditions of women's masque participation have not yet been addressed in any depth.[3] Masques have hitherto been read as literary rather than theatrical texts. By opening the masque form up to the politicised analysis of performance, this book sheds light on the forces which propelled female performers on to the stage and the gender dynamics of their silent performance once they got there. This in turn is highly revealing of the construction of masque performance, the genre's gender dynamics and its role in the construction of the identity of both the court and the courtier. Certain questions arise at this point. For example, why were women allowed to perform in the masque and in no other form of theatre (courtly or public) in early modern England? This raises further concerns, such as how this English embargo stood against the cultural construction of the performing woman in other cultures, such as that of Scotland, of which Anna herself had been a part. Furthermore, what were the results of masque performance for female cultural production, agency, and the perception and representation of the performing woman?

The answers to these questions lie in the study of masque performance itself, and *The Masque of Blackness* offers a useful starting point for an explanation of these issues. This is a performance text from which the fundamental principles behind Jacobean women's court performance can be gleaned and as such acts as a pivotal text to this study of Anna of Denmark's performances and cultural agency and of the development of early modern Englishwomen's performance more generally. *Blackness* had a forceful feminine presence. Jonson's incorporation of this presence within the masque text complicated the primary function of a court festival, the praise of the king as the privileged spectator. Although in theory the performative presence of the royal or courtly woman on the masquing stage was unproblematic, female performance nevertheless existed in an uneasy relationship with the masque genre; its dependency on the social and performative codes of the court, and on its historical and political moment, both required a female presence and laid the masque open to disruption when that presence was a transgressive one. The structure of the court masque, a synthesis of disparate genres of art and performance into a unified whole, left it vulnerable to a destabilisation which was compounded by Anna's active contribution to the feminine representative strategy. An examination of *Blackness* demonstrates the nature of female performance and of cultural agency as they related to the demands of the masque form, and reveals the controversial status of such performance within Jacobean society. In particular the tensions caused by Anna's active agency in commissioning and influencing this performance reveal much about her masquing career and the nature of female performance and cultural agency in the Jacobean court.

Blackness stands in the canon of the court masque as the first collaboration between Ben Jonson and Inigo Jones. It was also, however, the first of several interactions between Jonson, Jones and Anna of Denmark and not the first instance of the Queen's involvement with the court masque form. All in all, Anna of Denmark danced in six masques, Samuel Daniel's *Vision of the Twelve Goddesses* (1604) and *Tethys' Festival* (1610), and Ben Jonson's *Masque of Blackness* (1605) and *Beauty* (1608), *The Masque of Queens* (1609) and *Love Freed From Ignorance and Folly* (1611). She also participated, although did not masque as such, in Thomas Campion's *Somerset Masque* (1613) and was the privileged spectator of Robert White's *Cupid's Banishment* (1617). In all, Anna's masquing and commissioning accounted for almost the entirety of the English Jacobean court's female performance in the first two decades of the seventeenth century. Other than the above masques, women danced only in two double masques (which involved both male and female aristocratic performers): *Hymenaei*, written by Jonson in 1606, and Campion's *Lords' Masque* for the Palatinate wedding in 1613, in which the Queen was not involved. This relatively small corpus of performances had a substantial impact on early modern female performance in general. Stemming as they did from the traditions of courtly pageantry, Anna's masques will be complemented in this book by a consideration of a wider kind of performance: her Scottish coronation and entrances, the festivities for the baptism of her son, Prince Henry, and her second coronation in London all feed in to a more general picture of early modern female performance. As is clear from the above, most of the masques in which Anna was involved clustered in the first decade of the Jacobean reign in England. It is also apparent that Ben Jonson figured prominently in the Queen's career, scripting all but two of the masques in which she danced. However, the designer Inigo Jones was another constant in Anna's masquing career; indeed, his presence is more pervasive in this book than that of Jonson. Jones's work demonstrated a concern with the human body, a preoccupation which will illuminate the representation of the silent noble masquer, both male and female.

Despite the predominance of English Stuart entertainments in both Anna's career and this book, Anna of Denmark's career cannot be read in isolation either from her education in the Danish court or from her performances and political engagement in Scotland. To this end chapter 2 considers the Scottish precedents which influenced Anna's entire performance career, and reassesses the place of the English Jacobean court within the extensive network of European courts and courtliness. In doing so the book considers cultural transmissions between the nations in which Anna performed, and resituates her masquing and more general cultural agency within the networks of European courts. Take, for example, the motif of blackness in the masque of the same name. Anna was deeply involved in the production of *Blackness*; Jonson notes that he had to incorporate her demands in the conceit of the masque, saying that it was 'her majesty's will to have them [the women] blackamores at first'.[4] Given the remark's positioning in a transcript published after the fact of the performance, it is possible that Jonson was attempting to distance himself from the controversy surrounding that conceit, while being seen to have paid the appropriate lip-service to his queen. However, the motif of blackness, as will be seen, figured prominently throughout Anna's career and can be fully explained only by a consideration of her Scottish court career. For instance, the 1590 royal entry into Edinburgh is only one of several examples of the Queen's exposure to the performance of blackness, which suggests that the use of this conceit might indeed have been her idea.[5] Anna's performance career and her contribution to the process of masque creation in the English court must be read as part of a whole which extended well beyond the boundaries of early modern England and which was open to the influences of far more than simply English cultures.

Such networks of cultural transmission, closely concerned with the space of the court, also shed light on the gendered spaces of early modern female courtly engagement. The spaces of such an engagement are many and varied, but the dominant social space of patriarchy is that which Anna's masquing allows to be investigated and challenged, opening it up to a new configuration. Within this framework and using the information provided by the masquing of Anna and other women, other spaces are also redefined. For instance, the space of the nation figures prominently; as Anna's own career shows clearly, journeys between nations (in her case between Denmark, Scotland and England), which were figured in the exchange of the courtly female through the marriage networks of European courts, were themselves reworked within court performance and so helped to establish a notion of a courtly Europe. In the same way the movement of the royal woman between cities (Anna moved between Edinburgh, London and beyond to Greenwich) and between courts (Stirling, Whitehall and the Queen's court at Greenwich) are meaningful, readable trajectories. Such interpretable trajectories are also found within the detail of masque performance itself. Hence the female body in performance is examined, as it is defined in the motion of scenery or dancing, in the court's corporeal ideologies, in costume and in the juxtaposition of the courtly female body with the professional male transvestite performer. Throughout this book, the relationship of the performing female body to the space of the stage and the political actuality of the court community is reassessed.

The Queen's masques, as already established, were dependent upon their social, political and cultural context for their development and meaning, and one of the most significant contexts for these performances was Anna's own court. The status of what has been termed either a faction, a coterie or a court is addressed throughout the readings of the court masque performances undertaken in the chapters which follow. The historical, social and political contexts of these ephemeral moments of performance are used to ascertain the extent to which Anna of Denmark can be considered to have formed a queen's court. This, of course, itself has a wider context, that of the fractured Jacobean court in Scotland and England. The possibility of a queen consort's court challenges long-held assumptions regarding the nature of courts and courtiership and so also contributes to the reassessment of the status, perception and role of the courtly or royal woman. After all, women were necessary members of courts, and their status ensured them the chance of both an education and cultural agency. But what effect did these converging discourses of class and gender, courtiership and femininity have on the female courtier or royal woman and their performance in the Jacobean masque?

Perhaps the most useful way of answering this question is to address the ways in which elite Jacobean women actually gained access to the particular Renaissance stage of the court masque. Once again, *Blackness* provides important information, especially when illuminated by comments made almost two hundred years before it was danced, by Francesco Barbaro

in his early fifteenth-century treatise, *On Wifely Duties*: 'It is proper ...
that not only arms but indeed also the speech of women never be made
public; for the speech of a noble woman can be no less dangerous than
the nakedness of her limbs.'[6] Although it predated the performance of
Blackness, this statement remained representative of prevalent attitudes
which governed opportunities for women's performance in the early
seventeenth century; the danger of the female voice and body is powerfully
constant. Barbaro neatly encapsulated the perceived connection between
public female speech and a dangerously liberated female sexuality in the
open display of the gendered body. As they were denied access to speech
in the court masque, the aspects of the genre which allowed the female
nobility to perform were also those which simultaneously confined this
performative presence to the physical. Yet, as Barbaro's insistence on the
danger posed by the female body implies, such a presence, whether voiced
or silent, constituted a threat which had to be monitored and controlled.
From the familiar position of the silenced woman, the noble female
masquer found an expression through the second half of Barbaro's formulation, in the equally expressive and threatening presence of the female
body on the masquing stage. In the course of this process these tools of
apparent restraint were themselves rendered ambivalent and liberating.

The nature of the court masque genre was itself a prime factor in
allowing elite early modern women access to its stage. Performed by
members of royalty appearing alongside professional actors, the masque
form foregrounded the concept of performance itself and in particular
women's rather anomalous performance. Indeed, with aristocratic women
appearing alongside male actors playing female roles, the court masque
was the legitimate stage for the suggestive juxtaposition of the transvestite
male actor and the female masquer. Such female performance was possible
amongst the elite of the age only because it was dependent upon the
courtly norms and regulations of aristocratic behaviour. Elite female
performance, by definition, involved the intersection of class and gender
discourses which circulated within the masque and found a specific site
of expression in the performing female body. The gendered bodily
decorum of Jacobean society as manifested in the masque placed specific
restrictions on the male and female courtier and also permitted a feminine
expression through, rather than despite, these restrictions.

The masque genre contributed to female performance in specific ways.
The court masque was a form of elite social ritual rather than public
drama and it derived its performance conventions from its social environment. During the non-dramatic main masque, the stage was

imaginatively and physically continuous with the body of the auditorium and noble masquers were unified with noble spectators. Noblemen and noblewomen were judged on the masquing stage as they would have been were they watching instead of participating. It was the social nature of the court masque form that offered the royal and aristocratic Jacobean woman access to the masquing stage. Although this was complicated by the theatricalised nature of the ideologies of courtly behaviour, which themselves demanded their own concealment and which will be dealt with in detail in chapter 1, masquing was postulated simply as participation in court society rather than as performance. It may at first seem surprising to cite the court's social order as the motivating factor behind female performance in a society in which the conceptualisation of gender directly resulted in the exclusion of women from more usual theatrical performance. However, women achieved masque performance not through a lessening of social restrictions but rather through a firm, class-engendered imposition of controls upon both sexes of courtier, which set the strictly gendered aristocracy upon a more even footing.

Neither noblewomen nor noblemen were permitted to speak in the masque; as silent participants, Anna and her women can be more fruitfully considered as dancers than actors. When speech was required, as in the dramatic antimasque which worked in opposition to the essentially non-dramatic masque proper, these roles were taken by actors hired for the purpose. Although, as chapter 1 considers in more depth, to dance was the privilege of the nobility, Stephen Orgel points out that acting – which he defines as the adoption of an identity not one's own – was considered detrimental to the status of the courtier.[7] This becomes clear in the condemnatory response to the later role-playing of George Villiers, the Earl of Buckingham, when in 1626 he and two other prominent male courtiers took part in the Rabelaisian antimasque of an unidentified masque 'which many thought too histrionical to become him'.[8] It is extremely significant that there existed within the masque an equivalency of attitudes to the performance of elite men and women not found in other early modern theatrical forms. Noblemen and noblewomen were surrounded by the same limitations, the same restrictions. This equivalency of attitudes, the overpowering of gender definition by class concerns, may at one level have worked towards allowing women access to the masquing stage. Male silence actually created the possibility of female masquing; the genre's class-consciousness created a level starting point for the performance of the aristocracy through the defusing of the perceived threat of the garrulous woman.

Open and available to all members of the Jacobean court, both male and female, dance was the defining influence upon women's masquing. Dance was the courtly woman's primary point of entry to the masque form itself and its importance to the masque form cannot be overrated. Despite a certain amount of controversy over Andrew Sabol's definition of dance as the *'raison d'être* of the typical Stuart masque', what is clear is that the sheer length of the revels and their inclusion of the audience in the performance event meant that the dance, despite its scanty representation within the transcripts, was the most substantial aspect of the masque genre's structure.[9] In addition, just as the court masque was firmly based on the ideology and decorum of courtly society, so too was dance.

The early modern European court enshrined the dance as a necessary attribute of the courtly elite. Orgel states that it 'was permissible for masquers to be dancers, because dancing [was] the prerogative of every lady and gentleman'.[10] Skill in dance, attained through long years of training from an early age, defined what it was to be an aristocrat; it opposed the courtly against the non-courtly in an expression of elite community. The dance's social nature opened it to the female performer and sought to mark her as an acquiescent member of courtly society; dance training formed part of the literal incorporation into the individual of the controls exerted upon the noble body. The noblewoman's danced participation was intrinsic to the masque genre (at the very least within the revels) for it to offer the social affirmation necessary to its existence as state ritual.

Female participation therefore was not tolerated but rather was necessary, and was made inevitable by the essential theatricality of these governing codes of aristocratic behaviour. Mark Franko, in his analysis of the codes of the aristocratic body in dance and society, remarks that the Renaissance term 'grace' in fact referred to a kind of theatricality.[11] The masque dances were predicated upon a performative code of bodily display intended to win the praise or regard of a watching audience. This code was one in which virtue was defined as the creation of its appearance; the theatrical core of courtly behaviour entailed the creation of identity through performance.[12] The tensions of this correspondence between physical appearance and inner being will be significant later in my analysis of the feminine relationship to language in *Blackness*. At this point, however, what is important is that the dance of the female masquers was to some extent theatrical, a performance of their identities. Recognition of the identity of the noble performer was an intrinsic aspect of the masque form and one of the most important influences on female participation. The concept of masquing differed radically from that of acting, demanding neither the effacement of self nor the adoption of an alternative identity. Instead, the theatricality at the core of the courtier's identity, regularly enacted within the daily life of the court, was now performed upon the masquing stage. The body of the Renaissance aristocrat was itself a space of theatrical play – the leap from the performance of a courtly identity to a staged participation in the masque was not so great as it first appears.

Within this apparent parity of attitudes, there did, however, exist further distinctions in the conceptualisation of the gendered body in performance. Even within their shared silence, male and female courtiers were differentiated on a specifically bodily level through the same ideologies of dance that granted them access to the masque in the first place. Just as restrictions were imposed upon the speech of both male and female courtiers within the masque, so conformity to the codes of courtly grace was imposed upon both sexes. These constraints were, however, gendered ones; they differed in their details and in the nature of the limits they imposed upon the male and female courtly dancer. Any transgression in the corporeal realm, involving motion or not, was performed against the background of the stricter controls that operated on the female body. The process of analysing these distinctions and their ramifications is a central concern of this book.

The court masque, therefore, simultaneously demanded elite women's participation and the control of female representation during their performance. It is clear that the codes of social and gendered order and the court's demands of corporeal decorum and aristocratic community propelled the courtly woman into the masque, yet on her arrival on stage as a masquer she was trammelled by these very same codes of social convention and limitation. However, particularly in *Blackness*, these tools of control were also a means of expression for the masquing woman. The performative strategies of costume and face-paint opposed the requirements of court decorum, highlighting the ineffectual nature of female containment and emphasising the pre-existent tensions within the structure and form of this masque.

Commissioned by his queen to script a performance expressly avoiding female speech, Jonson was himself both confronted by and strongly implicated in the restrictions surrounding women's presence in this masque. The published text of *Blackness* lays out the poet's polarised categorisation of the disparate aspects that the masque form sought to synthesise: scenery, dance and costume he refers to as the 'carcass' and text and allegorical significance as the 'spirit'.[13] He writes of the elite audience of the masque, whose privilege it was to 'deface their carcasses' (that is, to tear down the enormously expensive scenery), and his fear that if he were not to immortalise the masque through the process of writing and publication the 'spirits' would also perish. This same concern, expressed in similar terms, is found also in the preface to the 1606 masque *Hymenaei*, often read as Jonson's definitive statement on the masque genre: 'So short lived are the bodies of all things in comparison of their souls.' [14] Just as tensions existed within the masque form, so too were they manifest in the relationship between masque performances and published text; Jonson's framing statement offers a theorisation of the masque not available in performance, but in the end it is one directly engaged with the representative strategies used to depict the female masquer on stage. Denied access to spoken text, the female masquer appears to have been aligned only with the carcass, with the physical aspects of the masque. This carcass is that which had no textual representation: music for which no text survives, the movement of the body, both danced and unchoreographed, scenery and costume (the designs for which were not included in Jonson's publications). Female masquers were on the whole granted access to expression only through the media of make-up, costume, dance and gesture; through the physicality of the body within which they were confined. This book is concerned with that carcass, with the performance of the masque and its definition of its female performers. Jonson's formulation has remained largely unchallenged in much masque analysis which, focusing upon the relationship of the published text to its political moment, neglects the more ephemeral performance text upon which this book centres.

Jonson's concern with the relationship of soul and body pervaded *Blackness*, recurring in Niger's commentary on the mingling of 'the immortal souls of creatures mortal / ... with their bodies'.[15] The poet's choice of terminology carries with it a value-judgement: the apparent inferiority of the body of the masque is in turn communicated to the female performers associated with that carcass through the commonplace alignment of the feminine with the physical. Connected intrinsically with the body and the bodily, the woman was considered the bearer, not the creator, of allegorical significance. Jonathan Sawday has described dissection (a literal 'de-facing') as the marker of sovereign power through the interpretation of the transgressive subject's body.[16] It is just this passivity that was challenged in *Blackness*. In what at first sight appears to be a further assertion of the monarch's centrality within the masque, these noblewomen took to the stage in order to be symbolically opened to interpretation; yet the act of interpretation revealed a feminine corporeality which posited an alternative ideology to that of the court's dominant faction. The relationship between the female performer and the linguistic dynamics of *Blackness* shows that the alignment of the feminine with the corporeal actually provided opportunities for a measure of female expression and autonomy within the masque, primarily since it was this very confinement of the female to the physical which allowed women to masque. Furthermore, although the female masquer did remain within a silent corporeality (with an important exception late in Anna's career in White's 1617 *Cupid's Banishment*, discussed in chapter 5), the physical expression of costume and make-up destabilised the restrictions placed upon her. Apparently constrained to submission within their physicality, the masquers in fact occupied an ambiguous, liminal position, transforming apparent tools of constraint into the means for near-autonomous self-fashioning.

As instanced in Carleton's description of the 'ugly sight' of the 'Troop of lean-cheek'd Moors', contemporary reaction to the costuming and make-up of the women was violent. The aesthetic sensibilities of the Renaissance held 'black' to be synonymous with 'ugly'. Niger's assertion that his black-skinned daughters were beautiful would, for the contemporary audience versed in the traditions of the black-faced devils of the mystery plays and the associations of tanned skin with outdoor and menial labour, have been a paradox. Importantly, both this blackness and the act of face-painting itself were held to imply a certain sexual voracity. Such an admission of sexuality complemented that found in the masquer's bare limbs, which Jacobean decorum decreed should remain covered and which Barbaro's statement classified as dangerously expressive (figure 1). Anna, six months pregnant with her daughter Mary at the time of the masque, her face and arms burnt by the heat of James's imperial sun, was an embodiment of consummated sexual passion. Carleton and the audience were, therefore, watching their queen perform in a garb of ugliness and sexual indecorum.

What was more, the white skin sought by the nymphs and promised by the monarch remained just that – an unfulfilled promise. The court had to wait for *The Masque of Beauty* (the complement to *Blackness* performed, after some delay, in 1608) to see the sun-bleached nymphs. The true dramatic action of *Blackness*, therefore, took place not on stage but in the court's lived experience of the controversy found in the years between the masque and its resolution. As a result of this lack of closure,

1 Daughter of Niger, from *The Masque of Blackness* (1605), by Inigo Jones

Blackness suffered from serious formal flaws; Anna's presence and the demands she placed upon the masque's content were problematic and unsettling. The restitution made for the transgressions of *Blackness* in *Beauty* demonstrates that such performances were linked in the memories of the watching and performing courtiers. This in turn means that female performance existed as a meaningful and interpretable activity which could be related both to itself and to male performances: the intertextualities between masques reveal the negotiations of power and authority in the light of previous performances. *Blackness* and *Beauty* not only were pivotal Jacobean female performances but also demonstrate the existence of a tradition of female masquing. Prominent in this canon of female performance was the ongoing development of a mode of female expression, and this book will use *Blackness* as a starting point to trace the emerging expressivity of the silent female performer through Anna of Denmark's court career.

The pervasive physicalisation of the feminine within *Blackness* extended in particular to the forms of language with which the masquers were associated. The tensions caused by the presence of the female performers as cultural agents were forcefully present within the discursive dynamics of this masque. Jonson describes the moment when the masquers began their dance:

> Here the tritons sounded, and they danced on the shore, every couple as they advanced severally presenting their fans, in one of which were inscribed their mixed names, in the other a mute hieroglyph expressing their mixed qualities. (Which manner of symbol I rather chose than imprese, as well for strangeness as relishing of antiquity, and more applying to that original doctrine of sculpture which the Egyptians are said first to have brought from the Ethiopians).[17]

Twelve silent women approached their peers holding painted words and symbols which purported to capture their very essences. Striking as this image of the dislocation of the female masquer from speech is, and however much it highlights the enforced silence of the noblewomen, it does not represent the endpoint of feminine discursive dynamics in *Blackness*. Denied verbal expression, the women were granted a physical medium of communication which was aligned with their constraint within the corporeal. The language of the masque was itself physical; it had become pictorial – the painted word and the painted hieroglyph.

Jonson's explicit choice of the hieroglyph over the *imprese* (which has been described as 'a personal badge', a 'representation of a purpose, a wish, a line of conduct') was more than just an appeal to the cultural authority of antiquity; in light of contemporary emblem theory it was extremely pertinent to the depiction of the female performer.[18] Michael Bath cites Bacon's discussion of the hieroglyph in *The Advancement of Learning*:

> hieroglyphics (things of ancient use, and embraced chiefly by the Egyptians, one of the most ancient nations) [...] are but as continued impreses and emblems. And as for gestures, they are as transitory hieroglyphics, and are to hieroglyphics as words spoken are to words written, in that they abide not; but they have evermore, as well as the other, an affinity with the thing signified.[19]

Bacon's alignment of gesture and hieroglyphs as physicalised forms of language is revealing; the physicality of the female masquing body existed on the same imaginative and discursive level as that of the hieroglyph – both participated in the creation of significance. Within the very discourse that attempted to constrain the significance of the female through confinement to the physical was a recognition of the corporeal creation of meaning which offered the female masquer expressive possibilities.

Even more striking is Bacon's assertion of the hieroglyph's 'affinity' with its referent. In contrast to the context-dependent *imprese*, emphatically rejected by Jonson, for which the association with the referent was felt to be merely conventional, the hieroglyph was thought to have a natural, single and readily available significance. The hieroglyph was seen to erase the gap between sign and signifier and to offer what Bath terms a 'natural, Adamic language'.[20] Similarly, Jonson's alliance of hieroglyphs and sculpture resonates within the dynamics of the physical confinement of the female and the ready availability of meaning within *Blackness*. In line with the neo-Platonic embodiment of the ideal within the physical and with early modern theories of sculpture which saw the artefact as pre-existent within the sculptural medium, the use of this physicalised discourse was an attempt to define the essence of the female masquers. The use of hieroglyphs – of linguistic sculpture – was an attempt to constrain the female to a single, predetermined and readily available authorial meaning, and to limit further the generation of significance through an apparently clear and available representation of what was defined as the feminine essence.

Against this conceptual background I would suggest that the structure and performance of *Blackness* complicated the straightforward interpretation of significance. The masque's fundamental conceit is the attempt to bleach the archetypal 'Moor', found in both Alciati and Whitney as an emblem of 'futile labour'.[21] Jonson cut this free from its original context of canonical textual authority by establishing its seemingly impossible fulfilment as the marker of James I's royal authority. This in turn means that, in a challenge to the interpretative authority of the emblem books, it was the failure to fulfil this proverbial impossibility that disappointed audience expectations. In much the same way the apparently unproblematic correspondence of the names and hieroglyphs to a single meaning was destabilised; their juxtaposition with the openly sexual bodies of the female masquers dislocated them from conventions of interpretative authority and opened them to a more various reading. The depiction of Anna and her partner, Lucy, Countess of Bedford, is a prominent example of this process. They carried between them the hieroglyph of 'A golden tree laden with fruit'.[22] The names painted on the second fan were 'Euphoris' and 'Aglaia' which, according to the studies carried out by D. J. Gordon, referred to the quality of fertility and to the first of the three Graces, herself associated with the fertility and abundance of the earth.[23] Gordon suggests one overall interpretation as being the representation of spiritual beauty fertilising the earth. His analysis also associates the theme of purity with these nymphs and with several of the other masquers' names and hieroglyphs. Yet the figures of the women holding these symbols of pure fertility were ones whose bodies were markers of a dangerous and open sexuality, destabilising the simplistic assumptions accompanying such emblems of purity and fertility. While the masquers, in particular the pregnant Queen, were indeed fertile, and while they did represent a form of feminine grace and beauty, once again it was not a form acceptable to the Jacobean court. Qualities of grace and fertility and spiritual beauty were represented through female corporeality, yet this did not accord with the interpretations imposed upon the openly displayed female body by the dominant ideology.

Such a failed attempt to constrain the meaning of the text of the readable female body with a literary text points to the problematic status of the correspondence between inner essence and outer representation, the dynamics of which resonate throughout *Blackness*. The codes of noble behaviour, the gendering of the aristocratic body and the discursive dynamics of this masque all operated in accordance with the notion of an unproblematic correspondence. Yet, as examination of the performative actuality of the strategies of female representation shows, this certainty was challenged by the female masquers' nonconformity, a departure which points up the constructed nature of these strategies. The female masquer's body was the nexus of issues of gender, discourse, the social conception and control of the body, and performance; all sought to control the feminine creation of significance by constraining her to the physical and seeking to simplify that physicality, and all failed. Gender, discourse and the grace of courtly behaviour are instead shown to operate through convention and consensus; they have no actual connection with that to which they gesture. More positively, the status of the female body as a powerful signifier becomes clear; despite the loss of a prelapsarian immediacy, the female body was not merely the passive bearer of significance but its active creator.

The masque audience would, therefore, have been witness to a problematic conjunction of the physical bodies of the female masquers and the physicalised language of the hieroglyphs which communicated two varying significances and which were forced together in the composite image of the women holding the painted words. The women, garbed in sexuality and danger, advanced holding meekly conformist symbols which purported to 'speak' their natures to those watching. This uncomfortable meeting of a physicalised language which sought (but failed) to be clearly available and the unsettling force of an openly consummated female sexuality would appear to ironise a straightforward reading of both the figures of the women and the nature of the discourse within this masque. In their enforced physicality the female masquers themselves became emblematic, their bodies themselves part of the discursive system of meaning-creation. Their presence was a disruptive one, however, exerting pressure upon the fractures already existent within the apparently stable linguistic system. The emblems existed in a reciprocal position of ironic commentary over the disruptive woman, a position which also allowed the transgressive female figure to commentate upon the canonical female ideal and upon the effort to constrain the abundance of significance – both gendered and discursive – to a single, one might say, absolutist, meaning.

The prohibition of female speech was a constraint of the masquing woman within her corporeality. Aristocratic women entered the masque through dance and were seen as physical beings, visions of beauty or shame robed in luxurious costumes. The performative status of dance as a substantial aspect of the masque meant that the only form of subversion open to the female courtier – that of the physical – was very close to the heart of the masque form itself. Tools of apparent constraint could be used to destabilise a simple acceptance of significance and were themselves rendered increasingly ambiguous; the physicality which seemed to enclose and inhibit the women itself provided an outlet for their expression. The open sexuality which shocked Carleton can be interpreted as an assertion of female sexual and political autonomy; twisted away from the simplistic flattery of the King to a statement of female agency, *Blackness* found no favour with its courtly audience. Costume and dance may have been two of the few means of female expression and were undoubtedly hedged around with strict conventions of female physical decorum. However, while masculine control can be instanced in the regulation of female bodily appearance, female rebellion against such restraints also took a physical form – the indecorum of bare and blackened limbs.

The physicalisation of language in *Blackness* demonstrates not that the corporeal female masquer was excluded from linguistic expression but rather that this resulted in the physicalisation of language itself and the textualisation of the performing female body. This performance denies Jonson's dichotomy of carcass and spirit, suggesting that this polarity is both redundant and reductive. In contrast this book moves beyond Jonson's static formulation into new and productive methods of analysing early modern female masquing.

Dance, gender and the politics of aristocratic performance in the early Stuart court masque

Sir John Chamberlain's description of the 1612 performance of Ben Jonson's *Love Restored* narrates a striking incident. This event, which occurred when the masquing courtiers led members of the audience out to dance in the revels, a moment known as the 'taking out', is now available to us only in a garbled form: 'When they [the masquers] came to take out the ladies, beginning ... of Essex and Cranbourn, they were refused, ... example of the rest, so that they were fain ... alone and make court to one another, whe ... was exceedingly displeased and spake low ...'[1] Frances Howard and her sister Catherine, members of the powerful Howard faction, refused to dance, all the more insulting to those involved given that the order of the taking out was pre-arranged.[2] Their performance of refusal suggests that the masque dance and the space associated with it could be realms of potential female assertion. Such a refusal, a significant strategy for the women of the Jacobean courts, is a useful starting point for an analysis of the nature of dance performance itself. If the expression found in the female refusal to perform is empowering, what does it then mean when a woman does not refuse to dance?

Traditional masque criticism has denigrated the dance. Writing about Jonson's *Masque of Queens* in the late 1980s, Margaret Maurer was of the opinion that 'it is hard to imagine a less consequential action than a dance graphically disposing letters spelling out the name of Prince Charles'.[3] Her statement is representative of criticism which, privileging the authorial poetic text above masque performance, regards dance as an inconsequential distraction, transitory and insubstantial in comparison to the permanent and meaningful written text. This apparent opposition between permanence and ephemerality is a prominent feature of the study of dance and the masque; both demonstrate an equal uncertainty and both are social forms, intimately connected to their historical moment of performance, making it impossible to achieve a full reconstruction of either.

The nature of masque texts themselves compounds the problems of assessing the dance. Published dance descriptions and those of contemporary observers tend to be subjective appraisals of the performance's quality and emotive impact. Dance was predicated on audience interaction, and the transcripts privilege this reaction even if, as Jonson's preface to *Hymenaei* (1606) suggests, that audience was less than ideal.[4] In *The Masque of Beauty*, for example, James I's pleasure in the dance altered the masque's structure; the dances were 'so exquisitely performed as the king's majesty, incited first by his own liking [...], required them both again'.[5] Early modern records of dance, the masque among them, suffer from the apparently insurmountable difficulty of rendering movement as text, and its reconstruction from such literary texts is also profoundly problematic. Although attempts to reconstruct either the dance or the masque are efforts to recover a past, unreachable moment, the ephemerality of the masque also means that any critical privileging of its literary text creates a false picture of the form. The importance of dance becomes clear when it is seen as an organising principle of the masque genre, almost a microcosm of the larger form, and some balance can be restored by examining the masquing dance in performance. Such a study clarifies the importance of the performing aristocratic body and the meaning it created on the masquing stage.

Unrecoverable though it may now be, the masquing dance staged the gender dynamics of both the masque form and the Jacobean court itself. Although cultural criticism has recently begun to reverse the neglect of dance and its categorisation as a primarily feminine practice through many periods of history, early modern dance has long been recognised as the attribute of the ideal male courtier and statesman. The Howard sisters' refusal to perform was in fact an appropriation of a male performative idiom – the dance – which resulted in the lords' humiliating enforced performance. The sisters' actions demonstrate that for the Jacobean courtier, male or female, performance and the refusal to perform were theatrical acts; each fashioned the aristocratic body (still or in motion) as the central focus of the audience's gaze. However, for those lords who found themselves turned down, this act had very different consequences. As my examination of early modern perceptions of the dance and of dance practice itself shows, this rejection robbed the lords of volition and inverted the social dance's usual gender balance.

Chamberlain's description is suggestive; forced to 'make court' to one another, the lords became unwillingly involved in a homosocial dance in an attempt to save face, but this violation of the dance's gender norms and the threatening female rejection of performance succeeded only in attracting the intense displeasure of those watching.

When elite women did dance, their performance created meaning. Contemporary records of the body in dance, sketchy and problematic though they undoubtedly are, provide a snapshot of the ideologies of bodily grace and gender which controlled the Jacobean aristocrat. As I have already suggested, female masquing was possible partly because of the theatricality of aristocratic behaviour in everyday social interaction. Similarly, early modern masquing dance practice demonstrates the extent to which its behaviour also mirrored that of everyday life, and, as a result, dance was an integral part of the forces which pushed the aristocrat towards the masquing stage. Once on that stage, however, the silent female body was an expressive force, and this body and its expression are the central focus of this chapter. Dealing with the most prominent masques of the first decade of the Jacobean court in England, I examine distinct forms of the masquing dance in turn. The antimasque of Jonson's *Masque of Queens* (1609) is considered for its embodiment of class discourses in the transvestite performance of the professional actors. The revels of *Pleasure Reconciled to Virtue* (1618) form the basis for a discussion of the distinct genderings of the male and female aristocrat in the social dance. The main masque dances of *Hymenaei* and *Queens*, among others, are examined for the physical expression of the silent female body in the textual motif of the graphic dance. This latter point is central: the female masquers' displacement of expression from the voice to the body is a significant aspect of the development of Jacobean female masquing, and indeed the development of female performance in early modern England. A reading of the expressive female body in these entertainments reveals that it pushed on the constraint of the aristocratic masquers to silence, giving them a means of expression which links these apparently uneventful Jacobean masques to the acting of Henrietta Maria in the 1630s, the female singers of Aurelian Townshend's *Tempe Restored* (1632) and William Davenant's interregnum entertainment *The Siege of Rhodes* (1656), and finally to the professional female actors of Restoration England in a progression which has yet to be fully integrated into the histories of the English theatre.[6]

Early modern concepts of the courtly dance

Jacobean perceptions of dance, and in particular of its class inflections, are an important part of establishing the nature and role of dance in the court masque. Masquing dances took several distinct forms; the performative dances of the antimasque and main masque climaxed when the spectators were taken out for the social dances of the revels. Further to these distinctions, the theatricalised antimasque dances differed also from those of the revels and the main masque because they were danced almost exclusively by professional male performers. In an echo of the practice of the city theatres, those players who took the parts of women were cross-dressed. The antimasque, designed to be non-courtly and occasionally grotesque, was intended to offer a contrast to the aristocratic decorum which, theoretically, was on display in the rest of the dances and in the performance as a whole. Built around such contrasts between the courtly and non-courtly, the masque form's performance conditions, where courtiers and actors, transvestite male performers and female masquers danced alongside each other, put a great emphasis on any distinctions in the class and gender of its participants, bringing them together on the masquing stage while simultaneously using differences in dance and speech to keep them apart.

Dance itself was an ambiguous act open to varying early modern interpretations. Given that dance's defining act is the movement of the body, later commentators are inevitably distanced from that body's forceful physical and social presence, the historical moment of performance and the reactions of spectators. However, contemporary perceptions of the human body in the Jacobean court masque and society are partially recoverable; we can deal with the aesthetics of bodily movement and the social perception of dance as a courtly attribute, two categories which strongly influence each other. The masquing and social dances of the Jacobean court were rigidly exercised, disciplined actions which demanded instruction, rehearsal and controlled movement. They were also an outflow of kinetic and emotional energy, the expression of constrained desires in the highly conventionalised release of the body into movement. In dance these two functions coexisted in 'un abandon controllé', a decorous means of signifying abandon without itself being abandoned.[7] In terms of its role in dramatic spectacle, dance also served two functions: on one hand it was a distracting interlude of pure aesthetic pleasure, on the other it also conveyed meanings which, as this chapter shows, demanded serious consideration. This is encapsulated in the masque genre's closing revels; though given minimal textual recognition, they lasted far longer than the action of the masque itself and without them the essential confirmation of courtly harmony could not be seen to be achieved.

As I have indicated above, detailed information on early modern performative dance is extremely scarce. Pamela Jones lists the few existing records of Renaissance performative dances, amounting to six, four of which are documented in Cesare Negri's social dance manual, *Gratie d'Amore* (1602).[8] Beyond the near-silent masque texts, there are few surviving contemporary British dance descriptions. Apart from six manuscripts of Inns of Court commonplace books and Robert Coplande's early sixteenth-century treatise, little has been discovered to date; those looking for more information must turn, with an eye to the dangers of unexamined continental borrowings, to continental manuals and treatises, such as Negri's, Fabritio Caroso's *Il Ballarino* (1581) and *Nobiltà di Dame* (1600) or Thoinot Arbeau's *Orchesography* (1588).[9] From the sources which are available, however, scholars have identified a pan-European elite dance discourse and practice defined in opposition to non-courtly dance: Dolmetsch writes that 'imported dances [were] more or less modified in accordance with their new environment, but without losing their fundamental characteristics'.[10] A shared etiquette and dance practice were disseminated through the pan-European culture of courtly entertainments, ambassadors' reports, and European travel and travellers' texts. Although neither the practical influence of the Italian manuals of Negri and Caroso on the style of Jacobean court dance nor the dates of their acquisition can be put forward with any certainty – and an unconditional acceptance of Arbeau's French manual *Orchesography* as a source for courtly dance is no longer possible, for reasons of its geographical and social distance from the European courts – Smith and Gatiss demonstrate their availability to the Jacobean court, and it is probable that a copy of Caroso's *Il Ballarino* was acquired by the Royal Library between 1608 and 1611.[11] Bearing these reservations in mind, it is possible to gather information on the dances of elite communities from the available sources and use them to interpret the Jacobean masque.

Although the kind of shared European discourse of courtly dance put forward by Dolmetsch certainly existed, important national variants nevertheless remained. As Erasmus's observation in *De civilitate morum puerilium* (*On Good Manners for Boys*), that 'among certain Spaniards to avoid looking at people is taken as a sign of politeness and friendship' shows, the meanings which could be read from the body were as socially specific as those of different languages, and dance too created different meanings in different contexts.[12] Dudley Carleton's comments on *The Masque of Blackness*, discussed in the introduction, are anecdotal evidence of the political impact of such differences in perception on the masque; although he praises the Spanish ambassador for taking Anna out to dance, he then compares his dancing to that of 'a lusty old Gallant with his Country Woman' – hardly the marker of a pan-European courtly discourse.[13] One interpretation might blame the skill of the individual dancer, another might point to the differences between Spanish and English courtly dance. The latter is supported by the apparently unconnected remarks of the French ambassador, who, referring to the revels of *The Masque of Queens*, commented that 'je ne voulois faire rire la compagnie, comme fit l'an passé l'Ambassadeur d'Espagne' (I did not want to make everyone present laugh, as the Spanish ambassador did last year).[14] It seems that the English courtier's judgement of dance was founded upon class; to dance like a country-dweller was to break the decorum of courtliness and to damn the dancer. Although any interpretation must recognise the hostility of the French and certain factions of the English court towards the Spanish, such an awareness merely reinforces the political nature of such readings of the masquing dance.

Whatever the differences between localised dance practice, the 1604 entertainment for the visit of de Velasco, the Constable of Castile, to the Jacobean court, in which Queen Anna and Prince Henry both danced, demonstrates that there was indeed a shared discourse of sorts, and balances Carleton's later hostility with a pro-Spanish compliment from Anna herself. Smith and Gatiss point out that de Velasco's account of the entertainment refers to a four-couple *brando*, a dance which existed only in this variant form in Negri's *Gratie d'Amore*.[15] This dance was performed much as it was at the 1599 Milanese court festival for the marriage of the Infanta Isabella, which Negri mentions de Velasco as attending. Smith and Gatiss see the recycling of a dance taken from an entertainment at which an honoured guest had been present as a typical humanist conceit. While this example hints at the potential currency of dance throughout the early modern European courts, when it is considered in conjunction with Carleton's concerns the extent to which dance was thought of as a class-inflected activity becomes clear; to dance as a courtier was to be recognised as a courtier and, equally, to break the codes of courtly dance was to be condemned. Such inflections become especially significant in a reading of the Jacobean antimasque, where the body was moved in a manner which highlighted the pleasure of broken aesthetic expectations and deliberately contravened courtly ideals. What is more, such violations as the transvestite dance of the witches of *Queens* also offer information on the dictates of a gendered courtliness and can help move towards a sense of courtly femininity.

The absence of grace:
antimasque, gender and decorum in *The Masque of Queens*

The dances of the antimasque, the repository of all that was un-courtly, can tell us much about the gender politics of the masquing occasion. The dance of the witches in *Queens*, a masque performed by Anna and her women, reveals the early modern conceptualisation of femininity through its construction in the dance and the juxtaposition of dancing noblewomen with the antimasque's transvestite male professionals. Entering from 'an ugly hell', the witches began to dance:

> with a strange and sudden music they fell into a magical dance full of preposterous change and gesticulation, but most applying to their property, who at their meetings do all things contrary to the custom of men, dancing back to back and hip to hip, their hands joined, and making their circles backward, to the left hand, with strange fantastic motions of their heads and bodies.[16]

Although Jonson's description goes further than most in its detail, avoiding the impressionistic accounts of the dancers' skill, costumes and audience reaction which masque texts often fall back on, it is of a kind with most descriptions of dance in Jacobean masque texts, which themselves cannot adequately represent the masque occasion.

What can be said is that the hags' costumes and the image of the witch itself were representative of the very antithesis of courtly femininity. In this sense the witches danced in opposition to the idealised queens 'personated' by Anna and her women, and as transvestite professional male players they were free to represent the inverse of aristocratic femininity with impunity. At certain points this opportunity seems to have been exploited; for instance, the Dame, 'naked armed, barefooted, her frock tucked', may have been reminiscent of Anna's scandalous appearance in *Blackness* when her display of blackened flesh impeached Jacobean propriety.[17] However, it is important also to note that the force of the witches' dance derived from its opposition to the court's expectations rather than from incompetent execution: non-courtly dance did not involve dancing badly, but dancing differently. In this sense, Jonson's description is remarkably revealing of the decorum of the dancing body;

a reading of the transgressive feminine dance can help us arrive at the construction of the ideal.

First, however, it is important to get a sense of precisely what characteristics of 'courtly grace' were violated by these antimasquers. Since the aristocratic masque dance was founded on the social discourse of courtesy, the answer is to be found in contemporary perceptions of the noble body and dance in courtesy manuals and educational treatises. These sources are especially pertinent since long years of dance training formed part of the courtier's education and led to a high level of skill; dance worked as part of the discourse of courtesy, both incorporated social corporeal controls into the individual body. In his sophisticated theorisation of the intertextuality of these two discourses, Mark Franko comments that there 'is nothing in [Arbeau's] description [of the simple basse danse] which would distinguish the simple or the double [steps] from walking in everyday life'.[18] Looked at in this light, elite dance, like the masque, is a place where the social and the dramatic converge. Certainly both dance and the masque were based on the same conventions which controlled the body within the everyday life of the court, and evidence for the overlap in these conventions can be seen in the similarity between the stance of Negri's dancers and the courtly greeting (figure 2). It is because of the existence of elite dance inside the discourse of courtesy that the latter ideology was literally incorporated into the dancers' movements, and because of this that those courtiers who danced and those who watched were governed and judged by the same standards. The masquer's body was constantly evaluated through the criteria of social grace, subject at all times to the demands of a *sprezzatura* which was also part of the masque genre itself. For example, the illusion of the masque's created world had to be as complete as possible and its artifice concealed; in the same way, the codes controlling the body had to be hidden, although all were aware of their existence. What this meant was that, for the courtier, dancing before one's peers was permissible but it was also fraught with the danger of censure if the decorum of the performing body was not observed.

Wrapped up in the construction of the aristocratic body through courtesy, the masque dance was also a bodily performance of power, the representation of the power structures of the court in movement. The way in which the body could express social order is perhaps most obvious in the reverence, or bow, which the Inns of Court commonplace books show began each dance. Lowering the body in this way was a gesture of respect to the dance partner which, when performed to the monarch, was

2 Social dancers, from Cesare Negri, *Le Gratie d'Amore* (Milan, 1602)

also an expression of the sovereign's elevated status. In *The Book Named the Governor* (1531) Thomas Elyot characterises the reverence as the marker of divine worship and royal homage; its use in dance was a bodily affirmation of the social order and, importantly for my discussion of the relationship between the dancing body and linguistic expression below, it was also an opening gesture of certain types of courtly conversation.[19]

Courtly dancers, therefore, embodied the social hierarchies of the court. Simultaneously, the overlap between dance and courtesy meant that aristocratic behaviour itself was both social and fundamentally theatrical, dependent on the performance of certain modes of conduct (such as the reverence) to create the courtly body as a spectacle for its audience. It follows that to dance before an audience did not breach Renaissance courtly codes. Since performance on the masquing stage was not substantially different from the performance of everyday courtly behaviour, the Renaissance court's codes of bodily behaviour drew the courtier into dance and provided the impetus for a more explicitly theatricalised participation in the hierarchies of the court.

How, then, did elite courtesy or dance manuals figure their subject? In general, courtly educational manuals favoured dance as a gracious and skilful aristocratic attribute; Elyot writes at length of dance as an exercise to sharpen the mind of dancers and spectators alike.[20] However, there was opposition to dance from beyond the court, and a distinct perception of its attributes which centred on the surveillance and control of sexuality, often equated with a threatening female desire. In *The Anatomy of Abuses* Philip Stubbs famously expostulates, 'what clipping, what culling, what kissing and bussing, what smouching and slabbering one of another, what filthie groping and vncleane handling is not practised euery wher in these dancings?'[21] It is not, of course, safe to draw firm dividing lines between courtly and Puritan discourses of dance, since the perceived threat of its possibility for sexual expression was in fact common to both, as is perhaps suggested in the elision of the body from contemporary dance treatises and courtesy manuals. Furthermore, contemporary treatments of the dance made the ambiguity of movement itself very clear. The commonplace comparison of Renaissance dance to the movement of the heavenly spheres and the accompanying equation of divine creation and social procreation, which were open to the court, staked a claim for the morality of movement in the face of such Puritan attacks. Even this analogy, however, faced the problems exemplified in John Davies's *Orchestra* (1596); Antinous, one of the protagonists, goes to great lengths to ascribe the motion of the dance to that of the planets and spheres, but he does so with the sole aim of seducing Penelope.[22] However, this commonplace did retain its force in the court masque, where the ideal dance was a kinetic incantation, drawing down blessings from the heavens upon the court. While those watching may not always have fully appreciated its nuances, the analogy of the dance to the constructing force of universal creation made it a central aspect of the masque.[23]

3 Satyrs, from *Oberon* (1611), by Inigo Jones

Costume designs are a rich record of the masque designers' vision of the body in performance and can provide much information on that body's controlling codes of grace and propriety. Though no designs for the antimasque of *Queens* survive, those of the male satyrs of *Oberon* (1611) contribute to an impression of the antithesis of courtly bodily grace (figure 3). The designs show the antimasquers' arms raised above the head in a way not usually found in courtly dance, while their skipping movements, twisted legs, bowed heads and body all contrast with the

more idealised courtly stance which can be seen in Jones's designs for
the masquers of *Queens* (figure 4).[24] A similar violation of courtly decorum
to that of the satyrs can also be seen in Jonson's description of the dance
of the witches of *Queens*. For instance the 'strange fantastic motions' of
the dancers' heads and bodies contravened the desired posture of the
courtly torso, which dance literature dictated should be flexible but should
not depart from the vertical; even in the reverence the torso remained
straight and bent only at the hips (figure 5).[25] Despite this rectitude, such
flexibility was a prerequisite of a body controlled by a concept of grace
which was itself governed by the Aristotelian virtue of the mean, and
related to the moralised interpretation of the dance and to the use of the
ethical term *measure* in dance terminology. A lack of flexibility would be
improper, since it would make the codes which governed the body
visible, when *sprezzatura* dictated that they should remain concealed. Just
as improvisation was an integral aspect of early modern dance, so too
the body had to be flexible. To this end, Caroso advocates that the
graceful body be slightly bent, the head still erect.[26] Claude de Calviac
lays out the ideal:

> la tête ne doit estre ni trop baissé [a sign of laziness], ny trop haut [a sign
> of arrogance] [...] Mais se doyt tenir droict et sans effort, car cela ha bonne
> grace. [...] Et ne faut point aussi que sa test pande d'un coste ny d'autre
> dessus son corps, a la mode des hypocrites.
>
> (the head should neither be too low, nor too high ... Rather it should be
> held just so and without effort, since that is true grace ... And on no
> account should the head hang to one side or other of the body, in the
> style of hypocrites.) [27]

These admonishments reveal the interpretative connection between ex-
ternal bodily grace and inner moral condition. After all, if the tilting of
the head could indicate hypocrisy, to move the whole body inappropri-
ately, as in the movements of the witches' heads and torsos and the
'sudden changes' of their dance, would mark that body as the antithesis
of the courtly ideal. Furthermore, since the performative dances of the
antimasque often used choreographic designs that 'open[ed] outwards
towards stage-front', the masque audience would have been encouraged
to take such a moralised interpretation from the witches' movements.[28]
In effect the hags were laid out before the audience as a negative model
for the construction of the court's norms of both dance and femininity.
    These antimasque dances put forward a transgressive representation of

4 Penthesilea, from *The Masque of Queens* (1609), by Inigo Jones

Reuerence.

5 Reverence, from Thoinot Arbeau, *Orchesography* (Lengres, 1588)

femininity in *Queens*. It is, however, important to note that any distinctions between masquers and antimasquers were based primarily on class difference; the witches' absence of grace was a marker of exclusion from the court. Such distinctions were not confined to Jonson's masque; for example, the rural morris dance of the antimasque of Beaumont's *Masque of the Inner Temple* (1613) juxtaposed elite and proletarian dance forms through the filter of the aristocratic court masque.[29] The idealised dancing courtier was fashioned in opposition to a non-courtly other that even at its most positive was either grotesque (the hags of *Queens*), sexually explicit (the satyrs of *Oberon*) or insane (the morris of Beaumont's masque).

In addition to the fundamental influence of class, the collision of class and gender inflections was also an integral part of the masque genre.

While, to a certain extent, class overrode gender to contribute to an equality of sorts for male and female noble performance within the dance, these gendered inflections were also fundamental to the genre and can be seen in the image of the witch in *Queens*, which exemplifies the masque's gendering of movement. The relationship between the dancers of single-sex performative dances, such as those of the antimasque, are especially pertinent to an exploration of such issues. Interaction between dancers had long been seen as part of the danger of the dance itself; in his attack on dance as 'an introduction to whordom', Stubbs proposed a gendered separation, suggesting that 'women are to daunce by themselues [. . .] and men by themselues'.[30] Yet Jonson's description of *Queens* sets up a transgressive relationship between dancers by emphasising the pairing of the dancers in the witches' back-to-back and hip-to-hip stance and joined hands, postures not found in single-sex courtly dance. While pairs of single-sex dancers were not unusual in Renaissance entertainments – an engraving of Dorat's *Balet des Polonais* (1563) shows a female geometrical dance in which some of the dancers held hands (figure 6) – the witches' movements do not adhere to the courtly norm.[31] For instance, 'back-to-back' dance, not found in any courtly pairing, was a reversal of the face-to-face stance of the social and performative dance.[32] The witches' hip-to-hip posture falls into the same category; though just this form of heterosexual contact occurred in the lavolta, its use by a group of transvestite male performers broke social and sexual norms. Other violations compounded the witches' gender crimes; they also seem to have been guilty of the violation of the ethical relationship between dance and the motion of the spheres. The Throne of Beauty in the 1608 masque of the same name moved in three simultaneous directions, one of which (left to right) was called *motum planetarum* and so was aligned with this celestial movement.[33] In contrast, *Queens* invoked this comparison through its transgression. At an unspecified point the dancers circled 'backward, to the left hand', breaking the dance's conformity to the motion of the spheres and aligning the witches with the earthly targets of anti-dance criticism rather than with the divine. In this particular antimasque, therefore, Stubbs's model of purity was challenged by a transvestite female community which, in a visual inversion of the court's hierarchical order, stood against the ideal order of the court.

Free to violate courtly norms because of its position in the antimasque and the transvestism of its performers, this dance also points up the self-conscious nature of this particular display through its performers' masculinity. The antimasque dance was a male recreation of female crimes

6 Geometrical figure from 'Chorea nympharum', in *Ballet de Polonais*, by Jean Dorat (Paris, 1573)

and an attempt to stage female submission in a complex consideration of femininity which developed in the main masque into the simultaneous demonisation and deification of the figures of the amazonian queens. Such transvestism and *Queens*'s central focus on femininity raises an important question: did these male performers dance as women or as men? Unfortunately the limited evidence does not make for any certainty. What can be said is that Jonson's description of the 'preposterous change and gesticulation' suggests a complex choreography, packed with sudden switches of direction, while evidence of female performative dances suggests that they were simpler and less active than those of the male, complying to the decorum of female movement.[34] It would, therefore, perhaps be plausible to suggest that these witches compounded their transgression by dancing in a masculine style.

While the witches' style of dance may resist straightforward categorisation, it is possible to outline what it means to dance 'as a woman', since the court's codes of grace were themselves gendered. Though predating the cultural production of the Jacobean court, Thomas Elyot's exposition of the gendered characteristics of contemporary social dance in the *Book Named the Governor* provides an insight into its conceptualisation at a time crucial to the masque form's development.

> A man in his natural perfection is fierce, hardy, strong in opinion, covetous of glory, desirous of knowledge, appetiting by generation to bring forth his sembable. The good nature of a woman is to be mild, timorous, tractable, benign, of sure rememberance, and shamefast [...]
>
> Wherefore, when we behold a man and a woman dancing together, let us suppose there to be a concord of all the said qualities [...] And the moving of the man would be more vehement, of the woman more delicate, and with less advancing of the body, signifying the courage and strength that ought to be in a man, and the pleasant soberness that should be in a woman.[35]

Elyot also suggests that the juxtaposition of masculine and feminine traits in the social dance created a balance of opposites which 'betokeneth concord'; gender balance led to social harmony.[36] Certainly, this equation was embodied in the Jacobean court masque, and in the distinct movements of male and female dancers. This is especially clear in *Hymenaei*, in which the threatening male masquers' dance culminated in the drawing of swords and seems to have exemplified a fierce masculinity which was then tempered by the balance of the noblemen and noblewomen in their ranked pairings. On a smaller scale this gendering also was found in the detail of dance steps themselves, most obviously in the peacock-like male display of the galliard. Caroso's *Nido d'Amore* held to Elyot's equation; the male performed galliard leaps and capers while the woman danced a tordion, the more solemn partner dance of the galliard.[37] Caroso's *Laura Suave* also laid out the decorum of feminine spectatorship during this male display; under constant scrutiny, the woman should not 'resemble a statue' but had to win the spectators' admiration with small and graceful movements in line with contemporary ideals of her gender.[38]

This rather simplistic model did not always hold true, however, and the exceptions are illuminating. The *Laura Suave* also contains details which complicate Elyot's gender equation. Caroso states that the woman 'should do the same variations as the gentleman has just done'.[39] Though he provides an alternative set of steps for the woman, this was done to help the less skilled dancer, and similar accommodations were made elsewhere for the less accomplished male. Despite these alternatives, and the constant possibility of improvisation, Caroso's model set both genders on a similar level of display. This trait was not confined to Italian manuals but was also documented in English practice in John Ramsay's spanioletta: 'heave upp ye woman in your armes, parte againe, pace, traverse meete againe, the woman heave up ye man, honor & soe ende'.[40] Rather than being an assertion of gender equality, these latter steps instead seem to have been the deliberate breaking of the norm which created aesthetic pleasure through a shocking break with expectation and the knowledge that usual conditions would soon prevail. Although occasionally suppressed, the gender codes of dance remained powerful; even in texts which sought to justify dance's respectability its erotic display was forceful, but that of the woman was necessarily more modest than that of the male.

The gender dictates of dance extended, of course, beyond dance steps to the body of the dancer. For the courtly dancer the locus of the ideal of the dancing body was found in the gaze and this, the marker of physical and sexual decorum, was also gendered.[41] While the gaze of both sexes had to be modest (Arbeau's male branle dancer glances 'modestly the while at the spectators'), the ideal male gaze was active and the female passive.[42] Despite his modesty, the gentleman was expected to throw 'a discreetly tender sidelong glance at the damsel', while both the female gaze and its object were carefully controlled; Arbeau's description of the pavan sexualises the woman's necessary acknowledgement of the audience as 'an occasional glance of virginal modesty at the onlookers'.[43] Furthermore, the female was prohibited from gazing at her male partner; she should not 'raise her eyes too high while dancing, [...] nor turn her head hither and thither in order to look at this or that gentleman, for this is a thing of vanity'.[44] Able to acknowledge the audience but not her partner, the ideal female dancer was complicit in the reification of her body, made a fetish by the impossibility of returning the active male gaze.

The early modern court's social dance was based solidly on the heterosexual couple. Given that such dances were an intrinsic part of the revels, it follows that these dances needed female participation in order to achieve the masque's goal of social confirmation. However, the Howard sisters' refusal to dance in *Love Restored* was not merely a simplistic rejection of courtiers considered to be too low in the hierarchy, or an enactment of factional court politics, but a potential rejection of the physical decorum which controlled the court. These codes themselves facilitated aristocratic masquing because of the status of dance as an extension of the theatricality of aristocratic daily behaviour into the public space of masque ritual. Dance drew aristocrats of both sexes into the court masque; as the following explores, although the gendering of the courtly body differed in its detail, that body gave male and female masquing a shared source and form of expression.

Dance and language: the dances of the main masque

Dance can tell us much about the early modern elite woman's problematic relationship to performance. Renaissance aristocrats gained a foothold in the masque for several reasons, not the least of which was that the masque was not created for the stage, with its problematic social status, but was a form into which a stage was later introduced.[45] Furthermore, as I have suggested above, the theatrical nature of the aristocrats' bodily behaviour meant that they were in fact required to dance in the masque to confirm their courtly identity. In order to safeguard the masquers' status, however, they did not speak, since speech was seen as the marker of the socially marginalised player. However, this distinction was not as clear-cut as it first appears. In the first decades of the seventeenth century the Stuart court masque became increasingly theatricalised; this process culminated in Henrietta Maria's acting, and the relationship of the dancing aristocratic body to language was one factor which pushed against the constraint to silence. The interpretative sign-systems of dance and language shared a common locus in the body, and, given the early modern period's perceived links between speech and the sexualised female body, this connection was particularly suggestive for women masquers. To some extent, therefore, the dancing courtly body destabilised the prohibition on aristocratic speech and was especially pertinent to the development of female stage performance.

This relationship between dance and language is especially clear in *Hymenaei*, where the performance of both male and female masquers in the double masque emphasised the genre's gender dynamics. The co-performance of male and female courtiers in *Hymenaei* altered the nature of the dance; with their swords now sheathed and having been joined by female partners, the men's aggressive dance became a pairing of martial males and reticent females which enacted Elyot's gender equation. Both *Hymenaei* and the other Jacobean example of the double masque, Campion's *Lords' Masque* (1613), were danced for weddings: Elyot's gendered equation suited the dynamics of the early modern marriage contract. By placing a version of the revels' heterosexual dance inside the main masque, *Hymenaei* illuminates the theatricality of aristocratic dance and the gender dynamics of the aristocratic body. Again, Jonson describes the dances:

> [the masquers] danced forth a most neat and curious measure, full of subtlety and device, which was so excellently performed as it seemed to take away that spirit from the invention that the invention gave to it, and left it doubtful whether the forms flowed more perfectly from the author's brain or their feet. The strains were all noticeably different, some of them formed into letters very signifying to the name of the bridegroom, and ended in manner of a chain, linking hands.[46]

This motif of writing-in-dance, the dancing of letters through the positioning of the dancers, textualised the body and made it language. Dance, a physical sign-system, communicated through the stance and posture of the body and allowed it an alternative outlet of expression to the singing or speaking voice. On this and other occasions, therefore, as argued in the introduction, dance formed part of the masque's alternatives to the literary text or language itself; dance, and indeed performance, along with painting, scenery, costume and make-up, were aligned with what Jonson's preface to *Hymenaei* called the masques' 'bodies', in contrast to the poetic text which he named their 'souls'.[47] In this way Jonson's contrast between ephemeral performance and the preserving act of publication identified the silent masquer with the 'carcass' of his masques.[48]

The importance of these danced names and words can be seen in the long-standing early modern connection between the body and language in the trope of the speaking or readable body. This relationship was grounded in Renaissance humanism and expressed, among other places, in Montaigne's *Apology for Raymond Sebond*; outlining the potential meaning created by the hands, head, eyebrows and shoulders, Montaigne concludes that there is 'no movement that does not speak both a language intelligible without instruction, and a public language'.[49] Such bodily legibility had great currency also within the dance's discursive context. Although denying its truth, Elyot grounds the origins of dance in the fable of the Sicilian tyrant Hiero whose subjects were forbidden speech and instead evolved a system of bodily communication.[50] Furthermore, Arbeau's comparison of the dance's steps to a linguistic grammar, which makes the systemic nature of this communicative code and its independent generation of meaning explicit, was only one of many such comparisons.[51]

One obvious reason for the connection between dance and language was their shared physicality; while dance is linguistic, language is itself physical. *Orchestra*, a failed dance poem documenting a failed seduction, provides a fine example of such physicality in this sensual description of Penelope's speech:

> the queen with her sweet lips divine
> Gently began to move the subtle air,
> Which, gladly yielding, did itself incline
> To take a shape between those rubies fair.[52]

In asserting speech's physicality, this passage also reinforces the contemporary association between feminine speech and sexuality. Though Penelope, the representative of the usually silent woman, does speak, the poem reifies her through its intense focus on her erotic physicality. In *Orchestra* speech is an act of kinesis which exists on the same level of physicality as the dance: 'all the words that from your lips repair / Are nought but tricks and turnings of the air'.[53]

In addition to poetic and humanist texts, dance manuals also acknowledged the equivalency of dance and language; in a famous comparison Arbeau states that 'dancing is a kind of mute rhetoric by which the orator, without uttering a word, can make himself understood by his movements'.[54] Early modern analogies between dance and rhetoric extended beyond shared terminology ('figure') to the performance of the dancer and the orator. Though there was a distinction between the written word and its oration, the performance of dance and language in the early modern court was fashioned through Renaissance courtesy, drawing on the shared gestures, stance and posture of the dancer and orator.[55] Furthermore, although not strictly the act of an orator, the reverence

which opened both courtly conversation and dance established a self-con-
sciously performative framework for what followed. Such an equivalency
between dance and speech gestures towards the extent to which the active
presence of the human body in early modern performance formed the
common ground for both language and dance.

Given this equivalency, the creation of legible symbolic patterned
images in the geometric dance intensified the interaction of dance and
language in the masque and needs to be considered as part of masque
performance. As already seen, Jonson's description of the main masque
dances of *Hymenaei* contains two important examples of such patternings,
the chain and the dance of the bridegroom's name. The former, a simple
chain figure, completed the masquing dance and was interpreted by Jonson
as Reason's 'golden chain let down from heaven'.[56] Perhaps more important than the specific meaning of this figure, however, was the status
of the dancing body as the locus of dance and language and a site of
interpretation. Discussing the entertainments of the Valois court, Franko
describes such dances as a legible text to be read by the monarch as part
of the power relationship between ruler and subject; the interpretation
of the geometric dance imposed a reading upon the dancing body which
could contribute to the power relationships of the court.[57] As far as the
Stuart court was concerned, the masque consistently asserted the legibility
of the body, and of the female body in particular. For example, Daniel's
Vision of the Twelve Goddesses describes the female masquers' bodies as
'beautiful characters of sense [...] easier to be read than their mystical
Ideas'; feminine corporeality made the abstract Platonic Idea available for
interpretation.[58] In this way the dancing body found both expression and
legibility in the graphic dance.

The late sixteenth- and early seventeenth-century French courts made
great use of the geometric dance. Perhaps the most fully documented
examples were those of the *Ballet de Monseigneur de Vandosme* (1610) in
which noblemen danced complex figures from 'l'alphabet des anciens
Druides' (the alphabet of the ancient Druids).[59] The *livret* distributed
before the performance reproduced these figures for the audience to
interpret (figure 7).[60] Although the dancers performed symbols taken from
a pseudo-language, the imaginative equivalency of dance and language
became intensified in this ballet: rather than simply performing graphic
patterns (such as the chain), here dance became a language of sorts and
the audience witnessed the bodily creation of text. In this, the closest
approximation of dance and language examined so far, the body itself
became language.

7 Danced figures, from *Le Ballet de Monseigneur le Duc de Vandosme* (1610), from Paul Lacroix, *Ballets et Mascarades de Cour de Henri III à Louis XIV* (Genève, Chez J. Gay et fils, 1868), I, pp. 265–8

Graphic dance had a place also in the Jacobean court's entertainments, such as the dancing of Prince Charles's name in *The Masque of Queens*, and was prominent enough to prompt Francis Bacon's assertion that 'turning dance into figures is a childish curiosity', a remark which chimes well with Maurer's disparaging opinion of the graphic dance which began this chapter.[61] Yet the graphic dance's physicalisation of language and linguistic potential perhaps had significances within the gender politics of the masque which go beyond Bacon's statement. The dance of the name of the 'most sweet and ingenious prince, Charles, Duke of York' was a patriarchal manipulation of the female body in its incorporation of the name of the future king.[62] Anna and her masquing women embodied Charles's name, the linguistic marker of masculine authority, in a manner which might seem to imply the public performance of female conformity. This is somewhat complicated in the performance as a whole, however, since female submission was far from given in *The Masque of Queens*. As I show in chapter 3, the bodies of the female masquers, which here seem to embody the court's patriarchal authority, were in fact the locus of conflict between alternative representative strategies of femininity.

The dances of *Hymenaei* form a useful counterpoint to the single-sex graphic dances of *Queens*, since they were performed by both men and women. *Hymenaei* was staged for the marriage of Robert Devereux and Frances Howard, whose scandalous divorce later caused Jonson to suppress the published text's references to the couple. Although *Queens* had danced the name of a royal male, in this earlier case the linguistic marker of male power was the name of the husband, the representative of marital authority. For those male masquers involved in this performance, their dance was a marker of the court's power structures and distinct from that of the women in that it was predicated along masculine paradigms. Just as the dance of Prince Charles's name was the expression of loyalty to a pivotal court figure (although, of course, his future status was as yet unanticipated), *Hymenaei* expressed loyalty to the Earl of Essex, fourteen at the time of his marriage and expected to wield substantial political power. Intended to heal the political rift of the thwarted 1601 Essex rebellion, this masque was both a celebration of heterosexual union and an expression of political intent.

Both these examples occurred in the first decade of the Jacobean court. It was not until 1617, in *Cupid's Banishment*, a masque staged at Greenwich for Anna of Denmark by the schoolgirls of the Ladies Hall, Deptford, that an English masque was recorded as dancing a female name. Robert White describes the culmination of his masque: twelve nymphs

pace with majesty toward the presence and, after the first strain of the
violins, they dance, [forming] Anna Regina in letters; [in] their second
masquing dance [forming] Jacobus Rex; [in] their departing dance is [the
formation of] Carolus P with many excellent figures falling off, by Master
Onslo, tutor to the Ladies Hall.[63]

The dance of a woman's name was not unheard of in the continental
courts; for example, the names of Cosimo II and Maria Magdalena were
danced by both male and female nobles in the 1611 Florentine *Mascherata*.[64]
As a mixed-sex dance, the Florentine entertainment differed from a purely
male or female performance, such as were mainly found in the English
court, and it is significant that the sole known example of a female name
in the English masque was danced only by women. What is more, the
mixed dances of *Hymenaei* and the single-sex performances of *Queens* and
Cupid's Banishment, the only Jacobean masques recorded as using this
technique, all involved female masquers. This might suggest that the gender
delineations of the English performances were more forceful than those
of the continent, and that writing-in-dance was, in England at least,
primarily a feminine practice. This and other issues form the subject of
the final chapter of this book.

In the dance of the names of the court's power elite, the identification
of the author of this physical text is rather problematic. Is the author the
choreographer who invented the dance, or the masquers whose bodies
performed the act of inscription? In *Hymenaei* Jonson claims that the
dancers performed so well that they 'left it doubtful whether the forms
flowed more perfectly from the author's brain or their feet'.[65] Though
this is perhaps mere flattery, the concealment of the rehearsed nature of
the dance's complex figures is also a part of *sprezzatura* and is tied up
with the status of improvisation in Renaissance dance. Although the
recourse to improvisation disguised both the author's and choreographer's
ideological control of the dancing body, Jonson's assertion also gave that
body a degree of autonomy. Once again the preserving act of publication
was put in opposition to the ephemerality of the moment and movement
of dance.

A similar undermining of the authorial control of the graphic dance
can be found also in the masque genre as a whole. In performance, such
control was dependent on the relationship between those dancing and
those watching. Clearly, danced figures such as the chain or letters were
best seen from above, and this is exemplified in the perspective of the
engraving of Dorat's ballet (figure 6). It is here that the power structures

of the court and the seating arrangements of the masquing hall come
into play. Although the monarch had a raised view from the royal dais,
the usual hierarchy of the court may, in this instance, have worked against
itself, since the less privileged spectators in the galleries may actually have
been better placed to read such dance patterns, while the elite who were
closer to the monarch were slightly disadvantaged in comparison. In the
light of contemporary emphasis upon the order of the masquing hall or
salle des fêtes, any nuance of the court's hierarchical arrangement was
important. It would seem that in this case the dance may perhaps have
disturbed this ordered hierarchy and, asserting the involvement of the less
privileged sectors of courtly society, destabilised the masque's implicit
aims.

Connections between the expressive female body and the inscription
of the graphic dance did, however, find their way under the auspices of
conventional authorial control in Jonson's published masque text. *The
Masque of Blackness* is one such example, as Aethiopia declaimed;

> Call forth thy honored daughters, then,
> And let them, 'fore the British men,
> Indent the land with those pure traces
> They flow with in their native graces.[66]

Within the poetics of this masque, text was created in the traces left by
the dancers' feet on the land, a text aligned with the interpretability of
the female dancers' bodies. In the masque form's ideal vision of the court
and *Blackness*'s specific discourse of an ideal 'Britain', the floor of the
masquing hall represented 'British' soil. When the blackened daughters
of Niger made their journey to 'Brittania', as described by Oceanus and
Niger, their movement to the Jacobean court reversed the usual trajectory
of colonisation, brought the colonised to the colonisers and complicated
the imaginative equation between the female body and territory found
in the sexualised images of early modern colonial discourse. This raises
an important question: what does it mean that these women used their
bodies to write on the homeland of the coloniser? In one sense it
demonstrates their conformity to the court's demands of the grace of
dance and was another public act of homage to James I. Alternatively
the combination of the masquers' subversive blackened faces with female
access to textual creation could constitute an assertion of female and
colonial independence.

The equivalency of dance and language was a feature of the early
Stuart court masque, but they were kept separate to a certain degree in

performance. In *Beauty*, for example, the 'time of dancing with the lords
[…] to give [the dancers] respite, was intermitted with song […] After
which songs, they danced galliards and corantos.'[67] It seems that, in almost
all Jacobean masques, song and dance were kept apart. The practical
explanation that the sound of dancing feet would overpower the speaker
or singer does not always apply, since speech or song were performed
during other choreographed movements; for example, the song of the
Graces in *The Vision* was performed as the goddesses processed to the
Sibyl's temple, and a song accompanied the chariot ride of *Queens*.[68] The
single Jacobean exception is Thomas Campion's 1607 *Lord Hay's Masque*,
in which the dance of the golden trees was performed to sung accompaniment. Campion's description states that there were special
arrangements made 'that the words of the song might be heard of all',
but he does not indicate their success or failure.[69] Significantly this
experiment does not seem to have been repeated in his later masques,
and the disjunction of dance and the vocal text implies that dance created
certain meanings which existed on a different interpretative level than
that of other co-ordinated movements and so was separated from the
linguistic text in a way that these other movements were not.

Such a separation seems to be a feature of masque performance. Vocal
expression occurred when the dance stopped, often in the moment when
its geometric symbols were completed. For instance, in *Beauty*, the
masquers began 'a most curious dance full of excellent device and change'
and 'ended it in the figure of a diamond, and so, standing still, were by
the musicians with a second song (sung by a loud tenor) celebrated' in
the immobility of the geometric figure.[70] It would seem that static symbols
and the bodies which made them were more readable than the body in
motion: movement made for a less stable legibility. This instability is
perhaps mirrored in the masque texts themselves, the problematic juxtaposition of dance and language within a single performance forming a
part of the masque texts' failure to document movement. The text of
Hymenaei, for example, gives few details except the masquers' initial
ranking and the concluding chain-figure. Although dance could create
text, text could not create dance motion: language could represent only
opening and closing immobility and the already textual name. While the
dancing body had a textual existence in geometric and linguistic symbols,
the resistance of dance motion to textual representation demonstrated
their essential difference. The moving body was not dependent upon
language, instead it generated meaning in complement to language and
formed a separate focus of the audience's attention.

It remains to be seen, however, what meanings these past, completed movements created in the Jacobean masque. If, as I have suggested, the endpoint of the change and motion of the masquers' dance of *Beauty* was stasis and that this stillness was celebrated in the masque's vocal text, then the opposition of dance and language paralleled the trope of motion and immobility common in European court festivals. This dichotomy was certainly central to the Jacobean masque in the much-used motif of the immobilisation of the masquers by the forces of the antimasque. Found in the image of the female masquers as statues in Campion's *Lords' Masque* and the *Ballet Comique de la Reine* (1581), and in the male statue in Beaumont's *Masque of the Inner Temple* and the *Ballet de Vandosme*, each instance resulted from the temporary control of non-courtly forces over the masquers.[71] In all of these entertainments the release of the masquers from stillness into dance signalled the renewal of divine and royal favour and allowed the confirming action of the revels or *grand bal* to take place.

More specifically, however, both the *Balet de Vandosme* and Beaumont's *Masque* released their dancers from the antimasquers' power through the controlling gaze of the monarch, the very ideological basis of the court masque. Inevitable though the final outcome may have been, this jostling for control of the masquers' movement or immobility fashioned their bodies as the site of conflict between courtly and oppositional forces. Staged for the interpretation of the audience in the geometric dance, the meaning which these bodies could generate was also up for appropriation. The most famous example of sixteenth-century French *ballet de cour* provides a useful example of this battle for the control of the body's significance. When, in the *Ballet Comique*, the enchantress Circe immobilised the dancing nymphs of the court in the middle of their patterning, she also froze the courtly generation of significance in mid-flow. When the dancers were released, they were again able to form a succession of figures for the court to interpret and, importantly, also able to dance out that court's codes of grace and civility which Circe had disrupted. However, since it was motion rather than stasis that resisted a stable reading of the body, this apparently desirable movement may potentially have undermined the court's 'safe' control of such meaning. It would seem, therefore, that both the masquers' bodies and their graphic dances were to some extent problematic; the court needed such an expressive form, but had to police its interpretability and its rejection of textual definition. Textually unrepresentable, the moving body was a space of unstable legibility.

The court masque staged the readable body of the aristocrat, expressive through dance in ways which complemented the other physical modes of expression, such as make-up and costume, available as part of the masque's 'carcass'. The duality of this legibility is clear in the female masquers' dance of the name; she danced her loyalty through the incorporation of the name, the marker of patriarchal authority. However, this dance also reflected the opportunities for expression offered by the female body; as the source of feminine language through vocalisation and dance, it was also the source of a destabilising sexuality and a site of conflict and potential opposition. Through dance women fashioned themselves as courtiers, using the performance which dance allowed them to create an elite female identity. The male dancer, too, danced his loyalty to the court hegemony, but his dance seemed a less complicated bid for political empowerment through the existing structures of courtly favour and advancement. The complexities of the male dance become apparent, however, when their nature is examined in more detail.

The social dances of the revels: the erotic politics of aristocratic performance

The court masque was based on the display of the performing body and the gaze of the spectator, and the eroticisation of both male and female dancers revealed the masque's gendered dynamics. Though aristocrats of both sexes were eroticised in the audience's gaze, important distinctions existed between their representation in performance. Perhaps the most important difference is revealed through a reading of the social dances of the revels, which we have seen were so important to the masque, where male dance forms a useful contrast to the perception of the female body. The infamous dance of George Villiers, Duke of Buckingham, in the revels of Jonson's *Pleasure Reconciled to Virtue* (1618) is a fine example of the male dances of the revels and the formation of the male body in the Jacobean court. Continuing where the male dances of *Hymenaei* left off, Villiers's dance was a means of gaining and holding power, and, present in the main masque and the revels, such aspiration would seem to have been a feature of the male dance. The theme of power is then continued in the perception of female social dance and its representation in early modern dance literature, where an interesting disparity between the literary and practical representation of women seems apparent. Just as the court masque itself was an expression of power, so too would this seem to be a fundamental element of its dances.

Thomas Elyot's balanced image of the dance depended on the certainty of male and female gender traits. The qualities which he ascribed to the male courtly dancer were perhaps seen at their most extreme in the tilts and barriers of the Jacobean court. Like the masque, these entertainments were displays of masculine power and courtly prowess. For example, the choreographed martial conflict of the barriers which were performed with *Hymenaei* pointed up the early modern conception of dance as part of a competitive elite masculinity, part of statesmanship. Contemporary educational manuals regarded accomplishment in dance as an attribute of the ideal warrior-statesman, and this was certainly present in Henry's representation in *Oberon* (1611).[72] What is more, this kind of idealised masculinity was evident in other masques. For example, the rebellious male masquers' dance of the humours and affections in *Hymenaei* concluded with the drawing of swords; dance expressed masculine courtly martial prowess, and the choreographed battle of the tilt was internalised within the dance in the athletic 'cabrioles and galliardes'.[73] Male dance was predicated on competitive display; Caroso documents a galliard variant in which the capers (stiff-legged kicks performed during high leaps) became a competition to kick a tassle.[74] Physical prowess and fitness to rule were also indicators of erotic attraction; the dynamics of power and sexual attraction were closely intertwined.

In contrast to the exclusively male tilt, women dancers were a necessary part of the masque's revels and their inclusion meant that the male courtier had to alter his dance, tempering such a forceful male display to offer a dance more akin to Elyot's gendered image of 'concord'. Such restraints on the male dancer are also found in Arbeau's warning against boisterous strides, 'as the damsel who is your partner cannot with decency take such long steps'.[75] As I have mentioned, just such an accommodation of the female dancer took place in *Hymenaei*, in the calming of the rebellious sword dance by the appearance of Reason and the women masquers, tempering gendered characteristics to form the Aristotelian mean.

When male courtiers took part in tilts and barriers, such competitive displays of athleticism helped to fashion them as objects of erotic attention. Certainly this took place in the entertainments which formed part of the chivalric revival of Prince Henry's militaristic Protestant court. In his engagement with court festivals as vehicles for his own personal chivalric ideology, Henry used the athletic (and choreographed) competition of the tilt or barrier to present himself as the erotic object of performative attention and, in doing so, as the ideal prince of early modern power and statecraft. As this description of the dancers of *Oberon* shows, this extended also into his masquing. The prince and his men were dressed in

> short scarlet hose and white brodequins full of silver spangles coming half way to the calf [...] They entered dancing two ballets intermingled with varied figures and leaps, extremely well done by most of them [...] then the gallards began, which was something to see and admire.[76]

Admiration is specular; dressed in revealing costumes which focused attention on the body, Henry and the spectacle of the athletic royal body in motion were the object of the watching court's gaze. Predicated on this display, masque performances like Henry's were also demonstrations of the fitness of the prince to rule. This is rather different from the reading of female dance, and suggests the inseparable nature of the dynamics of masculine eroticism and power for the male masquer.

Inigo Jones's costume designs for *Oberon* provide further information about the representation of the Prince and his men. Costume, a means of defining the body's potential movement and of directing the gaze of the spectator, expressed the conceptualisation of the masquing body. Dancing the role of Oberon, Henry's body was defined through a martial eroticism in the final design for his costume (figure 8). The display of the Prince's body is unmistakable; he was depicted in a close-fitting version of classical soldier's dress which clearly defined the musculature of his chest, stomach and legs, cut, as Jonson wrote in *Hymenaei*, 'to express the naked, in manner of the Greek thorax'.[77] In certain cases, however, this martial erotics merged with an effeminate quality; for instance, Oberon's attendant's flowing hair and beardless face, like that of his master, were the markers of an early modern effeminacy (figure 9). This impression was reinforced by his exposed abdomen, reminiscent of that of many female masquers, and the swathes of cloth which gave his chest a feminine silhouette. It would seem, therefore, that the eroticisation of these particular male masquers encapsulated apparently disparate masculinities in a martial effeminacy, all of which focused attention on the male body on the dancing floor.

The most extreme example of the erotic potential of the male masquer's dance is to be found in records of the performance of *Pleasure Reconciled to Virtue*. This much-quoted description of the revels is taken from the report of the Venetian chaplain Orazio Busino:

> [the masquers] did all sorts of ballets and dances of every country, such as passemeasures, corantos, canaries, Spanish dances, and a hundred other

8 Prince Henry as Oberon, from *Oberon* (1611), by Inigo Jones

9   Oberon's attendant, from *Oberon* (1611), by Inigo Jones

beautiful turns to delight the fancy. Finally they danced the Spanish dance once more with their ladies, and because they were tired began to lag; and the King, who is by nature choleric, grew impatient and shouted loudly, 'Why don't they dance? What did they make me come here for? Devil take all of you, dance!' At once the Marquis of Buckingham, his majesty's favourite minion, sprang forward, and danced a number of very high and very tiny capers with such grace and lightness that he made everyone admire and love him, and also managed to calm the rage of his angry lord. Inspired by this, the other masquers continued to display their powers one after another, with different ladies, concluding with capers, and lifting their goddesses from the ground. We counted 34 capers in succession cut by one knight, but none matched the splendid technique of the Marquis [...] The King then honoured the Marquis with extraordinary signs of affection, touching his face.[78]

James I's public signs of favour and Buckingham's prowess expressed the masculine erotics of power within what Orgel calls the 'play' of the court.[79] Following the heterosexual model of Christopher Hatton's attainment of political influence from Elizabeth I, Villiers's dance was simultaneously a public statement of power and a means to gain more.[80] Taking to the floor in an apparently spontaneous solo dance, Villiers was the focus of the audience's gaze and, with no partner and so no need to temper his athleticism, his was an unequivocal display of masculine bodily elegance and strength. Busino's account clearly highlights the dance's competitive nature and its use to attain political power; after their initial lapse of grace, the other dancers were 'inspired' to try to match Villiers's display, and failing in that meant loss of royal favour.

Written by an outsider, Busino's account identified the power structures of the English court. As James Knowles points out, Villiers's dance won both his king's favour and that of the audience; making everyone 'admire and love him', his skill gained him currency, both with the King and with those who needed to outdo him but also had to recognise his influence.[81] Just as his dance succeeded through the erotic specularity of his body, Villiers's achievement was confirmed also through that body, in the public marks of affection bestowed upon him by James I. These gestures, however, do not fit a simplistic interpretation; in the simultaneously public and personal space of state ritual, the public caresses of a king existed in an unstable interpretative space. Alan Bray has demonstrated the problematic interpretation of public displays of affection between men in the early modern period, arguing that they cannot easily be categorised as either purely political or sexual but instead existed within the complex dynamics of male sexuality, friendship and the display of political favour.[82] What can be said is that Busino's version of James's reaction suggests the eroticism of the relationship between courtier and king that was forged in this particular dance. In the insular social space of the Banqueting House the courtier's solo dance generated an intimacy with the monarch upon whose gaze the entire ritual was predicated, an intimacy which then extended into public signs of favour and affected the whole court. Furthermore, as Orgel points out, Buckingham's display both debased him before James and elevated him before the court in a conscious bid for political favour.[83] Through this self-abasing erotic display, Villiers gave his body up to the King's control, dancing at James's whim in a manner which almost amounted to puppetry; but he also asserted himself in his demonstration of the skill necessary to approach the site of power. James's outburst and Villiers's response demonstrate the extent to which the Jacobean masque displayed the body for the monarch's interpretation and manipulation; in the microcosm of the masquing hall, the ruler's power to move the dancing body was the counterpart of his actual power over his subjects. This performance, though similar to the ideal erotic sub-mission of the female in dance, differed in that it was based upon homosocial structures of courtly power.[84]

The exclusion of women from this particular dance between subject and ruler points to the power structures that underlie this exclusively male dance. Christopher Hatton's example demonstrates that the erotics of male dance were indeed related to the attainment of power, and the homosocial structures of Villiers's dance illuminate its distinct Jacobean circumstance. In direct contradiction to Philip Stubbs's pure same-sex model, the mockery which met the masquers of *Love Restored* demonstrates the problematic status of this kind of dance in the revels. Part of the reason for such mockery, however, must have been the shock of the lords' rejection and the disappointment of the audience's expectations. These were not the only causes of humiliation, however; another was the fact that, forced into a performance which was not quite like either the performative dance of the main masque or Villiers's solo display, the lords were perhaps guilty of an inappropriate use of the model of the heterosexual social dance and it was this which disempowered them. It seems that moving the same-sex dance from the stage and placing it within the revels disrupted the delicate balance which Elyot had extolled, itself now revealed to have as much to do with power and status as with gender alone, and damaged the dance's symbolic resonance in a way which was unacceptable to both audience and participants.

An interesting fictional counterpart to *Love Restored* is found in Davies's poem *Orchestra*, where its treatment suggests that a dissonance existed between the practice and the literature of the male dance. *Orchestra* describes the classical sex-changes of Tiresias and Caeneus in connection with dance. The ease with which Davies portrays the move between the gendering structures of male and female dance and the pleasure taken in dancing 'the woman's part' was belied in practice by the mockery which met the dancers of *Love Restored*.[85] The literary model, it seems, did not work in performance; few noblemen would have wanted to lower their status by dancing the female role. Dance won men power not through ease of gender-change but through the assertion of masculine prowess and virtues; in dancing the female part the lords were perceived not as women but rather as emasculated men. The clear water between practice and literary representation demonstrates also that women were a necessary part of dance and that their exclusion was not acceptable to the court. In a sense, therefore, the courtly woman held a position of strength; as the example of *Love Restored* shows, the withholding of her participation rendered dance itself invalid. While the lords' humiliation was an indictment of their failure to live up to the display of the male dancer's power and status, their rejection was a female statement of political intent which tapped into the same circulation of court favour which Villiers was later to exploit.

The relationship between dance practice and its literary representation is equally important for the early modern female dancer. Although distinct from those of the male courtier's dance, the erotics of display also operated in women's masquing dance, as the revealing costumes of *Queens* clearly show (figures 4 and 10). The definition of the female dancer as erotic spectacle occasionally attracted censure, and the interaction of the woman's dancing body and the audience's gaze certainly had the potential to destabilise the decorum of the court masque.[86] One aspect of the threat of female dance was expressed through a strand of dance criticism which centred on rape. Puritan criticism, and some contemporary drama such as *The Revenger's Tragedy*, depicted the court's masques as threatening female chastity, calling them 'so pernitious, that divers honourable women have beene ravished [. . .] by their means'.[87] The threat of violation was matched, however, by that of an active female sexuality which had been further heightened by the movement of the dance. Carleton's anecdote of the woman 'surprised at her business on top of the Taras [terrace]' on

10 Berenice, from *The Masque of Queens* (1609), by Inigo Jones

the night of *Blackness* figures this nameless individual as a sexual instigator stimulated by the dance.[88] Just as Stubbs's marker of the dance's immorality was the interaction of male and female, so in Carleton's anecdote the sign of the court's immorality is an active female sexuality within this dangerous interaction.

Of a kind with this perception, the representation of dance in contemporary literature robbed the eroticised female dancer of agency, fetishising her and privileging the male author and dancer. This was perhaps predictable given that dance texts, developed from educational manuals, were concerned primarily with training men; Arbeau, Coplande and the Inns of Court all depict dance from the male perspective, describing male dance steps and the ideal behaviour towards the female partner. Indeed, Arbeau's term 'dancer' applies only to men; he often refers to 'the dancer and his damsel', and his illustration of the *pieds largis oblique*, in the process of providing a teaching aid for the male dancer, marginalises the woman to the extent that she is represented only by a disembodied hand (figure 11).[89] It seems, therefore, that despite the necessity of women to the dance, theirs was a marginal and physical presence. Eloquently expressing her distance from representation, the female dancer was reduced to a bodiless hand at the edge of an illustration.

Such strategies of exclusion were embodied in other dance manuals in rather more subtle ways than in Arbeau's, concentrating instead on the management of the female body. For example, Caroso acknowledges the necessary presence of the female dancer and describes steps for both men and women. At the same time, however, he also controls the way in which the female body might move, extending beyond such dictates as the way in which the eyes should be held in dance, to recommend, among other things, silent walking in chopines and the decorous way to sit down on a chair.[90] It seems that as far as dance texts were concerned women were either excluded or operated under strict limitations. We should not lose sight of the fact, though, that such controls were similar to those imposed upon male dancers; both genders were constrained to prescribed forms of movement, and the differences which did arise occurred primarily in dance manuals rather than in dance itself. It seems that the representation of dance could differ importantly from its actual performance; male-authored texts excluded the woman who was necessary to performance and in doing so also placed the male at the centre of the reader's consideration.

Such distinctions between dance and its literature were carried through into the poetry of dance. Discussing Ronsard's *Sonnets*, in which the

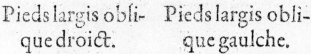

11 *Pieds largis oblique* from Thoinot Arbeau, *Orchesography*
(Lengres, 1588), fol. 42v

author describes himself watching his beloved as she danced, Margaret McGowan identifies the eroticisation of the female dancing body by the male poet and the way this inspired poetic creation.[91] Substituting the poet's emotional response for the dance itself, and so echoing the linguistic failure of the masque accounts, these poems reified the female dancer and made her powerless by appropriating the independent creative energy of her movement. Such traits were not confined to Ronsard, however; *Orchestra* draws on the trope of dance's creative energies (textual, sexual and universal) from Hesiod's classical dance of the Graces and Spenser's courtly version in *The Faerie Queene*, and embodies the energies of divine creation within the erotic vision of the dancing female body.[92] What is more, the forces of sexual desire and poetic inspiration are also aligned with the concept of universal creation. The woman (the divine Graces of Hesiod and Spenser, Ronsard's mortal Hélène de Sugères, and Davies's fictional Penelope) is figured as the inspiration for poetic and sexual arousal; her body channels celestial energies to the sublunary poet, resulting in the creation of a male poetic discourse.

    Orchestra offers what might be thought of as a culmination of female reification in its climatic vision of the Elizabethan court in Love's mirror. Now acting the part of the quintessential silenced woman, Penelope cannot articulate this sight; she

Fain would have prais'd the state and pulchritude;
But she was stroken dumb with wonder quite.[93]

The chance for speech is instead passed to the divine woman, Terpsichore, who, also faltering, is described as the victim of 'weak judgement'.[94] An admission of linguistic inadequacy in the representation of dance, this series of failed female vocalisations also reveals the poem's gendering of language. When the new Muse Urania finally does speak, this divine vocalisation does not rescue previous failures, so much as reassert male primacy by reinstating women as the passive inspiration of male poetic expression.[95] This model of inspiration, however, itself founders in *Orchestra*'s own failure as a poetic exercise. The unfinished poem never communicates its culminating vision, but ends instead with the limp phrase, 'Here are wanting some stanzas describing / Queen Elizabeth'.[96] Revealed as a patriarchal construct, the trope of the female dancer as a channel of divine energy is also an example of the male textual fantasy of control over the erotic energies of the female dance which the example of *Love Restored* suggests was less attainable in the reality of the court. The ambiguous status of the female dancer, both necessary and marginalised, resulted in practice in the restriction of the actively desiring female gaze through mechanisms of social censure, and in its literature in the compensatory textual fantasy of the passive woman who simply inspired the male poet.

The mockery of the homosexual dance of *Love Restored*, in contrast to *Orchestra*'s shifting conception of gender, highlights the dissonance of the literary and practical model of the gendered dance. To what extent, therefore, did this poetic model of the reified woman conform to the court's actual dances? Once again such a question is difficult to answer because of a lack of evidence, and we are forced to judge by what is not said. For example, eye-witness reports do not point out any apparently subversive activity in either the dances of the revels or the main masque. More than this there seems to have been an assumption that dancers would need to conform, and any attempt at self-fashioning by breaking the rules of the courtly dance would perhaps have been seen only as a failure in grace. This can perhaps be seen in Jonson's *Masque of Blackness*, where, despite the masquers' blackened faces, their dances seem to have been conformist. Perhaps the most that can be said is that there is no record of any such attempt, and that, although the potential existed for oppositional versions of the dance, this does not appear to have been attempted by either the men or the women of the court. This was also the case for the Howards in *Love Restored*; unable to dance differently, their only protest was the rejection of dance itself.

The slippage between literary representation and dance practice in the court masque highlights the tensions which were caused by its reliance on female participation. In contrast to her treatment in literature, the noblewoman could not be excluded from the social dance of the masque. In their display of courtly decorum and loyalty, these dances were the visual marker of the interiorisation of courtly ideology, and therefore needed female courtiers as much as their male counterparts. It was this need for the female dancer which allowed the courtly woman into the masque in the first place and also created the conditions for the Howard sisters' refusal to dance; dance gave both sexes the opportunity to manipulate the court masque for their own political purposes. Still, certain aspects of dance remained the realm of the male courtier; Villiers's virtuoso solo stands in stark contrast to the likely response to any female dancer who had indulged in such a display. In addition, although literary texts were predicated on the dancing female body, where the expression of female desire should have been there is only the amused condemnation of court commentators. Female desire was as divorced from representation in these texts as the motion of dance itself. In stark contrast to Buckingham's virile spontaneity and energy, *Love Restored* was the forum for what is reported as the silent female refusal of performance, narrated in the disjointed and damaged sentence of a male observer.

Governed by the demands of courtesy, dance was less a performance than an extension of the daily fashioning of a courtly identity through display, and it pushed the Jacobean aristocrat, both male and female, into performance. As a root of the masque, dance also played a large role in the emergence of women's masquing. Nevertheless, although it allowed women into performance, dance also restricted their necessary but none the less threatening participation through its gendering of movement, stance and posture, fashioning the female dancer into Elyot's ideal of the 'mild, timorous' woman. Such restrictions were reflected also in both the literature and the practice of early modern dance; the textual fantasy of female marginalisation was paralleled in the masque in the conformity of the dancing woman to the gendered controls over movement, stance, gaze and dance step. Perhaps the most extreme example of such restraints were found in the graphic dances, and the incorporation of the name of the king, prince and bridegroom into the female body.

In the dance of the name, however, the duality of women's position in relation to the masque dances also becomes clear. While these women were obliged to dance out the marker of patriarchal authority, these dances and the expressive potential of the textualised female dancing body to push on the constraint of the aristocrat to silence also gave them opportunities. Though this silence and the dance of the name applied to both male and female dancers, its implications were heightened by Renaissance conceptions of femininity and the perceived links between the female body and the female voice. Once again, however, although the court may have needed women dancers for the masque, their bodily expression had to be carefully controlled. This might explain why, while male writing-in-dance was a form of power-play designed to gain favour and advancement, the noblewoman's version of this dance was a more ambiguous event, granting them access to the power structure of the court and allowing them to fashion their identities as courtiers while constraining them to the bodily dance of, on the whole at least, the patriarch's name. Whatever the case, the frail tradition of the elite woman's approach to linguistic expression in the graphic dance was of the greatest importance to the development of female performance. The status of writing-in-dance, the access it granted to female corporeal expressivity and the tradition of the textual and linguistic female body all pushed upon the restraints of the Jacobean masque.

Given the importance of the dance to the male masquer's court career, the significance of any female appropriation of the dance, like that of *Love Restored*, was greatly heightened. It is rather ironic that, once the dance had given women access to performance and expression, the refusal to perform became an empowering statement of female choice. However, the Howards' refusal to perform in 1612 was not an isolated incident but was reminiscent of Anna of Denmark's similar refusal in her London coronation several years earlier. In each performance the strategy was the same; women used non-participation as a means of undermining the reifying obligation of female presence, since, after all, enforced performance could be as disempowering as exclusion. In a performance genre which prohibited female speech and in which the female body was expected to be given up willingly to the dance, such refusals were particularly eloquent. Yet it should be kept in mind that women such as Anna of Denmark and the Howard sisters relied on their powerful family status and royal favour for their own security to act in this way, and such apparent acts of autonomy can in fact be seen also as an expression of factional loyalty and status.

Marriage and the performance of the romance quest: the role of the queen consort in the early modern European court

Anna of Denmark's first recorded participation in court ritual was her civil marriage by proxy at fourteen years of age to James VI of Scotland on 20 August 1589 in the Danish royal palace of Kronborg. By no means unusual in early modern court practice, this proxy ceremony marks Anna's first engagement with the rituals of royalty and of courtly identity, her own, her future husband's and that of the nobleman who stood in his place. This sparsely documented first performance, which has previously slipped so easily from scrutiny, gestures briefly towards Anna's status within the Danish and Scottish courts.

The proxy wedding took place with the Scottish ambassador, George Keith the Earl Marischal, taking the place of James VI. A comprehensive Danish account of the marriage festivities in both Denmark and Scotland briefly plans the proxy ceremony, describing an event which seems to have been a mixture of state and religious ritual:

> In the third hour after noon in the royal palace there will be a solemn promise of marriage. Then there will be an address in the German language, made on behalf of the most serene king of Scotland by the illustrious and noble lord earl [the Earl Marischal] as head of this delegation. This will be followed shortly by mounting the bed. Since it is the custom of kings and princes in these ceremonies that wedding torches are brought in, twelve nobles from one side and twelve from the other will be chosen to bear them before the bride. And because particular colours are customarily assigned to the torches, the illustrious and noble lords ambassadors are to be asked which colours should be assigned to their torches, according to their pleasure.

These ceremonies having been completed, the illustrious and noble lords
will again be led into their chamber and not long after to the royal table
in order to take a meal.[1]

With its processional, symbolic torches and above all the proxy's impersonation of the groom, this moment bears strong similarities to later
English nuptial masques, such as Jonson's *Hymenaei* (1606). The marriage
ceremony's inconclusive nature is somewhat ratified by unsubstantiated
claims that, in addition to the actual ceremony between Anna and James
himself, which took place on 23 November 1589 in the Great Hall of
the Old Bishops' Palace in Oslo, James later demanded another enactment
of the ceremony at Kronborg on 21 January 1590.[2] If nothing else, these
claims show the way in which marriage was perceived to be a repeatable
performance. Such a tendency is embedded in the heart of the proxy
marriage plan in the symbolic mounting of the bed by Anna and the
Earl Marischal, enacting the deferred consummation which would eventually finalise the marriage but which, in not ruling out its re-performance,
hints at the representation at the heart of royal marriage and identity.

This moment of deferred consummation, and the way it would later
be recalled by English Jacobean marriage masques, illuminates the performances of Anna and Keith as bride and groom. The masque most
obviously brought to mind by this structure is *Hymenaei*, itself a ceremony
of deferred consummation. Revealingly, *Hymenaei*'s main conceit used
the symbol of marriage for the territorial and political union of Scotland
and England under James I, and referred both to the Howard–Essex
match it celebrated and to the founding royal union between James and
Anna sixteen years earlier. When *Hymenaei* reassessed the Scoto-Danish
marriage, in a self-conscious masque which operated as 'an extended
apologia for ritual', Jonson called on tropes shared between specific courtly
performances.[3] Of course such back-referencing is the reason for the
similarities between the two ceremonies, and points up the intertextuality
of aristocratic ritual. It also suggests, however, that the staging of a masque
such as *Hymenaei* was merely an extension of the role-playing at the heart
of the proxy ceremony.

Such role-playing is nowhere more evident than in the roles of the
bride and groom, played in Jonson's masque by transvestite male actors
and in the proxy marriage by Anna and Keith. Taking the monarch's
role upon himself, George Keith occupied a heightened position used
primarily to effect royal marriages, where, since the ceremonies were
usually conducted in the bride's court, her presence was necessary but

the authority of the groom could be transferred to an impersonator. Since the Earl's identity remained intact during the civil marriage ceremony, his performance was in fact closer to the 'personation' demanded of a masquer than to the assumption of a different identity undertaken by a professional actor. Such shared performativity of proxy and monarch, while perpetuating sovereign power, also acted as a threatening demonstration of the transferable nature of royal identity. As in both the Danish ceremony and later English masques, the need to impersonate the king and bridegroom was caused by James VI's withdrawal from performance, a stance which would become a feature of his career. This sustained withdrawal throughout James's reign suggests that the pattern of the proxy maps on to his own performance career more naturally than does that of the romance quest hero which, I suggest, he attempted to claim for himself.

Of the two main protagonists of the Danish civil marriage ceremony, therefore, Marischal took an identity upon himself, while Anna performed her own. As far as the Danish plan for the ceremony was concerned (and there is no evidence to confirm that it was carried out), Anna is rather written out of the proceedings, given a utopian representation of silent passivity befitting the nature of the early modern queen consort and bride. Yet despite this, Anna's physical presence and participation in the state marriage service prefigures her active relationship to performance in the English court. In her ceremonial creation of queenship Anna's presence and her husband's absence established a pattern that would run throughout their careers.

There are further good reasons for attending to Anna's marriage celebrations, as they are helpful in understanding her performances in both Scotland and England. The influence of both her Danish and Scottish backgrounds on the totality of her career can perhaps be best understood though Louise O. Fradenburg's articulation of the nature of the early modern queen consort. Necessarily foreign, initiated into sovereignty through marriage, the consort moved between courts, bringing with her the influences and material traces of her previous culture, and for this reason Anna's career cannot properly be understood without a consideration of the rituals and entertainments of the late sixteenth-century Danish and Scottish courts.[4] Although both James and Anna were distanced from English culture, Anna's difference was intensified still further by the convoluted process of cultural transmission from Denmark, through Scotland to England; her career cannot be read only from the vantage point of its final location but should instead be seen in totality. The trajectory of the royal female body within Anna's journeys was conceptualised through the male-authored articulation of the romance quest. This trope, found initially in the performances and documentation of the 1589–90 journey of James VI from Scotland to Denmark to 'rescue' his wife-by-proxy from heavy seas, governed Anna's representation within Scottish court culture. The motif of the romance quest addressed the movement of the aristocratic woman through the spaces of court and nation as part of the networks of courtly exchange instanced in the negotiations of royal marriage. Furthermore, it fashioned the markers of performance which created the identity of the queen consort in both her home and marital court. To begin the task of assessing this representation, it is necessary first to switch our attention from Anna to James, and to his actions following the proxy wedding.

In late autumn 1590, shortly after the proxy marriage ceremony was successfully completed, James VI got word of an unexpected delay to his bride's journey to Scotland and embarked upon an undertaking anomalous in both the history and the historiography of his life. Faced with insurmountable seas and the potential destruction of their ships, the Danes had taken shelter on a part of the Norwegian coast under Danish control. Frustrated, James took the remarkable decision to fetch Anna himself, braving the Baltic's winters seas in a gesture which startles commentators accustomed to the image of James as a timorous man.[5] Though out of character for its protagonist, both the act and its documentation had all the components of the literary romance quest. The underlying pattern of James's journey is that of the prince's voyage over perilous seas to a distant and enchanted land to claim his prize, avoiding the malevolence of both Danish and Scottish witches. This model is found in literary form in Jason's voyage 'to *Colchos* in the Galley that was first devisde in *Greece*, / Upon a sea as then unknowen, to fetch the golden fleece'.[6] The statement in which James declared his reasons for his departure from Edinburgh is itself also a reinscription of the heroic quest of romance: 'for as to my awne nature, God is my witnes, I could have abstenit langair nor the weill of my patrie could have permitted'.[7] James, the monarch sacrificing himself to the adventure of matrimony for the good of the nation, figured himself as the active, questing warrior-hero whose sexuality is directed not by personal desire but by the common weal, a sentiment echoed in his verse on his Danish journey in which he presented himself as under the control of God's will – 'to eschue his destinie in no man's hands it lies' – an intelligent stance for a king with little personal inclination towards marriage.[8]

The motif of the romance quest common to the documentation of James VI's journey and to the ensuing performances in Denmark and Scotland was closely tied to Anna's representation in Stuart court ritual. Found both in James's self-representation and, as I discuss below, in court performance, the ways in which this romance narrative was reconfigured shows how this voyage and its gendered components were contained within the Stuart court's communal self-expression. Identifying Denmark as the other of the Scottish court and the repository of exotic feminine forces, such a reworking of the romance trope was an attempt to assimilate and defuse the threat of the foreign royal woman, which had perhaps intensified in the aftermath of the rule of the French-educated Catholic Mary Stuart. Such perceptions of the nature and role of the queen consort defined the parameters within and beyond which Anna herself could operate.

James VI's stance as the questing romance hero was echoed in his adoption of the role of 'raging Roland' in 'A Dier at her M:ties desyer', one of his *Amatoria*, Petrarchan love verses which fall comically short of their intended ideal and which Anna, who in 1589 as yet spoke no Scots, would not have been able to read.[9] James's pose as the romantic lover was again that of the ideal Renaissance prince, the private manifestation of the public role of the monarch sacrificed to marriage, and he went on to fulfil this constructed role in his quest to rescue his endangered beloved. Sailing from Edinburgh on 22 October 1589, in a journey which was the logical outcome of the pressing Scottish political situation and of the roles James had chosen to perform, he was sighted off the Norwegian coast at Flekkerøy seven days later.[10] It is true to say, however, that the Scottish King's self-representation as questing hero stemmed as much from shifting perceptions of marriage itself as from his own need to refigure his marital reluctance into the sacrifice of the benevolent monarch. The gendered quest motif which James called upon was connected with the discourses of early modern marriage. Post-Reformation conduct books rejected the Pauline view of marriage as only marginally superior to damnation, and sought to ensconce it within a discourse of heroism; marriage, wrote Alexander Niccholes 'is an adventure, for whosoever marries, adventures; he adventures his peace, his freedom, his liberty, his body; yea, and sometimes his soul too'.[11] Though she denies the concept of a monolithic Protestant discourse of companionate marriage, Mary Beth Rose has concluded that the female marital adventurer was elided from these texts, which existed primarily to emphasise masculine courage.[12] What is more, James's ocean 'venture' bore a strong relation to the perceived commercial heroism of the first colonialist ventures to exploit the 'New World'. Marriage, it would seem, and royal marriage in particular, was an explicit negotiation of danger and threat, commercial in the commonplace commodification of the bride in negotiations and heroic in the actions of the groom. This gendered trope of the marriage quest is embedded within the performances created by James's marital exploit. Interesting in its own right for its relationship to the cultivation of chivalric myths by Elizabeth I, the southern female monarch to whose throne James aspired, the fashioning of the Scottish monarch as the questing hero also reveals the perception of Anna of Denmark as queen consort within Scottish court performance. For if James VI was inscribed as the sanctified warrior-king, what scope did this leave for female self-representation? What representational strategy portrayed the object of the quest, the wife?

The immediate conclusion would seem to be that there was relatively little room for feminine agency in the entertainments surrounding Anna's marriage. In general these spectacles displayed Anna as the passive prize of the quest, and her spectatorship as conforming to courtly perceptions of queenship. However, one moment during James's voyage uncovers the tensions in such representation. On reaching his new bride, the King continued to play out his self-scripted roles; David Moysie records that, when he finally arrived at Oslo, James ran to Anna 'with buites and all', in a display of energetic masculinity fitting to both the impatient lover and hero.[13] Yet on this occasion James's role-playing was threatened with unmasking when Anna refused to play her part:

> His Majestie myndit to give the Queine a kisse efter the Scotis faschioun at meiting, quhilk scho refusit as not being the forme of hir countrie. Marie, efter a few wordis priuely spokin betuix his Majestie and hir, thair past familiaretie and kisses.[14]

Depending on interpretation, Moysie paints either a picture of blushing female chastity or a less attractive image of a woman persuaded to concede to the demands of her new 'lord'.[15] Although, as has been noted, this incident formed the sole expression of Anna's will in the documentation of her marriage, even this rare glimpse is revealing. As Moysie implies, Anna's rejection of James's advances resulted from a clash of culturally determined manners. Yet it also prefigures Anna's later, more meaningful rejections of her husband; as the example of Frances and Catherine Howard in *Love Restored* would suggest, the refusal to perform would, paradoxically, resurface as an integral part of Anna's performance career and those of Jacobean courtly women in general. Whether in this particular instance Anna was adhering to Danish custom, feigning feminine modesty or enacting true shyness, it is significant that her will found its sole documented expression in a gesture of non-co-operation. In general, however, the narrative image of the queen consort as 'reward', the necessary outcome of that of the king as questing hero, shaped the entertainments which celebrated her entrance into Scottish queenship and, as I suggest, it also resonated through later English performances.[16]

However, before it is possible to arrive at an understanding of these later performances, it is necessary to assess Anna's experience in the Danish court. The court of Frederick II and Sophia of Denmark into which Anna was born in December 1574 contributed to her sense of queenship and offered a specific model of royal femininity which was a central influence on the young girl who initially refused to co-operate with her new husband. Raised by her grandparents at the court of Mecklenburg, Anna's early education remains somewhat obscure. However, she was certainly educated in German (the Danish courtly language), vernacular Danish and Latin, as the account of the 1590 Edinburgh entry reveals when it describes the Netherbow tableau as 'spokin in Latyne becaus the queane understood na Scotis'.[17] The appointment of a French schoolmaster in March 1589 confirms that Anna had begun to learn French to communicate with James (French was also her language of choice with her close friend Henrietta, Lady Huntly, in Scotland) and demonstrates the existence of an educative structure within the Danish court.[18] This, and the fact that Anna would also learn both Scots and English (advancing rapidly in the former), dispels preconceptions of her lack of education and ability, and implies that she benefited from the educational structures available for royal women in the Danish court.[19] Beyond such information, little is known about the extent of female education or the influence of women within Danish court circles. However, one clear instance of female political and cultural commitment in the Danish court is to be found in Anna's mother, Queen Sophia.

Sophia's career shows clear evidence of her cultural and political involvement. In addition to patronising Vedel's publication of Danish ballads, supporting the astronomer Tycho Brahe's investigations (to a greater extent than had Frederick II before his death) and visiting his observatory on Hven, the 'mighty queen and regent of Denmark' of the Danish marriage account was also involved in a long-term struggle to rule as independent regent during the minority of her son, Christian IV, an effort which perhaps constituted a pattern for Anna's own later attempt for the English regency in 1617.[20] Despite Sophia's failure to obtain the regency, the joint authority she held with a specially established regency council, headed by Niels Kås, was, given the recent Danish practice of electing a regent from the male *rigsraåd* or parliament, something of a victory.[21] In the light of this struggle, it is perhaps revealing that, in her correspondence with James VI, Sophia should chose to style herself as 'Regina'.[22]

Anna certainly seems to have been influenced by Sophia in these broad terms of cultural and political engagement. She was perhaps working within the model of Danish femininity adopted by her mother when she actively created her Scottish court as 'a centre for contact with Denmark', manipulating her political and personal favour with Christian IV, interceding for Scottish prisoners and making recommendations for filling certain posts.[23] In the light of Sophia's influence on her daughter, it would seem logical to look there for precedents for her later performances. However, although Mara Wade's research has made inroads into the uncharted territory of performance at the Danish court, at this point all that can be said is that Danish noblewomen were, on occasions, the instigators, although perhaps not the organisers, of court entertainments; the Danish account mentions that on 5 November 'the well-born Fru Ide remarked that [Bishop Jens Nilssøn] should arrange something for the entertainment of her ladyship [Princess Anna]'.[24] The account, however, never expands on this incident and its outcome is never revealed.

Anna was married again to James, this time in his presence, on 23 November 1589 in Oslo, and the couple left to return to Denmark by land in December. They stayed in Denmark for the remainder of the winter, leaving on 21 April 1590 after attending the marriage of Anna's sister Elizabeth to the Duke of Brunswick and arriving back at Leith on 1 May.[25] Anna's coronation as Queen of Scotland took place on 17 May 1590, accompanied by Danish frustration at its delay, and was followed on 19 May by her official entry into Edinburgh.[26] These events, and the continuing definition of the queen consort and bride through the ritual of state and church, offer ways of finding Anna's constructed identity. In unravelling such constructions it is important to bear in mind the discourse of early modern queenship. When she married James, Anna became imaginatively aligned with the dowry which she brought to Scotland; furthermore, although a gift in herself, the queen was also the medium through which the marital adventurer attained the deferred prize of the heir. But beyond the tangible gifts of money and heirs, Anna was also the passive bearer of yet another, equally valuable reward; her marriage forged international networks of political, dynastic, cultural and religious bonds between the courts, links more enduring than the quickly spent dowry.

Anna's coronation and entry: creating the Queen of Scots

The coronation ritual which defined Anna of Denmark as queen consort of Scotland took place in Holyrood Abbey several months after her various Danish marriage services and was followed by her presentation to the Scottish nation in her entrance into Edinburgh.[27] Following from Anna's construction in the proxy wedding and James VI's own self-fashioning as romance hero, the Scottish state and civic ceremonials contained instances of representative strategies, and, perhaps most importantly, female performance which were to have a profound influence on Anna's career.

The impact of both Scottish and Danish court cultures on Anna belies their long-standing marginalisation from the mainstream of early modern cultural studies. It has often been noted that Henrietta Maria imported concepts and practices of female performance from France, but less attention has been paid to the Danish and Scottish precedents which informed Anna's masquing in the Jacobean court. Scottish court and civic practice had a particular impact. Despite the preconception that Scotland was not a performance culture (and the misguided belief that its single theatrical expression was Lindsay's *Satyre of the Thrie Estaitis*), early modern Scotland in fact had a flourishing aristocratic culture, intensely open to continental and especially French influence, and a relatively vibrant court culture. For example, the court of Mary Stuart hosted the first 'British' *magnificence* of the Renaissance, and James VI was himself the author of a masque for the 1588 marriage of the Marquis of Huntly and, in one noted instance in 1599, a supporter of a touring company of English actors against the objections of the kirk.[28] Both Mary Stuart's involvement and the documented existence of the female poet Christian Lindsay, who was a member of the Montgomerie circle and referred to in James VI's own verses, highlight issues of female courtly education and cultural engagement within the Scottish court.[29]

Perhaps most importantly for my purposes, early modern Scotland was a relatively more open site of female performance than contemporary England. In fact female performance is documented throughout the distinct phases of early modern Scottish court culture which preceded the 1589–90

Stuart marriage. Accounts for the progress entertainments of James IV and Margaret Tudor, for example, detail proletarian female dance, and an entry for November 1501 records a payment to 'the madinnis of Forres that com to Ternway and sang'.[30] Non-aristocratic women also occasionally performed professionally in the court of Mary Stuart; James VI's mother employed two female jesters, Nichola la Jardinière and Janet Mouche, whose names hint at the extensive French influence on Renaissance Scotland's flourishing domestic court culture.[31] Sited within an official discourse of praise and royal acceptance, such entertainments operated outside the greater restriction on female performance in contemporary English practice. What is more, Mary Stuart's court, influenced by the intense political and theatrical female engagement of the Valois court, also sanctioned the involvement of aristocratic women in Twelfth Night masquing and the playing of the Queen of the Bean. Such entertainments provide a striking example of female court performance and of the Scottish court's occasional practice of cross-dressing. In January 1565–66, for example, a banquet for the French ambassadors was followed by a masque in which Mary and her women presented daggers to their guests while 'cled in men's apperrell', an incident of Scottish courtly aristocratic female performance and elite transvestism which was extremely significant for the 1594 Stirling baptismal tournament, below.[32] It seems, therefore, that early modern Scottish culture had a frail tradition of silent performance by female courtiers and of a vocal one by women from beyond the nobility. What is less clear, though, is whether elite performance, which crossed the barriers of transvestism, also crossed those of speech or song.

Early modern Scotland's relatively liberated female performance fed directly into the formation of Anna of Denmark's career in the Scottish Stuart court. Given that so many of the documented instances of female performance took place in royal entertainments, Anna's Edinburgh coronation and entry are fertile ground for further investigation. While women performers from beyond the courtly classes were found in the pageants for her entrance into the city, the coronation was an example of Anna's own performance in court ritual. Once the clergy's objections to the proposed Sunday coronation were overcome, James processed into the church at Holyrood, followed by Anna, who was accompanied by the English ambassador, Robert Bowes, the Countess of Mar and other Danish and Scottish nobles.[33] The rather straightforward coronation ceremony not only tells us about Anna's depiction as queen consort but, when considered against her later London coronation, as at the end of this chapter, is revealed as an influential early performance. In isolation, however, the Scottish coronation is equally important for its dependence upon the body of the queen consort for its ritual meaning.

The importance of Anna's coronation is apparent in the religious controversy which it caused. Apart from the problematic Sunday coronation, the clergy's main objection was to the ritual anointing of the Queen, which kirk ministers regarded as idolatrous. The King prevailed, but the presiding minister, Robert Bruce, made it clear that he was performing James's orders against his own will.[34] A surviving Scottish account describes this moment:

> The preiching being endit, the Duik of Lennox, and the Lord Hamiltoun . . . and Maister Robert Bruce and Mr Dauid Lindsay, tua ministers, goes, all four togither, to the Kingis Majestie, that, according to his publict directioun, to be given to theme, they might performe that quhilk wes injoynit to theme of befoir, quhilk wes to proceid unto the act of Coronatione.
>
> Therefter Maister Robert Bruce declaires that quhilk wes directit be his Majestie to be done concerning the ceremonies of Coronatione.[35]

There then followed the cause of the controversy, the ritual anointing of the Queen's body:

> The Countis of Mar immediatlie cumis to the Quenis Majestie, and taks hir richt arme, and openes the craige of hir gowne, and lyes bake ane certaine pairt of boithe.
>
> Mester Robert Bruce immediatly puires furthe upon thois pairtis of hir breist and arme, of quhilk the clothes wer remowit, a bonye quantitie of oyll; quhilk's pairtis efter the annoyntment therof, wer coverit with sum quhyt silke.[36]

Anna then retired, emerging in new robes of purple velvet and white taffeta to mark her altered condition.[37]

Anna's performance here indicates the extent to which the ceremonies of marriage and crowning were intertwined. Her coronation, like her marriage, was the public display of the legal fact of queenship; hence the Scottish coronation was referred to as a 'mareage', and for her later 1603 London coronation, during which James's relationship to his nation was indicated by placing a ring on his wedding finger, Anna was described as wearing her hair loose like that of a virgin bride.[38] Anna's elevation to queenship by union with James related complexly to his own future self-construction as metaphoric husband to the nation, since, as his 'actual' wife, she was placed in a necessary but unacknowledgeable position which perhaps threatened the conceptual base of James's power.[39] However, the coronation ritual clearly defined the queen consort's sovereignty as dependent upon that of the king. Holyrood Abbey became a theatricalised space in which James was pre-eminent, his power emphasised in the movement of the crown and sceptre from the King, through the ranks of the most exalted lords (a reminder of the consort's dependence on masculine power structures), before reaching Anna.[40] Hierarchical seating created a symbolic order similar to that of the later English court masque, and movement was used to signal distinct states of being; for example, after Anna's crowning, she was raised to a higher seat. As this suggests and as the Scottish account records, the coronation rendered Anna intensely corporeal; 'hir Majestie wes raisit up aff the saitt [. . .] and be convoy of the Duke of Lennox and Lord Hamiltoun wes brocht unto ane heicher place'.[41] Such passivity was also mirrored in Anna's silent acquiescence to the coronation oath, during which she is described as signalling her affirmation by 'twitching [touching] the Bible with her richt hand' after the oath was read to her, a physical gesture of submission to the written law of king and kirk.[42]

Anna's sacramental anointing as queen was controversial primarily for its implications of royal divine right. James VI attempted to use the display to reinforce the doctrine of the divine selection of the monarchy, sanctified through ritual anointing, but Bruce's disclaimer and the absence of prayers during this part of the ceremony demonstrate the ministers' attempts to empty the ritual of such quasi-sacramental significance. This struggle was staged over, or rather through, the body of the queen; the physical display of the queen's passive body in the coronation positioned that body as the site of dispute between the conflicting ideologies of king and kirk. Royal and clerical will converged on and in the reified body of the queen.

The disputed performance of the monarch's will over the passive female body illuminates later Stuart performances; the sacramental exposure of Anna's body to its display to king and court was strikingly similar to her later performance in Jonson's *Masque of Queens*. This shared bodily display was also the erotic submission of the queen to the king, although, as I argue in chapter 3, this passivity is overturned in *Queens*. Perhaps more importantly though, such an erotic submission enacted in the display of the female body destabilised the coronation's idealisation of the crowned queen. In the baring of Anna's skin the coronation's gendered vision of sanctified queenship prefigured the definition of the female masquers through their eroticised bodies, and through a display of their sexuality. In this sense the coronation's legitimate exposure of the royal female body eroticised the queen consort and complicated any simplistic reading of Anna's representation in this ritual. The queen's body was the locus of ideological conflict, and itself variously interpretable.

The problematics of this bodily text are evident in the variant readings which opposing factions imposed upon Anna's corporeal assent to the coronation oath. There are striking discrepancies in Bruce's articulation of the demands of the populace upon their queen, implicated in the oath to which she was to swear. The Scottish description includes Bruce's statement, 'we creave from your Majestie the confessione of the faith and religion quhilk we professe', absent from a Danish account which avoids representing a religious conformity which Anna had not in fact embraced.[43] Again we see the royal woman as a disputed site, the text through and on which conflicting ideologies were expressed. Yet, passive as she undoubtedly was, Anna's silent participation offered her also the opportunity of a reinterpretation in her second coronation in England thirteen years later, in which such conditions of bodily passivity and religious conformity were turned around to suit the purposes of the woman who was by then the queen of both Scotland and England.

In 1590, however, in her role as the new Scottish Queen, Anna was presented to the nation in the entry into Edinburgh. As a civic ritual the entry complements the royal self-presentation (on James's part at least) of the coronation ceremony and reveals the dynamics of queenship, and in doing so substantially expands accepted notions of female performance in early modern Scotland. This female performance, and its correlative of the staging of blackness, are both important precedents for later English performances and importantly revealing in their own right.

The 1590 Edinburgh entry followed a similar route to that established by the entries of Mary Stuart in 1561 and James VI in 1579.[44] Entering the city at the West Port, her coach surrounded by men dressed as 'moors', Anna processed to Bow Street, the Butter Tron and the Tolbooth, to the Mercat Cross, entered St Giles's Kirk, proceeded to the Salt Tron and the Netherbow and finally completed her journey at Holyrood Palace.[45] The positioning and significance of the pageants which greeted the new Scottish Queen also owed a great deal to those constructed for her predecessors; all three entries shared pageants at the Tolbooth, Mercat Cross and St Giles's, the Salt Tron and the Netherbow. However, while Anna's entry shared a dualistic representation of such royal pageantry, balancing panegyric with the reassertion of the monarch's duties to uphold the city's rights in the way that previous entries had, the 1590 entry differed from those of James VI and Mary Stuart in the distinct negotiation of power necessary for a queen consort. For example, the opening pageant of the angelic child who descended from a globe clutching a bible and the keys to the city is suggestive of both the power and the dangers of sovereignty:

> You shall have the power to do to us
> whatever law and justice suggests to you
> and to bring justice to all men.[46]

In contrast, the Butter Tron pageant, which involved female performers, expressed the mutual contract and obligation of sovereign rule in terms of maternal shelter – 'We will treat you as our mother / And you shall be our brave refuge.'[47] Pageants such as those of the holy woman at the West Bow and the female virtues at the Tolbooth were designed to flatter, but they also placed a burden of action and decorum at the feet of the consort, addressing her as a political creature and demanding her intercession in the affairs of the nation.[48] The speech of the holy woman placed the burden of the creation of the heir at Anna's feet and clarified her status as intercessor between people and king:

> You are to remember that God has created you, [...]
> you will bear royal children with honour,
> and also become a woman of intelligence
> whose virtues will shine both inwardly and outwardly.
> You will inspire your lord to good deeds
> and convert the people to the fear of God.[49]

Later in the entry, recalling the pageant of Solomon's display of wisdom in James VI's 1579 entry, the 1590 East Port pageant of the Queen of Sheba's visit to Solomon further clarified the consort's intermediary position. Submitting to the superior wisdom of the king, Anna's dependence upon her husband's sovereignty reworked the motif of Solomon which was to become an integral aspect of James's self-presentation.

As noted, the 1590 Edinburgh entry had a documented female presence. Johnston describes the nine muses at the Butter Tron: 'Thairefter com to a skaffald at the butter trowne qlk was plenisht with the fairest young wemen of the toun coistlie apparellit with Orgenis playing and musitionis singing, qr ane bairne maid ane Latine oresoun.'[50] The Danish account also notes the performance of 'nine worthy daughters of the citizenry [...] They were most splendidly dressed and they had beautiful gilded books in their hands. When her majesty arrived they curtsied deeply and a young person addressed her majesty on their behalf.'[51] The 'young person' has been identified as the son of John Craig, who took on the role of chorus, and whose participation implies that female speech was not permissible.[52] These boys, as young as eight according to the Danish account, were the children of the citizenry; youth and social position perhaps freed them from restrictions which may have operated on the aristocracy.[53] The silence of the women is contradicted, however, in *The Receiving of James the Sixt*, which notes that the women 'sung verie sweete musicke'.[54] Despite these discrepancies, the tradition of female singers in early modern Scotland suggests that female performance was possible within the kind of civic pageantry in which these women, the daughters of citizenry, took part. Although not offering comprehensive answers to the question of Scottish noblewomen's performance, the entry does demonstrate that, in her initial experience of Scottish pageantry, Anna was exposed to female performance.

In addition the entry also shows that Anna witnessed another means of representing women in performance. Transvestite boy actors formed a striking presence in the entry: 'At the tolbuith was young bairnes on ane skaffald in wemenes cleithing representing peax plentie, polacie – Iustice Liberalitie and temperance qr euerie ane schew thair selfis and Naturallie in Latyne.'[55] Their speeches presented Anna with a male performance of familiar female virtues, closely connected with the Queen's political involvement: Virtue reminded her to 'be virtuous and pious towards your subjects'.[56] While not mentioning the Tolbooth transvestites, the Danish account does, however, describe the Mercat Cross pageant of Bacchus and Ceres which involved 'four young lads in maiden's clothing' and the pageant of the astronomer at the West Bow, in which the transvestism is revealed to the reader only by the actor's description of himself as a 'holy woman'.[57] From this evidence it would seem that, as in England, transvestite actors in Scotland enjoyed a less controversial relationship with speech than did 'actual' female performers.

Anna's own participation in this entry seems to have been primarily as the recipient of Edinburgh's demands to its new queen consort. Certainly Anna showed little of the agency demonstrated by Elizabeth I in her coronation entry of 1559, although her passivity might be partly attributed to the very different demands on a queen consort than on a queen regnant. Such differences are perhaps most clear in the pageant of the Queen of Sheba's visit to Solomon, which was informed with both Anna's own foreign royalty and her dependence on James. Yet, while her dependency was made clear, her own royalty and her responsibilities within the contract of rule with the city were also emphasised.

The liminality of Anna's position was perhaps, however, most obviously depicted in the escort of blackened performers who surrounded her carriage. Within the romance genre the exotic other is figured through femininity and through blackened skin, the marker of another group marginalised from the centre of mainstream culture. Although not novel in Scots court performance (almost a century before Anna's arrival in Scotland the court of James IV employed such imagery to express the problematic relationship of the Scots to their English queen, Margaret Tudor), blackness, enacted by 'actual' black performers or by the impersonation of blackness by white performers, is a marker of difference closely connected to Anna's performance career.[58] And, of course, images of blackness were not confined to the Scottish court but surfaced most forcefully in Jonson's masques of *Blackness* and *Beauty*, problematic because of the over-intimate association between this imagery and the person of the Queen. However, Anna's liminal status as both woman and foreigner is also signalled very clearly in these earlier performances through the consistent presence of blackness.

The 'moors' who cleared a path for Anna's coach through the crowd on her way to Holyrood are relatively mysterious figures. However, although it has long been known that most of the men were not really 'moors' at all, the Danish account reveals that one of the figures, the leader of the group who carried a ceremonial sword, was in fact a 'real' black man.[59] This assertion is backed up by the reference to 'Ane Moir' in Anna's household accounts of February 1590 and by the presence of a black performer at Stirling in 1594, more of which below.[60] The Danish account, distanced from Scottish performance conventions and in awe of the 'absolutely real and native blackamoor', strips down the markers through which blackness was performed:

> These people were masked with faces of lead, iron and copper which were made so cleverly that it was not easy to tell that they were made of these materials, so natural were they. Some had blackened their faces so that their heads were just like those of blackamoors, but an absolute real and native blackamoor was their leader.[61]

The Danish account is so revealing simply because the commentator's eye seems not to have been trained in the same way as the Scottish observers, who would have perhaps been more accustomed to both the presence of black performers in the Scottish court and the symbolic performance of blackness. Through this description, however, the Danish observer uncovers the conventional nature of the performance of blackness in much the same way as the descriptions cited above reveal the presence of women or transvestites.

A brief consideration of the most contemporary examples of the performance of black and blackened players in Scotland shows how such associations clung to Anna and indeed were taken with her into England. The history of black performance and the performance of blackness in Scottish court entertainments establishes precedents for the 'moors' of Anna's entry. Most contemporary and intriguing is an apocryphal incident in Norway during the Stuart marriage celebrations. Both Ethel Carleton Williams and Kim F. Hall report an unsubstantiated incident in Oslo on the day of the wedding. Williams, in an unexamined expression of colonialist discourse, states that

> James arranged a curious spectacle for the entertainment of the people of Oslo. By his orders four young Negroes danced naked in the snow in front of the royal carriage, but the cold was so intense that they died a little later of pneumonia.[62]

Hall unpacks the racial assumptions of the description and performance, yet evidence for it remains purely anecdotal.[63] Although the fact that this incident is mentioned by neither the Scottish nor Danish marriage accounts does not guarantee that it did not take place, I have been able to trace the incident only as far as John Gade's 1927 *Christian IV*.[64] Gade also offers no source for his information but makes a further, unsubstantiated, assertion that James brought the exploited black performers over to Denmark in his ships. It is possible to make a suggestion such as this partly because of the proven presence of black performers in Scotland and, more significantly, because of the currency of the association of blackness with Scotland itself. I would suggest that it is this correlation between Scotland, femininity and blackness which really needs to be unpacked.

The anecdote of the doomed Oslo performers is useful in that it emphasises the high-profile presence of black or blackened performers in Anna's career (both English and Scottish) and in particular in the 1590 Edinburgh entry. The performance of female royalty in the entry or in later court celebrations was imaginatively linked with the performance of an otherness marked through racial difference. Such a link is substantiated through the strong presence of blackness as a motif in Scottish royal performance, notably in Mary Stuart's 1558 marriage celebration when 'moors' served a similar function of crowd control and again in her 1561 royal entry, when fifty townsmen in black masks escorted her coach. Unfortunately neither performance can demonstrate the presence of 'real' black participants.[65] That this motif was apparently not included in James

VI's 1579 royal entry intensifies the connection between blackness and femininity as markers of otherness and difference intrinsic to the perception of the royal woman in Scotland.

As far as Anna's 1590 entry was concerned, this remarkable form of crowd control was associated only with the alien figure of the queen consort, and this points to the specific associations which existed in Scotland between blackness and royal femininity. Such associations emerged from one of the founding myths of Scottish national identity. An early chronicle figures Scota, the daughter of the Egyptian pharaoh Chencres (the Greek term 'skotos' translates as 'darkness'), as the founding figure of Scotland.[66] In donning black make-up in the later *Masque of Blackness* therefore, Anna was not merely performing her difference from the English court into which she had travelled but was in fact embodying a specifically feminine and royal difference that was intrinsically connected to and defined against a sense of Scottishness. In bringing such layerings of other cultural identities to the heart of the English court, this masque perhaps also complicated a sense of the Jacobean court's purely 'English' identity, connecting it too with a royal and foreign femininity.[67]

In addition to bringing the presence of a black man to our attention, the anonymous Danish account also provides significant information about the kind of performance in which this man and his companions were involved. While Scottish commentators merely describe the 'moors' as dancing, this foreign observer remarked that these men 'had been assigned a particular and special gait in imitation of various sorts of people'.[68] This brief comment denaturalises the dance, emphasises that these men were involved in a performance and, in describing Scottish dances apparently unfamiliar in Denmark, also demonstrates the specificity of early modern dance. Unfamiliarity meant that the Danish spectator went into greater detail than most about the kind of movement he observed; some 'moors' danced jerkily, some low to the ground, and some with their heads down in disregard of their audience. By dancing in this way, the 'moors'' gait became a means of crowd control; more effective than violence, it was the physical performance of the aesthetic violence of difference, taken into the bodies of the performers and in conscious violation of the conventions of courtly movement. As we have seen, to dance difference is not to dance incompetently but unconventionally; the movements of the 'moors'' dance were associated with the antimasque dances and were imaginatively equivalent to their bodily performance of blackness.

Such a bodily marker of difference kept order by maintaining the symbolic performance space around Anna as she moved through the city.

In one sense the 'moors' were antimasque performers who presaged Anna's appearance as the transcendent vision of the idealised court, from which the spectators were distanced. And yet, at the focal point of this spectacle of difference, the Queen presented an ambiguous figure of order and threat whose otherness had to be assimilated into Scottish society. Marked by a display of racial difference, Anna was also positioned as an intercessor between king and subjects as the white audience identified with their blonde queen over the heads of the performance of blackness.

Focusing closely upon the physicality of the performers' bodies, their short, tight-fitting trousers, their blackened skin and their copious adornment, the Danish account also expresses the erotics of the male body in performance. These men's blackened bodies were jewel-laden showcases for the Scottish nation's wealth. John Burel's commemorative poem describes

> the Moirs ... Quha dois inhabit in the ynde:
> Leving thair land and dwelling place,
> For to do honour to hir Grace.[69]

The seamen's tunics worn by the performers established the conceit of the submission of the exotic to the authority of the Scottish throne. This same conceit – the crossing of great distances by black performers to honour the monarchy – is also that of *Blackness*, where it was transferred to the blackened bodies of Anna and her ladies. Though by no means original, what is striking (and clearer still from the Stirling banquet entertainment, below), is the extent to which *Blackness* called on Anna's previous performances, refiguring her position within them to assert her performative and cultural agency. The English masque saw Anna's emergence from performative passivity; she took the marker of difference upon herself in order to assert her own oppositional stance in a statement of female cultural agency. Blackness was unproblematic when associated with the body of the lower-class male performer, but was subversive when assumed by the female aristocratic body. This statement gains in impact when seen in the context of Anna's career, within which performances and motifs bear an intertextual relationship to each other.

The next significant phase of courtly festivals associated with Anna took place in 1594, for the baptism of her first child, Henry Stuart. In the entertainments surrounding the birth of the heir (one of the defining moments of a queen consort's life) the motifs of blackness, femininity and cross-dressing again loom large in the figures of blackened male performers and cross-dressed knights.

The Stirling baptismal celebrations:
the queen as mother and Medea

In 1594, four years after her marriage, Anna fulfilled her marital role and delivered a healthy son to the king and the nation. 'The right Excellent, High, and Magnanime, FREDERIK HENRIE, HENRIE FREDERIK, by the grace of God, Knight and Barron of Renfrew: Lord of the Yles, Erll of Carrike, Duke of Rosay, Prince and great Steward of Scotland' and future heir to the throne of England, was born on 19 February 1594.[70] Henry was baptised at Stirling on 30 August 1594, after prolonged delays caused by the total reconstruction of the Chapel Royal and the absence of ambassadors from the English court. Grand festivities along the lines of continental *magnificences*, though dogged by financial and practical restraints, accompanied the baptism, scripted and arranged by Anna's secretary, William Fowler, and by Patrick Lesley, Lord of Lendores. Fowler also kept a record of the events in his *True Reportarie of the Baptisme of the Prince of Scotland*, a text which, unsurprisingly given that Anna had just provided an unstable nation with an heir, documents the entertainments' preoccupation with the perceptions of royal marriage and of the queen consort.

Despite its rushed and improvised air, Fowler's festival was designed to signal the magnificence of the Scottish court and advance James VI's succession to the English throne, and both Scots and anglicised contemporary variants of the text exist. It is not insignificant that it was the absence of the Earl of Sussex, the English special ambassador, which delayed the christening; when he did arrive he was prominent in the ceremony, carrying the baby to the altar. Fowler's detailed description conveyed the politicised theatricality of the ritual. Once James VI was seated in the chapel, the ambassadors were taken to the 'Princes Chalmer of presence where the Prince was lying on his bed of Estate, richly decored, and wrought with brodered work, containing the story of Hercules and his trauels', a statement of intent for the child's supposed future possession of the English throne.[71] During the ceremony of baptism the prince was passed on through a hierarchy of guardians, which was first established in the child's chamber. Held initially by the Countess of Mar (whose role was of great significance), Henry was then taken by the Duke of Lennox to Sussex (who was assisted throughout by Robert Bowes). The English officials carried the prince into the Chapel Royal under a canopy surrounded by visiting ambassadors. After sermons by the bishop of Aberdeen and Patrick Galloway, the moderator of the general assembly, and the singing of the twenty-first Psalm, the prince was returned to Sussex from 'the Mistress Nurse' for his naming.[72] The ceremony concluded with the Bishop of Aberdeen's declaration of the close ties between Scotland and the visiting states, significantly privileging those of England above the others. The court then removed to the King's Hall, where James knighted and then crowned his son. Within such a political text Anna's role must also be read in politicised terms; nowhere outside the baptism of an heir does it become clearer that the queen consort's position and status depends upon maternity. The obvious consequence of this is that Anna's representation as both queen and mother in the performances which Fowler scripted for her to watch and participate in are of the greatest importance.

Fowler's published text contains a fascinating elision, and one which concentrates attention on Anna's role in these festivities. Despite the clear advantage gained by the queen consort in keeping close connections between herself and the heir to the throne, Anna is never mentioned in connection with Henry's baptism. None of the variant texts notes either her presence or her absence from the ceremony; a plan for the ceremony does not mention her and she goes likewise unmentioned in the reports of Bowes and Sussex, the English ambassadors. Although she was prominent at the banquet held on the evening of the baptism, as far as the records of the ceremony itself show, Anna was not there.[73] Whether she was excluded from the performance or its textual record, there is no suggestion of illness on the part of the Queen (the excuse used most often to explain her absences from court events in England) and her conversion to Catholicism was still in the future: what might be the reason for her absence?[74] Although non-aristocratic mothers (at least in England) usually did not attend baptisms because they had not yet been churched (a ceremony which allowed women to re-enter church once a suitable period had elapsed since childbirth), Henry's baptism took place at about six months of age and so this reason seems unlikely.[75] However, given Anna's later conversion to Catholicism (more of which below) it is perhaps possible that she had wished to be churched and, in the light of the Catholic resonances of such an act, had been prohibited from doing so. In this case a refusal to enter the chapel for the baptism would be in line with Catholic practice. It is clear that Anna's absence from Henry's baptism was not an isolated incident, since in 1600 she was absent from Prince Charles's baptism in Holyrood Palace. It seems that such an absence might, then, be due either to a religious protest on Anna's part or to the model along which Scottish royal baptisms operated.[76]

Anna's place in the christening ritual seems to have been taken by the dowager Countess of Mar. Described by the Danish account of Anna's coronation as the woman 'who had brought up His Majesty King James of Scotland during his childhood', this proximity to the King now extended to Prince Henry and the next generation of rulers.[77] In line with Scottish court tradition, James VI had in fact entrusted the care of Henry to the Countess's son, the Earl of Mar, and the role of guardian which the Countess enacted in carrying Henry to and fro in the baptismal ritual was part of that duty. I stress the Countess's role in this ceremony because Anna's later struggle with her for custody of her son in 1603 has recently become a central aspect of a growing critical awareness of the Queen's agency.[78] Arriving at Stirling Castle to take Henry south to England in 1603, Anna was denied by the Countess, who was still acting as the child's guardian. Accounts vary, but the consensus is that Anna, then pregnant, miscarried from the force of her distress: 'The Queen flew into a violent fury, and four months gone with child as she was, she beat her own belly, so that they say she is in manifest danger of miscarriage and death.'[79] If nothing else, this moment, in another instance of Anna's bodily performance, demonstrates the importance of the heir to the consort, and highlights the significance of the Queen's absence from his baptism. What has often been elided, however, is the extent to which the baptism acted as a precedent for the later confrontation between the Queen and the Countess, and the roots of this struggle in the workings of the Scottish court. It is worth comparing Anna's later actions with her possible exclusion from the 1594 baptismal ceremony.

The baptism of a royal infant was a powerful ritual moment from which to exclude the queen, whose status was defined through her motherhood. The Countess of Mar had appropriated the foundation of Anna's authority as queen consort, either excluding her from the baptism ceremony by convention or forcing her to adopt a strategy of self-exclusion. Evidence suggests that Anna breastfed Henry, and it is significant that the issue of Henry's education becomes pressing when he is weaned from his mother and moves from the maternal space into the seemingly more political one of court society.[80] Anna's struggle for custody of her son, which began as early as 1595, and her eventual success have previously been interpreted only in terms of a clash of James VI's political ambition with his wife's maternal instinct.[81] While such impulses clearly cannot be ignored, Anna's conception of queenship and James's own response construed her actions as political: 'though he doubted nothing of her good intentions yet if some faction got strong enough, she could not hinder his boy being used against him, as he himself had been against his unfortunate mother'.[82] The Queen did not raise the same objections over the educations of her other children. This might, however, have had more to do with a factional balancing of guardians, since Elizabeth was raised by the Protestant Lord Livingston and his Catholic wife, and Charles by Alexander Seton, the future Chancellor of Scotland and a prominent church papist.[83] Whatever the case, Anna's lack of opposition does imply that there are further reasons for accepting a politicised awareness of Henry's status on the Queen's part. However, it seems to have been precisely the power of Anna's politicised maternity and her necessary proximity to the heir to the throne which, in being threatening to the King himself, demanded her exclusion from the baptism ceremony.

But what of the festivities in which Anna could and did take part, the banquet and its interlude? Given her absence from the baptism, these moments carry a greater importance, and the banquet entertainment which she watched later that day carries a particular representative burden, not least because of its female performers. Given this powerful female presence, the representational strategies used in the interlude are of the greatest significance for both those women performing and the watching queen consort. Fowler's entertainment staged the quest narrative in its visual use of maritime imagery and in the written text's reworking of this trope; the banquet entertainment embodied an image of women, and particularly of the queen consort, as the exotic, threatening other of the romance quest. Femininity and the female body itself (both watching and performing) were markers of exclusion and liminality within Scottish court culture, an association achieved partly through their juxtaposition and conflation in performance with another such marker – that of blackness. The 1594 entertainment, shedding light on Anna's status as queen consort and the conceptualisation of the female body, in particular its relationship to language and the voice, also reveals the discourses of the Stuart court's self-representation in performance.

One of the highlights of the banquet entertainment which Anna witnessed was the entrance of a tableau of goddesses upon a chariot, pulled by a 'Moore'. The presence of this performer was a hasty contrivance: the original intention was to use a lion to draw the chariot, but the plan was dropped for fear of an adverse reaction on the part of either the animal or the audience.[84] The analogy, not lost on critics, is one between blackened skin and bestial exoticism as a marker of sovereign power; the black man and the lion were used as interchangeable symbols of exotic physical strength.[85] As the 'real' black performer of Anna's 1590 entry shows, the performance of blackness was far from unknown in Scottish entertainments. The first recorded presence of black performers in Scotland dated back to 1505 and the court of James IV, where perhaps its most significant appearance was in the tournament of the Black Lady (1507 and 1508) in which a black woman, celebrated in Dunbar's 'parodic blazon' as the 'ladye with the meckle lippis', performed.[86] This exotic antithesis of courtly beauty was the prize of a tournament which juxtaposed performing slave with spectating noblewomen. Aligning himself with the exotic other against which the court defined itself, James IV fought for the Black Lady as the Black or Wild Knight: two symbols of the non-courtly and non-civilised converged, as Fradenburg sees it, to defuse courtly anxieties concerning the alien energies of femininity and of an exotic foreignness.[87] The black female performer was represented, there-fore, as something simultaneously to be striven for and vilified, a polarisation clearly posited by Dunbar in the humiliation awaiting those who fail to win the Lady's more conventional favours of having to 'cum behind and kis hir hippis'.[88]

The recurring motif of blackness in Scottish court culture contributes to the Stirling baptismal entertainment's representation of a courtly femi-ninity. The figure of the Black Lady, an early and rather heightened example of the perceived proximity of the markers of racial and sexual otherness found in sixteenth-century Scottish court performance, can illuminate the representational strategies employed in 1594 and the limi-nality to which such markers gesture. The place of ambassadorial exchange in the interaction of continental and Scottish court cultures is further evident in the impersonation of femininity and blackness of the French ambassador Monsieur de Foys at the Scottish court in 1561. The ambas-sador and his group of nobles ran at the ring 'dysguised and appareled thone half lyke women, and thother lyke strayngers, in straynge maskinge garmentes'.[89] In this, and in the instances of racial and gendered imper-sonation in the Scottish court, we can see the close approximation of the feminine and the foreign as symbolic markers of difference.

The tournament held immediately preceding Henry's christening also contained such a juxtaposition of the exotic and the feminine. Organised by Fowler and Lord Lendores (the latter also ran at the ring), this tournament costumed its participants in a manner which would, in English aristocratic performance, have degraded their noble status. The Duke of Lenox, Lord Home and Sir Robert Ker were dressed as Turks, and Fowler outlines a plan, later discarded when they failed to appear, to costume three other unnamed noblemen as 'moors'. Most striking, however, is the appearance of Lendores, Walter Scott, Lord of Buccleuch, and John Bothwell, the Abbot of Holyrood (the aristocratic holder of the abbey benefice), dressed as 'three Amazones in women's attyre, verie sumptuouslie clad'.[90] This tournament performance unpacks the intense concentration of significance within the figure of the Black Lady, as the qualities of blackness, religious diversity and femininity are dispersed throughout a group of aristocrats personating these marginalised elements of courtly culture. Yet these two performances are in dialogue, pointing to a consistent defusion of the threat of diversity through its representation within the Scots court.

Although this kind of impersonation contrasts sharply with English models of noble performance, it is important to contextualise this against a wider European background. As the adoption of moorish and Turkish disguises by Christian IV and his noblemen in the tournament for his coronation in 1596 demonstrates, the use of this kind of role-playing and its effacement of aristocratic identity was a common factor between James VI's court and that of Denmark.[91] Rejecting the English practice of performing only roles which contributed to the high standing of the noble, both James's and Christian's courts used aristocratic disguise as a means to express and defuse anxieties of divergent and threatening masculinities within a discourse of chivalry. Returning to the Scottish context of this particular moment, however, it is useful to bear in mind that the compact symbols of blackness and femininity initially encapsulated in the body of the Black Lady were dispersed throughout Fowler's tournament and, later, through the banquet interlude. Aspects, or perhaps pieces, of this emblem recurred separately throughout the baptismal entertainments rather than occurring only in a single figure. And these differences in Scottish and English courtly performance are important in distinguishing between the ideologies which governed them. Indeed, in the face of the reaction, founded on intersections of class and gender discourses, of the English courtiers to Anna's later performance in *The Masque of Blackness*, outlined in the introduction, even the unfulfilled intention of the noble impersonation of blackness in Fowler's entertainment resonates with these distinctions. In one of her pivotal English performances, therefore, Anna took upon herself the Scottish trope of royal or aristocratic disguise, in this case blackened skin (although gender is clearly also a significant difference here), in an English masque form which condemned such disguise, demanding instead the ready identification of masquers in the act of personation.

The appearance of the 'moore' of the Stirling baptismal celebrations was made in close physical and thematic proximity to that of women performers. The black man and the 'goddesses' whose chariot he drew into the hall were both presented to the court as silent spectacles of strangeness. In this presentation it can be seen that, almost ninety years after the appearance of the Black Lady, the same markers of difference, foreignness and liminality were in place in the court of James VI, where they inscribed Anna of Denmark's liminal status as queen consort.

Present at the banquet entertainment after her absence from the church service, Anna witnessed a mode of female performance that illuminates her own later English masque performances. One moment from the earlier tournament is especially pertinent; when she offered diamond rings to the victors as a mark of royal favour, Anna, like the Black Lady of James IV, was figured as the tournament's prize. In fact, in a neat mirroring of her metaphorical status in James VI's dash for Norway four years earlier, Anna here became the passive prize of chivalry. However, this moment is not a simplistic one; although the handing out of the rings reified Anna, it also meant that she was, to some extent, a participant in the tournament. In fact, if we follow Fradenburg's analysis of the influence of the female gaze on the tournament form, which postulates that this gaze allows male performers to 'constitute themselves as "men", who fight for and are watched by women', Anna's presence as a spectator simultaneously empowered her to fashion the nature of male tournament participation and was also a defining influence upon the women performers of the banquet interlude which was to follow.[92] In his account of the banquet entertainment Fowler describes the entry of the chariot and its tableau of 'six Gallant dames, who represented a silent Comedie'.[93] The women performing at the Stirling banquet represented the conventional mythic figures of interludes; Ceres and Fecundity, the goddesses of fertility and plenty, celebrated Anna's success in providing an heir, and Faith, Concord, Liberality and Perseverance embodied virtues of statecraft. The duty of fertility which Anna owed to the state, was also, therefore, closely associated with the attributes of successful rule.

Given the presence of female performers, Fowler's description of the women, and of Ceres in particular, is worth examining in some detail:

> In the first front stood dame Ceres, with a sickle in her right hand, and a handfull of Corne in the other, and vpon the outmost part of her thigh, was written this sentence, *Fundent vberes omnia Campi*, which is to say, the plenteous Fields shall affoord all things.[94]

Perhaps the most striking aspect of this description, especially given the prominence of the body as a critical concern in recent years, is the glimpse of writing on the body. Often hinted at in Anna's career in the juxtaposition of the female body with language, as in the hieroglyphs of *The Masque of Blackness* discussed in the introduction, this earlier example is more extreme in its practice. In the inscription of language upon the female performer herself, her body became both device and motto, the emblem's components of written word and pictorial device conflated in the body and offering the silent woman a corporeal means of linguistic expression. Nor was Ceres an isolated example of such expression; the pattern was repeated throughout the female figures of the tableau and these silent women were living emblems, abstract personifications identified by the objects which they held – Ceres by her corn and sickle, Faith by a basin in which were 'two hands ioyned together', Concord by 'a golden Tasse' and an horn of abundance, Liberality by the two crowns and two sceptres which she held, and Perseverance by a staff and anchor.[95] Furthermore, this particular kind of expression would seem to be reserved for the women performers in this interlude; the noblemen of the earlier tournament also formed emblems of sorts to be read by the audience, but they did so via a threefold structure in which, although the nobleman himself was part of the pictorial device, the emblem was displayed on fans by his page. This implies that the juxtaposition of physical imagery and pictorial language was conflated into a more intense relationship within the bodily expressivity of the silent woman.

The comparison between the expressive female bodies of the Stirling banquet interlude and Jonson's *Blackness* is instructive. In contrast with Jonson's staging of transgressive fertility in the blackened body of the pregnant queen in 1605, the representational strategy used for the female performers in the banquet conformed to a more naively available representation of the courtly ideals of feminine fertility. In the context of the christening Ceres herself, for example, was obviously an idealised image of that aspect of Anna which fulfilled the public duty of providing heirs for the nation. It is clear, therefore, that the subversively open sexuality signalled in the bodies of the masquers of *Blackness* ironised a simplistic interpretation of the emblems which they held.

At this point, however, my interest lies in the fact that these devices (both pictorial and linguistic) were indeed held, not inscribed upon the masquers' costumes or bodies. In the Stirling entertainment's condensation of device and motto, the bodies of the female performers actually became emblems, but the bodies of the performers of *Blackness* maintained an ironised distance from language, undermining the pictorial and linguistic representation of the feminine through their corporeality. To a certain extent, therefore, the performance of *Blackness* unpacked the intensely layered imagery of the Stirling entertainment, ironising its more simplistic use of the relationship between the ideal female body and corporeal linguistic expression which operated as a compensatory device for the enforced silence of the female masquer. In both instances we find women engaged in the performance of language, but in *Blackness* its painted form existed at one remove from the gendered body. It seems that, in these cases, language sat easier on the female body in an unironised context, and that the distanced juxtaposition of *Blackness* was integral to an ironised representation. However, these moments contribute also to our wider understanding of the performance career of Anna of Denmark; it is extremely important to recognise that the Stirling entertainment operated as a context for the later Jonsonian masque. Such female bodily expressivity was not conjured up solely for Anna's English performances, rather this later masque drew on and subverted an initially unironised and essentially conformist motif from the Queen's own earlier experience.

However, while the representation of the feminine in the 1594 entertainment has so far been read as relatively easily available, such a simplistic response can be problematised through an examination of its ambiguous representation of Anna herself. In this interlude the queen consort was witness to a vision of virtuous femininity to which the court dictated she should subscribe, but to which she herself existed in a rather more complex relationship. This is perhaps again best demonstrated through the motif of the romance quest, which was most prominent in the pageant car of the ship, which in its detail once again recalled James VI's Norwegian voyage. Fowler has this to say:

> The Kings Maiestie, hauing vndertaken in such a desperate time, to sayle to Norway, and like a newe Iason, to bring his Queene our gracious Lady to this Kingdome, being detained and stopped by the conspiracies of Witches, and such deuillish Dragons, thought it very meet, to followe foorth this his owne invention, that as Neptunus ... ioyned the King to the Queene.[96]

The reference to James as Jason incorporates the narrative image of the journey and of the marriage quest into courtly entertainment through the fashioning of Anna as the quest's reward. Surfacing in Fowler's literary text through the recourse to classical quest narrative, the juxtaposition of this allusion with the direct reference to the consort's perceived enchantment by figures of female evil gestures towards the anxieties which centred on Anna's presence at the performances of the Scottish court.

While the entertainment fêted the Queen's fertility and the masculine quest which facilitated it, James's aggrandisement to Jason in the interlude's literary text hints at the uneasy convergence of the discourses of the quest and the feminine ideal upon the representation of Anna herself. Here, as so often, the depiction of the husband defined the ambiguity of the wife. The most obvious source for the figure of Jason is Ovid's *Metamorphoses*, which describes Jason's triumphant public combat against the enchantments of Aeetes, and his return with the golden fleece,

> Of which his bootie being proud, he led with him away
> The Author of his good successe, another fairer pray.
> And so with conquest and a wife he loosde from *Colchos* strond,
> And in *Larissa* haven safe did go againe a lond.[97]

The Ovidian myth operated as a narrative archetype for many Renaissance court entertainments and their documentation. In this particular instance we see that Jason's quest of epic and romance was enacted inside the public ceremony of the tournament, which transfers on to the 1594 *magnificences* which included precisely that form. In this sense the test of Jason's power against the forces of a distant enchanted land underlay James VI's representation as the romantic questing hero who braved out the Berwick witches. However, the end result of figuring James as Jason is the simultaneous inscription of Anna as both the golden fleece (the dowry which was the physical prize of Jason's quest) and as the wife whom Jason brought home; Anna became both the process through which the dowry is attained and the result of that process. The association with the golden fleece commodifies the Queen as the tangible prize attained by the active questing male hero; Jason's wife was, after all, the medium through which his goals were achieved.

Jason's wife was also, of course, Medea, the prize which destroyed the victor. Ovid depicted her as first inspired by sexual desire to help Jason and betray her father and homeland, and later as driven by sexual jealousy to murder the very heirs she was required to provide. Such was the narrative trajectory of the queen; the betrayal of father and homeland through union with a foreigner, the journey to the husband's country and the importation both of the gifts of the dowry and of the constant threat of the repetition of betrayal.[98] Through her incorporation in the literary text of the banquet entertainment at which Anna was a spectator, Medea became a pattern for the perception of the queen consort. In part as a result of the queen consort's liminal position in relation to her new court's power structures, Anna became associated, through the embedded figure of Medea, with a powerfully alien and threatening knowledge and experience, the source of witchcraft and adultery.[99]

It is indeed this embedded allusion to Medea's witchcraft which most threatened Anna's idealised representation, as it linked her with the illicit experience of a woman of threatening alien subjectivity, knowledge and agency. Such an alignment also bound Anna to those unfortunate Berwick witches accused of cursing her journey to Scotland in 1590. Although accounts of the episode, including the witches' confessions, figured Anna as the precious gift or talisman which had to be prevented from reaching Scotland if evil was to prevail, in the light of the later published record of the Stirling entertainment the implicit textual association between the literary Medea and the actual queen consort refigured Anna as intimately associated with supernatural enchantment and forbidden knowledge. Accusations of witchcraft and the discourses of female difference which it encapsulated were, of course, a recurrent aspect of the early modern European perception of women. Such associations surfaced also in Anna's English career, most prominently in the demonised witches and virtuous queens of Jonson's *Masque of Queens*. Diane Purkiss has described the depiction of witchcraft in this masque as an attempted appropriation of a motif of transgressive femininity on the part of the seemingly virtuous queens, their apparent difference from the witches of the antimasque simply disguising an intimate bond.[100] Such a bond was established between Anna and the dual representations of the queen consort which were incorporated into the literary documentation of the banquet interlude; the golden fleece was always accompanied by the threatening promise of Medea. Whether this representation was related to the extreme doctrinal differences already apparent in 1594 between Fowler, the fervently Protestant former employee of the spy-master Walsingham, and Anna, his soon-to-be Catholic mistress, remains unclear.[101] Regardless of such speculation, however, the duality of the representative strategies surrounding Anna in this entertainment demonstrates the ambiguity surrounding the position of the queen consort, the foreign woman always fluctuating between states of trust and suspicion.

The constant tensions surrounding the notions of national and courtly community and its opposite, the outsider, were marked also in the interlude by the recurring presence of maritime imagery and, again, they were wrapped up in the figure of the woman who moved between courts. The queen consort's positioning inside the quest motif created an association between Anna, the golden fleece and Medea, and also bound Anna to the representation of alien femininity through the symbol of the sea, the barrier between Scotland and other nations, but also the means through which danger could reach its shores. Through the ritual entertainment of the court in which Anna spectated and performed, royal female difference was reinscribed in motifs of sea voyages and blackness and through female performance itself. The Stirling entertainment reworked the romance quest motif of Anna's marriage and childbearing as representations of her difference, ranking alongside those of blackness and femininity itself. It seems that foreign women (even pale blonde ones) embodied the threat of the other.

The modes of representing the Queen found in the ritual of the Scottish court have a wider relevance also to her career as a whole, since the motif of the quest also found clear echoes in her English masquing. Although the quest trope was perhaps a commonplace of the English masque, once again, it is in the masques of *Blackness* and *Beauty*, stagings which seem intimately involved in the consideration of Anna's experience of performance in the Scottish court, that one of the most prominent examples is to be found. Anna's 1605 and 1608 commissions presented the events of 1590 not as the journey of the King to his wife, but of a queen marked as foreign by her skin colour to the King's native shore.[102] This appropriation of the imagery of difference reversed the trajectory of the quest. Although the masque's conceit made it clear that the masquing women were drawn to the shore of 'Britain' by the power of James I, Anna's performance in the masque ensured that James's inscription as romance hero was here relinquished for his preferred role of spectator. Where once he had been depicted as the heroic lover, warrior and prince, in *Blackness* and *Beauty* James I became the goal of a female quest led by the queen he had previously purported to rescue.

The transformation of the tropes of the questing king and the prize he sought between their representation in Scotland and England leads to another moment of cultural transmission, the re-performance of Anna's coronation in England. Such transitions point up the influence of Anna's Scottish career on her later English performances, showing how tropes of blackness and the idea of performance itself read in distinctly different ways when positioned against their Scottish context.

In her second coronation Anna reworked her previous passivity within a new cultural context. However, although it is tempting to characterise Anna's journey to London as a clean break with Scotland and the beginning of the sustained independent cultural programme upon which she then embarked, such a reading is both oversimplified and anglocentric. Although Anna's Scottish performance career does seem to be characterised by passivity and conformity, this was not true of her other pre-1603 activities. For one thing Anna's time in the Scottish court demonstrates a continuous political engagement, in her pursuit of Prince Henry, her struggle for her lands at Dunfermline Abbey, her involvement in factional politics or her conversion to Catholicism.[103] Rather than simply being passive in Scotland and active in England, the evidence suggests a shift not in the level of Anna's agency but in its direction; Anna's London coronation demonstrated a shift in her attitude to the possibilities of performance. Whilst her previous engagement was expressed primarily through factional politics, it would now be expressed through court ritual in a way which called upon and actively reworked Scottish notions of royal femininity in a new cultural context. There is no simplistic divide between Anna in Scotland and Anna in England, and certainly no sudden epiphany at the border, but instead a more complex model of the re-enactment of the performances which surrounded European queenship within a distinct cultural setting. In 1603 England the celestial banquet of the church sacrament was, like the terrestrial banquet of the Scottish baptismal celebrations, the forum for the royal woman's performance of difference.

The year 1603 was one of great change for both England and Scotland. The death of Elizabeth I and James VI's assumption of the English throne had given England a male monarch with a consort and family of heirs, security the likes of which the nation had not enjoyed since the time of Henry VIII. The move from Scotland to England was also the opportunity for Anna's most explicit expression of difference from her husband so far, and the maturation of her independent stance as queen consort.

Initially Anna's agency was focused on her dealings with her children and seems to have been a continuation of her long-standing struggle for Prince Henry. As a result of the confrontation between the Queen and the Countess of Mar, described above, Anna left Edinburgh in 1603 accompanied by her son. Significantly, no such battles were waged over Elizabeth or Charles; in fact the latter, too weak to travel, was left behind in Scotland.[104] Alongside Henry, however, in a striking emblem of the power of royal motherhood and of the queen's ability to revoke the gift of the heir, Anna also kept with her the body of the child she had miscarried in her clash with the Countess. Revealingly, the French observer, the Duke of Sully, documented the rumours that Anna's miscarriage had been faked for political effect.[105] Certainly Anna's actions seem to have been read as political by the newly created James VI and I, and they caused him great concern during the move south. He disapproved strongly of her choice of chamberlain, the favour she displayed towards Lucy Harington Russell, Countess of Bedford, and her rejection of the senior women of Elizabeth I's bedchamber, all of which were the actions of a woman keen to cast off the trappings of Elizabeth I and to define herself through her own coterie.[106]

At an early point in her new reign, however, Anna's energies were redirected towards performance. The coronation of James VI of Scotland as James I of England took place on 25 July 1603 and, although not the first English performance Anna was exposed to after the entertainments of her progress south, contained the first definite gesture of active self-representation of her English career.[107] Scaramelli, Venetian Secretary at the English court, described the moments following the crowning of the King:

> The Archbishop then proceeded to crown the Queen, and placed the sceptre and staff in her hands, and then without further functions they conducted her to the throne. Up to this time she had been seated near the altar, without taking any part in the ceremony. Then the King approached the altar, and from the hands of the Archbishop he received the Lord's supper in bread and wine out of the chalice, which had been borne before him. The Queen did not receive the Sacrament, nor did she move from her throne.[108]

The refusal of the Protestant sacrament was a striking statement for an incoming queen consort to make and one which, as Scaramelli's report shows, was intended, despite the enclosed nature of an elite ceremony held during a time of plague, to reach an aristocratic and diplomatic audience throughout Europe.

Prime among the cultural differences between England and Scotland which must be fed into this moment are those of religious belief, since in Anna's second coronation the images of otherness so prominent in her Edinburgh entry were subsumed into those of religious difference. Anna's conversion to Catholicism has long been acknowledged by historians and most recently has been confirmed by Peter Davidson's research in the Vatican archives.[109] Ambassadors' accounts document the intense suspicion that she had converted or was swaying towards doing so.[110] In fact her conversion took place in the Scottish court, perhaps under the influence of the Catholic aristocratic faction, instanced in Anna's friendships with Henrietta, the Catholic Countess of Huntly, and Jean Drummond, sister-in-law of the Catholic Lord Seton, Anna's favourite lady-in-waiting and Prince Charles's first governess.[111] Women's role in the survival of recusant Scottish Catholicism was a strong one, and the presence of a vigorous female Catholic community may well have aided Anna's conversion. Anna's own Jesuit priest, Father Robert Abercromby, documented both her change of faith and James VI's awareness of its occurrence. Although such a high-level conversion would obviously have been valuable Jesuit propaganda, Anna's correspondence with Pope Clement VIII and Cardinal Borghese clearly demonstrates James VI's knowledge of her new faith and, importantly, his willingness to exploit it to approach European Catholic powers in his bid for the English throne. Anna's letter to Borghese, 'the protector of the Scottish nation at Rome', dated 31 July 1601, is frank in claiming James VI's authority. Documenting a previous correspondence between James and the papal powers, and warning of the danger of Elizabeth I's spies, the letter is open in its embrace of Catholicism.[112] Despite warnings and the return of illegal Papal gifts in 1603, Anna's expression of her Catholicism continued throughout her time in England, with evidence suggesting that she received communion at the house of Alonso de Velasco, the Spanish ambassador in England.[113]

The manipulation of Anna's religious difference, by both James VI and the Scottish Catholics, depended upon Anna's equivocal position as queen consort; she was close enough to the throne to cultivate Catholic interest, distanced enough to be a controllable threat. And such a controlled difference was made further possible by the rather blurred and shifting early modern religious categorisations applied to the individual. For example, attendance at Protestant ceremonies is not enough to define someone as Protestant, since such behaviour was problematised by the need to display conformity. James VI, for instance, was content to allow the Catholic Alexander Seton to remain as chancellor in Scotland, on the proviso that he swore the oath of allegiance, attended Protestant services and took the sacrament.[114] Both Catholics and Protestants engaged in a pragmatic expediency. So conversions like Anna's were hidden, and accepted on the condition that they were concealed. Under less heightened circumstances Anna herself had conformed to the practice of church papacy; two days before the coronation Scaramelli wrote that Anna 'is most obedient to her husband, and goes with him to the heretical services'. However, he adds an important caveat: 'all the same she endeavours to place in office as many Catholic nobles as possible, and as the King is extremely attached to her she succeeds in all she attempts'.[115]

Anna could enjoy less freedom of religious expression in England, however, and her coronation was a public display of her conversion which was not tolerable in her new circumstances. Anna's gesture was similar to that of the Catholic ambassadors at whom it was partly aimed, who were content to attend the Stuart coronation but who left Westminster Abbey during James's communion in order to avoid attendance at a 'heretic' service; but by remaining in the Abbey Anna also became a physical reminder of her own refusal to participate.[116] Before accepting this at face value, however, there is another interpretation which must be considered. Given the difficulty of reading acts of religious affiliation in this period, it is not terribly surprising that Anna's refusal of the Protestant sacrament cannot be taken as purely Catholic, but that its resonances alter when it is set against Scottish religious experience. In the context of the Scottish Reformation and its aftermath, the refusal to take the sacrament of any kind was in fact a marker of a truly reformed faith; James's twofold crime of kneeling before the altar and of taking the sacrament would, perhaps perversely, have branded the King as closer to Catholicism than the Queen.[117] Anna's refusal to participate offered the Catholic ambassadors evidence of her conversion, but simultaneously, in calling upon the codes of the powerful Scottish reformed faction, hid that conversion from sight in the moment in which it was most clearly displayed. Whatever one's reading of this moment, it is clear that while James was careful to signal his conformity with his new subjects, Anna's refusal, whether an act of Catholic or Protestant allegiance, was above all a display of her difference from the English.

By remaining silent and still at the altar while refusing to accept the Protestant sacrament, Anna's gesture was a display of physical withholding, of remaining outside the coronation service while making her presence felt within its parameters. This contrasts with her passivity in her Edinburgh coronation, when she touched the Bible to assent to the oath of allegiance, was moved around the kirk and was exposed in erotic subjugation to the will of the King. The Queen's autonomous immobility in the London service was a marker of her rejection of the ceremony; confined to silence, Anna exploited the physical expressivity of stillness, refusing movements (kneeling, accepting the sacrament) which would confirm the power of church and court, and instead choosing stasis. And although stillness does have connotations of reification, to choose to be reified is after all to subvert reification by making it an act of will.

Whether her stillness is read as Catholic or Protestant, what can be said is that on this occasion Anna stood outside the central ritual of the coronation. In the early modern period such a gesture of withholding had peculiarly feminine associations found also, for example, in the Catholic religious woman's rejection of childbearing. Anna's performance of refusal was also a prefiguring of that of Frances and Catherine Howard in *Love Restored*, and both instances highlight the real risk which a sanctioned female performance entailed for patriarchy and also suggests why such performance was, in England at least, still relatively rare. The necessary presence of royal and aristocratic women in court performance allowed the space for the self-representation of that elite community to be questioned through, among other tactics, the public refusal to perform as one should or, as in these cases, the refusal to perform at all.

The strength of Anna's gesture is demonstrated by a description of an argument between Anna and James on the morning of the coronation, narrated by Scaramelli.

> The King earnestly besought the Queen to take the Sacrament along with him, after the Protestant rite, on his Coronation Day, and that same morning the Archbishops also endeavoured to persuade her. They urged that if she did not, she would be living without any religion at all, for no other would be permitted in this kingdom. Her Majesty, after very quietly saying 'No' once or twice, declined to make any further answer.[118]

As it was extremely unlikely that he would have been present at such a moment, Scaramelli must have reported the incident second-hand, offering a glimpse into an intimate moment of state. In doing so Scaramelli employs a degree of narrative shaping, depicting a heroic female resistance extremely attractive to his Catholic sponsors. Indeed, in narrative terms, this retelling has much in common with another rendering of female resistance, although on this latter occasion the moment was recorded and scripted by the woman herself. Anne Clifford's 1616 confrontation with George Abbot, Archbishop of Canterbury, among others, concerning her disputed inheritance bears several similarities with the description of her Queen's earlier encounter.

> my Lord Archbishop of Canterbury, my Lord William Howard, my Lord Roos, my Coz. Russel, my Brother Sackville & a great Company of Men of note were all in the Gallery at Dorset House, where the Archbishop took me aside & talked with me privately one Hour & half & persuaded me both by Divine & human means to set my Hand to their Arguments. But my answer to his Lordship was that I would do nothing till my Lady & I had conferred together. Much persuasion was used by him & all the

Company, sometimes terrifying me & sometimes flattering me, but at length it was concluded that I should have leave to go to my Mother & send an answer by the 22nd of March next.[119]

Again surrounded by male representatives of church and state, the elite woman was once more involved in a narrative representation of resistance. Despite the differences in authorial agency, what is especially interesting is the possibility that a narrative trope for female resistance existed to document courtly women's agency. That such a rhetoric was available is telling; offering a means of representing female opposition, this trope perhaps demonstrates the availability of such opposition as a strategy for the elite or royal woman's political involvement. While this demonstrates that Scaramelli's account records Anna's agency in a way which cannot be taken at face value, it also suggests that a means existed to document her chosen mode of resistance, a narrative figuration for the articulation of courtly female opposition.

Anna's English masquing, for so long seen as her only performances, reads rather differently when positioned against her Scottish and Danish contexts. Blackness, religious expression and female performance itself must all be reinterpreted to a certain degree when they are considered against the totality of Anna's life, education and career. In particular, the images of blackness which clustered around Anna in Scotland, an intimate aspect of the perception and representation of the queen consort, were not easily assimilated into a new English court environment. As *Blackness* and *Beauty* backfired in their reworked presentation of female royalty within an English context, so the London coronation of Anna of Denmark reconfigured the perception of the queen consort through an ambiguous depiction of religious difference: difference, that is, from England. Anna's status as both outsider and insider is undeniable; a Danish princess who became queen of Scotland and then of England, she moved between courts carrying cultural practices with her. In this sense the performance of Scottish ritual fed significantly into that of the English court, and English rebellion can explain Scottish conformity: Anna of Denmark's English career was founded upon the active reinterpretation of Scottish performance.

CHAPTER THREE

'Spectacles of strangeness': the performance of the female body in the major Jacobean masques

Against the background of the prohibition of female participation in other contemporary English theatrical forms, Jacobean female masquing emerged as a unique and exciting staging of the early modern female body. Certainly a great deal of the significance which early seventeenth-century English female masquing holds for late twentieth- and early twenty-first-century critics derives precisely from this unparalleled prospect of a legitimate female presence on stage. Technically speaking, of course, the entertainments of the Stuart court in Scotland and its first recorded London masque, Samuel Daniel's *Vision of the Twelve Goddesses* (1604), were not actually staged at all. A raised stage was not introduced to the masque form until the collaboration of Jones and Jonson in *The Masque of Blackness* in 1605. Until this point these masques and entertainments were enacted on moveable pageant cars and the floor of the hall. The move to a raised stage brought a more centralised perspective, moving the visual lines of the masque closer to the contemporary performances of the London city theatres, and in particular the indoor private stage. At the same time, the introduction of shifting scenery formed a striking visual and conceptual distinction between the stages of the city and court. The imaginative status of the masque stage altered with these developments; its spectacle was now centred on the gaze of the watching king, which was itself directed towards the bodies of the performing courtiers and witness to the novelty of a shifting scenery which could also move them around the stage. Such developments in staging, playing space and scenery profoundly affected female performance. The early modern English noblewoman did not gain access to an existent stage, rather a stage was placed beneath the feet of women who had already been accepted as performers. Even before these radical developments, however, the female masquer was a central component of the visual picture of the masque genre, and the introduction of the raised stage formed only part of her continuing and altering relationship to scenery, costume and theatrical space.

It seems that developments in the staging of the masque in the English Stuart courts significantly altered the gender dynamics of that stage. Despite the striking nature of this alteration, the extent of the impact of the masque's shifting staging strategies upon the gendered aristocratic masquing body has not yet been investigated. So, what can an assessment of the performance conditions of the court masque add to a reading of these entertainments? To answer this I want to pose a successive question: to what extent were the perceptions, representation and expressivity of the performing female body – the main component of these early Stuart masques both before and after Jones's and Jonson's intervention – altered by the shifting staging conditions in which these women danced?

The court's gender dynamics and the way in which these conditions shaped and configured the female body were embedded in the masque's stage conditions; through an assessment of these conditions and constraints, a clearer image of the developing nature of Stuart courtliness and the court's perception of both femininity and female performance can be reached. A consideration of the masque's staging affects the reading of the female body partly because it allows for the reinstatement of this ephemeral moment of performance within the discourses of courtliness and the aristocratic body, which I have discussed in previous chapters and which is one key to the perception of the courtly and royal woman. Female masquing was enacted within restrictions imposed by the masque genre's playing conditions and the sheer novelty of the legitimate performance of the female body; my aim is to uncover the extent to which the material representative strategies of the masque were affected by and in turn affected those women who performed on that stage.

Two texts which crystallise exactly these debates are Daniel's *Vision* and Jonson's *Masque of Queens*. These texts are additionally pertinent as they stand at either end of the masquing activities of the first decade of the Queen's court in England, and so allow for analyses of the interaction of staging and gender during one of the most influential periods of female court performance. Daniel's masque, the first of Anna's English career and the first of the English Stuart court for which a text survives, was danced at Hampton Court in 1604, whilst Jonson's commission, regarded as the 'apotheosis of queenship', took place in the second Whitehall Banqueting House in 1609.[1] The fluidity of the staging of the female body found in the distinct approaches of each entertainment reflects the political and social moment of their performance, and ties them to the masque career of Anna of Denmark. The importance of social and political context is particularly apparent in those masques staged in the first decade of the Jacobean court in London, a period of considerable cultural and political sway for the queen consort. Anna's dominance over the masquing stage in this first decade of English Stuart rule can be seen in the fact that, with the exception of Jonson's *Hymenaei* (1606) and Campion's *Lord Hay's Masque* (1607), the court's masquing stage was occupied almost entirely by women. This recognition opens up a number of significant questions. For instance, do the shifts in female performance and representation between the initiation of the female Stuart court's English masquing activities and their highpoint in *Queens* reflect a parallel movement in the perception and status of courtly female performance and cultural engagement? Furthermore, what is the relationship of the expressive female body to language, stage architecture, spectacle and the discourse of courtly magnificence in these two performances? When the gendered stagings of these masques are examined, the extent to which their physical conditions impacted upon the bodily and conceptual presence of the performing aristocratic woman becomes apparent. Examining these conditions makes possible the identification of the shifting politics and aesthetics of the gendered body on the female masquing stage.

One significant aspect of female masquing was its juxtaposition with the transvestite male actor. Bringing the cross-dressed male and the 'real' female body together in the same stage picture instead of maintaining the separation found in other theatrical forms led to a clear distinction being made in the masque between these co-existent markers of the female body, and this further emphasised the legitimate presence of the 'real' female body on the masque stage. In a culture accustomed to transvestite male performance, and within which the staging of the female body was a rarity not legitimately witnessed beyond the confines of the court community, tensions surrounded the performance of the aristocratic female body. Such anxieties manifested themselves in an intense focus on the physicality of that body within these entertainments, constraining the masquer of both sexes to silence and allowing expression only through physical and bodily means. Yet as both Daniel's and Jonson's masques demonstrate, the central status of the female masquer's corporeality was itself empowering; allowing the elite woman access to theatrical spectacle also permitted her entry to the court's display of grace in the political arena of the masque and so to the currency of favour. In turn, however, this specularity was problematised by the transgressive nature of the female masquing body. Anna's appearance as Pallas in *The Vision* and that of the amazonian masquers in *Queens* demonstrate the liminal nature of female performance, in that they positioned the female masquer in opposition to the idealised femininity of the mainstream Jacobean court. Whatever the duality of female performance, when these masques are read as part of a tradition of performance in Anna's English court they establish the courtly women's masquing as the meaningful and self-conscious practice of culturally engaged female courtiers and royalty.

'The best-built temples of beauty and honour': *The Vision of the Twelve Goddesses* and the female body in Hampton Court Great Hall

During Christmas 1603–04, while the court sheltered from an outbreak of plague in London, Samuel Daniel's *Vision of the Twelve Goddesses* was danced at Hampton Court. Writing to the contemporary chronicler Sir John Chamberlain in December 1603, his long-time correspondent Sir Dudley Carleton looked forward to 'a merry Christmas at Hampton Court, for both male and female maskes are all ready bespoken, whereof the Duke [of Lennox] is *rector chori* of th'one side and the La: Bedford of the other'.[2] The gendered divisions of the Jacobean court are clearly underlined in Carleton's projections for the festival, but equally significant here is his singling out of Lucy Russell as the leader of the women. As Daniel's dedicatory letter acknowledges, it was at the instigation of Lucy Russell, Countess of Bedford, that he obtained the masque commission.[3] Russell's patronage of female masquing, which would become a regular feature of her court career, suggests the availability of such strategies of courtly advancement to the female as well as the male courtier. Her prominence in her new Queen's court meant that she was central to the initiation of Anna's English performance career.

In commissioning Daniel for the first of Anna's English masques Russell was supporting a poet of the former Pembroke circle as well as a writer previously patronised by Elizabeth I.[4] At the same time the Countess was initiating a creative relationship which would endure the varying fortunes of Daniel's career. Despite Daniel's contentious role as licenser for the Children of the Queen's Revels (the troop of boy players whose staging of plays openly critical of James I, such as the scandalous 1605 production of *Eastward Ho!*, eventually lost the company Anna's patronage), and his entanglement in the political controversy over his play *Philotas* (the action of which seemed to bear too close a resemblance for comfort to Essex's conspiracy of 1600), his relationship with Anna continued.[5] Though Daniel was to write only one more masque for Anna, *Tethys' Festival* in 1610, in 1605 his 'Pastorall Trage-comedie', *The Queen's Arcadia*, was presented to the Queen at Christ Church, Oxford. His career also shows signs of Anna's continuing favour; from 1607 he was Groom of Anna's Privy Chamber; by 1613 he was Gentleman Extraordinary and in 1615 he secured his brother a patent for the Children of the Queen's Chamber of Bristol, all perhaps evidence of a fruitful relationship with the Queen. Perhaps more importantly, at his death in 1619 he was compiling a prose history of England under Anna's patronage, a significant record of female literary and historiographical engagement which mirrored, in its impetus, the commissions of Anna's mother.[6] Daniel's career is evidence also of Anna's involvement with the London theatre companies and of the extent of her cultural engagement beyond the Jonsonian masque.

The masque which Daniel wrote for his Queen, her participation and her ongoing involvement in patronage and performance demonstrate Anna's willingness to exploit the political capital of the state occasion of a masque. Carleton's description of *The Vision* and the ambassadorial haggle for precedence reveals that the Queen's Twelfth Night masque had pride of place in the Christmas festivities.[7] *The Vision*, a negotiation of female power within the hegemony of the Stuart court, was the coveted Twelfth Night performance of that court's inaugural festivities in England. Although critical assessment is influenced by the chance nature of textual survival, it is still significant that Anna's first masque should have apparently initiated the masquing life of the English Stuart court with a performance which would establish a pattern of controversial female performance for the remainder of her career.

Despite the defining nature of this masque, analysis of *The Vision* has tended to focus on its affiliations to Tudor court entertainments, contrasting it unfavourably with the future innovations of the Jones/Jonson partnership. In their seminal early twentieth-century work Herford and Simpson call Daniel's masque 'structureless and old-fashioned' and go on to describe what they considered an outmoded form of staging: 'The action was dispersed between a Cave of Sleep at the upper end of the hall, a Temple of Peace near by it, and a mountain at the lower end, from which the masquers descended.'[8] Though it is important to avoid privileging the staging innovations of the Jonsonian masque, both this dispersed scenery and the dancing of *The Vision* in the Tudor Great Hall at Hampton Court do point unmistakably to its affiliations with the past.

The dispersed scenic items, reminiscent of the pageant cars used in the Elizabethan masque, formed the basis of the masque's conceit and action; the goddess-masquers descended from the raised mount, processed through the hall to present gifts to a Sibyl, danced the measures and revels with audience members and returned to their divine mountain.

Since *The Vision*, together with White's *Cupid's Banishment*, was one of only two major Jacobean court masques to be performed outside Whitehall Palace, it is worth considering how this difference in venue might have affected the meaning of the masque danced there. The ephemeral moment of *The Vision*'s performance is illuminated and clarified through an awareness of the allusive nature of the performance space in which it was danced – the particular resonances surrounding the building and playing space participated in the creation of the masque's meaning. Before 1606, when James I ordered the Whitehall Banqueting House to be rebuilt in stone, Stuart masques were mainly performed in the semi-permanent 1581 Banqueting House.[9] For Daniel's inaugural Jacobean entertainment, however, the court danced in a structure which predated both the Stuart and Elizabethan reigns. Built for Henry VIII in 1532–34, just after the Eltham Ordinances of 1526 which restricted the keeping of hall to six select royal residences, the Great Hall at Hampton Court was a remnant of feudal practice. Remaining largely unaltered in the years after its construction, the striking gilded oak and blue panelled hammer-beam roof of the heavily decorated Great Hall was the elaborate backdrop for the prominent display of the arms, emblems and initials of Henry VIII.[10] The inaugural masque of the new Stuart court, then, that moment which signalled the transition from Elizabethan to Jacobean rule, was danced in a Henrician context; plague forced *The Vision* into an allusive dialogue with the tradition of English royal power. In its depiction of the union of Scotland and England, found among other places in Iris's mention of 'mighty Brittany', Daniel's masque was a validation of the incoming Stuart rulers' negotiation of English monarchical authority and its existing physical and conceptual structures of power.[11] Complementing this, the Great Hall's ties to medieval feudalism represented a continuity of specifically English experience appropriated by the Stuart courts in the moment of performance as markers of dynastic continuity. Daniel's masque suggests a resonant series of ties between Elizabeth I and Anna of Denmark, England's new queen consort, which gain weight and relevance from their performance in a Great Hall built by a major figure of the Tudor dynasty.

Distinctions between the social and performance spaces of the first

Whitehall Banqueting House and the Great Hall suggest that further resonances attached to this performance space. Stemming from a tradition of spaces designed for a specifically social and communal purpose – the gathering of the court for meals and sleep – the Henrician Great Hall was a precursor of the purpose-built performance spaces of Stuart court ritual, the series of Whitehall banqueting houses. Though they cannot be categorised as theatres, the 1581 Banqueting House and its successors were purpose-built performance spaces, avant-garde in comparison with the 1532 Great Hall. Built over wine cellars, these later buildings all served the dual function of communal entertainment and dining, but to a degree differing from that found in the reign of Henry VIII. Although some Henrician halls were the communal dining room for the 'lower members of the Court', this function had become somewhat obsolete in the stylised constructions of later reigns; Jacobean masque banquets were not held in the banqueting houses themselves, and those ceremonial meals which were held there, such as those for St George's Day, were infrequent.[12] All these spaces repeat the symbolic distinction between the upper and lower hall, achieved through the raised dais and increased illumination.[13] However, perhaps the most important consistency between these constructions was their theatricality; these halls existed as performance spaces for courtly ritual. Despite not being specifically designed for this purpose, the Great Hall was consistently used for entertainments 'as it alone of the components of the house provided sufficient space, its gallery a place for minstrels and the dais a viewing point for the King'.[14] Furthermore, the Hampton Court Great Hall was converted into a theatre in the 1620s and the great hall in Whitehall Palace itself became a permanent theatre in 1665, gesturing to the theatricality inherent in these spaces.[15] Despite these intertextualities, however, the coexistence in Whitehall Palace of a great hall and the banqueting houses demonstrates their distinct imaginative status. Most importantly, therefore, *The Vision* was danced in a retrospective space, resonant of a style of monarchy and court which fitted neither the Elizabethan nor the Stuart reign but which offered the new rulers an opportunity to appropriate the physical reality of previous English government.

The siting of Jacobean masque performance in the Hampton Court Great Hall impacted upon the performance of the gendered body in *The Vision*, as did the specific performance conditions of Daniel's masque. The Great Hall, which still stands today, is a large rectangular room, at the lower end of which is an oaken screen with two openings. On the wall above the screen is a gallery, which was often used to accommodate musicians; on this occasion, however, the music was positioned to the side of the hall in full view of the audience. At first glance, then, the masquers performed within a hall which did not differ markedly from the later Whitehall Banqueting House. Yet an important distinction existed in the arrangement and use of gallery space in each location. Here configurative differences had a substantial impact upon the dynamics of the performing female body, fundamentally altering the relationship between that body and the audience's gaze. Unlike the banqueting houses, which were galleried on three sides, splitting the audience to allow one section – the less privileged – an elevated view of the action, the Great Hall has only one gallery, not used for seating.[16] This meant that the audience of *The Vision* were seated in two sections of equal height, and that, while they were fairly unified, their viewpoint was also restricted. With the musicians excluded from the gallery, the vertical axis was exploited only by the masquers as they descended from the summit of the mount to the lower world of the court. Though the tiered seating at either side of the Great Hall was raised, it did not afford the gallery's elevated perspective down on to the action of the dancing floor; the audience's eyeline would have been restricted to the horizontal plane, gazing across the communal space of the dance floor at the performers and at each other. The configuration of the Great Hall for Daniel's masque, then, demanded that the audience witness the display of the female body against the backdrop of their peers. In itself this was not radically different from the Whitehall banqueting houses, whose audiences also faced each other, but when this seating arrangement became the setting for the processional movement of the female body between dispersed scenery, as it did in the Great Hall, a new dynamic emerged.

Significantly, the audience's gaze was further fixed on the female masquing body by the fact that *The Vision* did not use a single raised stage, but instead used dispersed free-standing scenic units reminiscent of Tudor pageant cars. Daniel's introductory text details the scenic arrangement of the mountain from which the goddess-masquers descended, Sleep's cave and the Temple of Peace; the action, then – the movement of the female masquers – was staged on the floor of the hall between the pieces of scenery.[17] As a genre the masque was dependent upon the visual, and the heavily emblematic *Vision* was almost entirely predicated upon the visual interpretation of the performing female body in a physical display found in the later Jonsonian masque only in the measures and the revels. The obvious but forceful distinction between the use of the floor in this and later masques lies in the masquers' crossing and recrossing of the floor, a movement not found again within the court masque's central conceit until the 1613 performance of Campion's *Somerset Masque*. The goddesses' horizontal travelling motion displayed their bodies, costumes and movements to the audience, which meant that *The Vision* had an intense focus upon the spectacle of the female body within the social space of the dance floor.

It would seem that, for both *The Vision* and the masque genre as a whole, the travelling motion of the masquers as they descended from the mountain, crossed the floor and returned to their starting point was a significant movement. Danced before Jones's shifting scenery was first used in *Blackness*, Daniel's masque did not stage the aristocratic body in the same way as such later masques. Rather than being moved by the shifting scenery and presented to the audience – which is, as we shall see, a primary trait of a masque such as *Queens* – these masquers emerged from the static scenery under their own power and, decked in elaborate costumes, gave these individual scenic items motion. The performance in the Great Hall was a circular procession of the royal and aristocratic female body on the hall floor, which held its performers in the gaze of their peers or subjects in the audience for as long as possible. The upright figure of the female as she processed, itself a movement governed by courtly grace, focused the audience's gaze upon the female body which was structured not by stage scenery but by costume.

As we have seen, Daniel's masque placed the female body at the centre of the audience's gaze, establishing an intense focus on that body which was to be a feature of the Jacobean masque genre. However, although this relationship between the spectators and the display of the courtier's masquing body formed a precedent for those masques which followed *The Vision*, the later Jonesian/Jonsonian masque predicated that relationship along very different lines. The recognition of the crystallisation of the later Jacobean masque around the physical dialogue between James I's gaze from the raised dais at one end of the hall and the perspective stage at the other end is a commonplace of masque criticism. The later Jacobean masques put on in the banqueting houses replaced Daniel's creation of the ideal court on the social space of the dance floor with a centralised vision which focused on the twin spectacles of the King on the dais and, among others, the royal female body on the perspective stage. A post-1605 masque audience, therefore, had a radically different view of performance from that of *The Vision*. While the former witnessed the female body within the strict hierarchy of the banqueting houses' perspective sightlines, offering a full view of the stage only to those of high enough rank, the latter were presented with a communal vision of the procession of the goddess-masquers, clearly visible to all in the shared space of the hall floor. While such a communal spectacle did form a substantial element of the measures and revels of the Whitehall Stuart masques, it made up the main action and conceit of *The Vision*; as its title suggests, Daniel's masque was a visionary spectacle, the common masque trope of the idealised court (later confined behind the proscenium and on the stage during the main masque) was made real in the shared visual and symbolic space of the hall floor. From this perspective the Great Hall was a less strictly hierarchical space than the banqueting houses would become under the Stuarts. Flanked by the court, the space of the dance floor was an intensely social one. Positioned in this specific performance space and before an audience which gazed in self-absorption at itself, *The Vision* placed a very definite weight on the display of the female body. This, after all, is a masque which presented the female body as a readily readable text and, in the introduction to the goddesses, as the Platonic Ideal Form, 'for that those beautiful characters of sense were easier to read than their mystical *Ideas* dispersed in that wide and incomprehensible volume of nature'.[18] In particular it seems that this Tudor-style masque danced by the incoming queen consort used the display of the female body to set up a dialogue between Anna and her predecessor, Elizabeth I, drawing on the recent history of the English court to explore its future with its new queen.

In its display of the female body, its position in the masquing hall and its representation in costume, this inaugural Stuart masque gazed back at Elizabeth I's female community and forward to Anna's court. Leeds Barroll has interpreted the Stuart Queen's court as offering greater opportunities for female advancement than her Elizabethan predecessor, but in its configuration of its female performers *The Vision* looked both back to established female power and forwards to potential female opportunity.[19] Validating Stuart performance through Elizabethan tradition, Daniel's masque employed certain aspects of Elizabethan imagery while reconfiguring it for its new Stuart context; as part of this alteration, this imagery had to negotiate the shift of female authority from queen regnant to consort, authorising the new court's altered circumstances. Unsurprisingly then, as with so many of Anna's performances, *The Vision* was concerned with the role of the consort in general and with the nature of Stuart queenship in particular.

The Vision most clearly signalled its pivotal position between Tudor and Stuart performance through its visual text. Costume had a vital role in constructing meaning in the masque and in defining and representing the gendered body, and this is borne out in a reading of *The Vision*. There are no extant masquers' costume designs for Daniel's masque because it was danced in clothes taken from the late Queen's wardrobe. Arbella Stuart wrote that 'The Queene intendeth to make a mask this Christmas to which end my Lady of Suffolk and my Lady Walsingham have warrants to take of the late Queenes best apparell out of the Tower at theyr discretion'.[20] Audrey Walsingham's position as Keeper of the Queen's wardrobe implicated Anna herself in the raiding of the clothes and in the appropriation of their riches and iconographical significance. What is interesting in this case, however, is the way in which, in much the same way as the commonplace and coincidental outbreak of the plague shifted the performance of *The Vision* into an allusive framework, so happenstance had a further influence on the meanings of this masque in the use of the dead queen's clothes.

In many ways the use of Elizabeth's clothes to provide masquing costumes for the Christmas entertainment was not exceptional, since aristocratic clothes were commonly used in private and public theatres.[21] The reuse of existing clothes was itself far from remarkable in early modern England; due to the high cultural status accorded to textiles and embroidery, and their astronomical financial value, it was common practice to reuse such materials. Indeed Elizabeth I occasionally had her own dresses remodelled as gifts for her ladies-in-waiting and Anna herself, on arrival in England, had the former queen's dresses remodelled for her own use.[22] However, in the case of Daniel's masque, the ramifications of this recycling are more forceful precisely because the choice of the new queen consort did not light on aristocratic clothes, or on those of her own wardrobe, but on those inherited from Elizabeth. Elizabeth's clothes were a valuable and prized part of the new Queen's possessions and their use would signal Anna's status as Elizabeth's female heir. We should, however, also be wary of reading the later role of the masque designer and his centralised control over the masque (which itself developed over time) into pre-Jonsonian masques. Too much weight cannot be given to the decision to use existing costumes since, after all, the role of the costume designer seems also to have been an innovation, for the Stuart masque at least, of the Jones/Jonson partnership. Anna's actions, therefore, had their basis in elite practice. However, although perhaps mitigated by its mundane nature, one result of Anna's adoption of the former queen's costume was the appropriation of her predecessor's corporeal existence; in a visual reminder of the physical presence of female rule, Anna shaped her body as Elizabeth's had been shaped.

The theme of the construction of the female body in costume and staging is prominent in Daniel's masque. Speaking while descending from the mount, the choric figure of Iris informed the audience that a coterie of goddesses, descending to the mountain 'found there the best [...] of ladies [Anna of Denmark], disporting with her choicest attendants [her women] whose forms they presently undertook as delighting to be in the best-built temples of beauty and honour'.[23] This statement is significant since it highlights both the possession of the female body by a divine force and the comparison between that body and architecture; both run through the masque and impact on the representation of the women who danced in *The Vision*. As will become clear below, this relationship between the gendered body and architecture figured more prominently in the staging of Jonson's *Masque of Queens*. However, the gendered early modern discourse of architecture was one of the underpinning principles of the Jacobean masque's representation of the female body and was also present in *The Vision* in Iris's description of the masquers as the 'best-built temples of beauty and honour'. The link between this divine possession of the masquers and the structuring of the female body is found in their costumes. The recycling of earlier costumes and the appropriation of a past physical presence could be interpreted as the possession of the dead queen and her corporeal actuality. Indeed, the text does suggest that clothes and bodily identity are available for appropriation; at one point Iris, referring to the masquers' bodies, notes that the divine Powers 'clothed themselves with these appearances'; the female body, like clothing, could be taken up and worn by others.[24] The image of the female body as costume, given material existence in the appropriation of Elizabeth's clothes, points to the constructed nature of gendered ideals while simultaneously expressing the passivity of that body. But despite the connotations of female passivity in divine possession – connotations of puppetry and manipulation which invoke the dichotomy of the corporeal soulless woman and her incorporeal divine counterpart – Anna's performance of Elizabeth's mortal body and body politic can be read as empowering. Just as Anna and her ladies were supposedly possessed by the spirits of the goddesses whom they personated, they themselves were the inhabiting spirits of the now defunct Elizabethan courtly body. Female physicality was adopted and adapted as a means of reconstituting feminine power within the performance of the gendered body in the masquing hall.

Nowhere is Anna's possession of the former queen more obvious than in her personation of Pallas, a singularly Elizabethan icon. Anna's personation of the classical deity so often associated with the virginal Elizabeth avoided a more conventional alignment with Juno, queen of the goddesses and deity of marriage. As such the masque eschewed any representation of the incoming royal couple through the gendered construct of the patriarchal family and distinguished itself from the later formulation of Stuart authority in masques such as Jonson's *Hymenaei* (where Anna was figured as Juno to James's Jove). The lengths to which Daniel went to represent Anna/Pallas as *The Vision*'s ruling goddess – Iris calls her 'the all-directing Pallas' – draws attention to this unconventional choice and underlines the associations between the helmeted queen consort and her amazonian predecessor.[25] Furthermore, other female characters encapsulated similarly Elizabethan resonances; Lucy Russell's personation of Vesta – 'purity' – also harks back to a learned Elizabethan virginity.[26] The piety and cultural engagement of both Russell and Elizabeth were represented through the visual markers of the book (the Bible) and the burning lamp of the wise virgin, an image resonant of the former queen's sexual self-representation. Other characters added to the reworking of Elizabethan imagery within the performance of this first English Stuart masque. The inclusion of Diana, for example, signalled a return to an image prominent in Elizabeth's iconographical career (and to be equally prominent in Anna's), while the performance of Astraea by Lady Walsingham, personating a figure intimately related to the dead Queen, marked the return to the fold of one of Elizabeth's ladies.

Anna's reincarnation of Elizabeth I instated the new consort and her noblewomen in a continuous tradition of female courtly authority. Perhaps more intriguingly, this duplication of the Elizabethan aristocratic body also reworked that corporeality to express the shift between Tudor and Jacobean female power. This refashioning, signalled primarily through casting and costume, centred on Anna herself. Certain alterations made to Anna's costume signalled the significant distinctions which existed between Elizabeth I and the new Stuart queen. Dudley Carleton's comments are well known: 'Only Pallas had a trick by herself, for her clothes were not so much below the knee that we might see a woman had both feet and legs which I never knew before'.[27] While such an alteration in Elizabethan skirt-length might be explained by the need to allow the performer to dance, such alterations were clearly not made for all the masquers. Both Anna's unique royal status and her difference from Elizabethan femininity are signalled through the transgressive display of the royal female body. Though the new queen assumed her predecessor's corporeality, Anna exhibited the marital sexuality of the queen consort, the woman who must gift the nation with heirs. Moreover, as is suggested by Carleton's assessment of the performance ('Pallas bore the bell away'), the contrast between the Stuart Queen's youthful grace and the ageing Elizabeth must have been particularly arresting.[28] Consummated female sexuality distinguished the queen consort from the former queen regnant and the latter's negotiations of power. The open display of the consort's eroticised body was taken further in *Blackness* and *Beauty*, but here the resulting controversy served only to indicate the partial success of such bodily demonstration.

Such multi-levelled resonances confirm a special relationship between this masque and what came before. Certainly, danced in Tudor costumes in a Henrician great hall and performed within an Elizabethan scenic configuration, Daniel's masque had an undoubted allegiance to the past. Yet, as the refashioning of Elizabeth's clothes demonstrates, *The Vision* was a Tudor masque which looked to the future, even if it did so through what one critic, discussing a later masque, has described as 'a powerful and potentially subversive nostalgia'.[29] Gazing back at the previous reign, *The Vision* also looked forward to the court of the new consort. The familiar Tudor marker of the politicised woman was reworked to legitimise the potential for Stuart female power – Elizabeth's authority made Anna's viable. Daniel's explicit attribution of political qualities to the female masquers is significant in this light; they are 'imperial' and 'war-like', even Venus is not the goddess of romantic love but, in a clear reference to Anglo-Scottish union, has the power 'T'engird strange nations with affections true'.[30] As the Stuart consort inhabited the body of the former English queen, and as the Great Hall was appropriated for the inauguration of a new, legitimated dynasty, so this masque itself expressed the appropriation and inhabitation of structures of English rule by the Scottish royal family. For example, through her costume's colour symbolism, the personification of Concordia, 'the union of hearts', signalled the union between Scotland and England, and the motif of travel to the new 'Britain', 'the land of civil music and of rest', was an arresting feature in a masque which negotiated the arrival of the Scottish court in London.[31] Sibylla's question to the masquers, 'will the divine Goddesses vouchsafe to visit this poor temple?', demonstrates the synthesis of issues of royal authority, performance space and the gendered body.[32] The temple she refers to represented both the masquers' bodies and the Great Hall itself, both possessed and visited by divinity in the evocation of the journey of the Scottish court to London and of memories of the dead queen. Borrowed clothes and borrowed performance spaces expressed the reality of the shift of monarchical authority.

The staging of the refashioned Elizabethan female body within the Henrician performance arena points to the prominence of the concept of costume and the perception of the body in this masque. Although Daniel's masque displayed the female body, powered through its own kinesis, as the central, social spectacle of the performance, this trait was radically altered by the introduction of shifting scenery into the masque form in *Blackness*, the next performance commissioned by Anna. This innovative transformation, which took place in 1605 in the Jones/Jonson collaboration of *Blackness*, had a profound impact upon the representation of the female body as self-motivated spectacle.

Part of the scenery:
The Masque of Queens and the gendering of stage, architecture and costume

Danced by Anna and her ladies in the second Whitehall Banqueting House in 1609, *The Masque of Queens*, with its amazonian queens and humiliated witches, is fertile ground for the investigation of the gender dynamics of the Jacobean masque text. Recent feminist criticism has found *Queens* inviting, but disagrees on the extent to which the masque should be seen as a proto-feminist text.[33] The term 'text' is significant here, since many readings of this masque are just that – textual interpretations which do not account for performance. However, the gender dynamics of the Jacobean court were inscribed also in the performance text and stage picture of *Queens*. For instance, reports of Anna's involvement in the rehearsals for this masque suggest the importance of performance to a study of *Queens*. In January 1609 the Venetian ambassador wrote that Anna 'held daily rehearsals and trials of the machinery', a phrase which suggests that, for those involved in the creative process, both masquers and stage scenery needed to be rehearsed in the smooth completion of their tasks and held a similar imaginative status.[34] In this way the human body and the masque scenery, encapsulated by Jonson's term 'carcass', were conceptually bound together in performance. Jonson's masque, then, foregrounds questions about contemporary femininity not only through its textual ramifications but also through its performance text of stage machinery, costume, and the relationship of the performance of the gendered aristocratic body to each.

The relationship between this body and the masque's performance conditions takes on a particular urgency when placed alongside the relative absence of their description in the text of *Queens*. Although in the annotations which Jonson made for Prince Henry after the masque had been danced he stated his intention to describe the appearance of the masquers and 'the persons they presented', where this should be the reader finds instead a summary of the ways in which these characters have been treated by literature.[35] Jonson describes both fictional and historical women solely through their literary representations, stressing the fictionalised nature of the masquer's assumed identities and perhaps telling the reader more about literature than about the characters themselves. For example, Camilla's description is in fact a paean to Virgil's verses, than which 'nothing can be imagined more exquisite'.[36] Similarly, Jonson's climactic rhetoric in the description of Anna as Bel-Anna – 'if I would fly to the all-daring power of poetry, where could I not take sanctuary? Or in whose poem?' – again replaces the physical description of the masquer with a panegyric to poetry.[37] Literature and literary history certainly had a prominent place in contemporary entertainments, where the figure of the male poet/scholar was typically given precedence; echoes of Jones's House of Fame are found in Webster's Temple of Honour in his 1624 Lord Mayor's pageant, *Monuments of Honour*, in which Chaucer, Gower, Lydgate, More and Sidney were represented, and in the Parnassus of Scottish poets and scholars in Drummond's 1633 *Entertainment* for Charles I in Edinburgh.[38] In contrast, *Queens* placed women in a construct typically occupied by male authors and described them only through their representation in the male-authored texts of poetry and history; written about rather than writing, these women were subject to the authority of the male canon. This treatment is especially clear in the case of Anna herself. Though the only living woman among the fictional and the dead, Anna's role was also taken from literature; her name, 'Bel-Anna', is a quotation from Jonson's first royal entertainment of the Stuart reign.[39] The almost complete elision of the masquers in favour of their literary representation allowed Jonson to quote from his own work to describe Anna as the sum of all queens, and in doing so to present himself as the sum of all poets. It seems, therefore, that the literary text of the masque performance, written at the request of Prince Henry, records both the performance and the court's shifting loyalties and alliances. Moving from Anna's patronage to that of her son in the time between performance and publication, Jonson used the scholarly authority of the printed text to elide any traces of the female body and its performative agency in favour of his own authority as poet and that of the man who it was then thought would be the future king.[40]

What physical description Jonson's transcript does deliver is reserved not for the queens but for the scenery; the masquers' physicality is glossed over in favour of that of the House of Fame (figure 12). It seems that the female body is described not in literature but in design, in the texts of scenery and costume. Unlike the House of Fame, the costumes are not described by Jonson, but both their designs and that of the House make up another record to rival the literary text. After all, the sheer fact of female performance meant that the scenic and corporeal text of *Queens* could not resist a direct engagement with the representative strategies of female corporeality. In this way the visual text's necessary focus on the bodily can be seen to unsettle the primacy of the scripted text. By offering this alternative account of female textuality, the visual script works to deny Jonson's linguistic construction of the feminine, and stands in contrast to the published text of the masque. Such a reading allows for a recognition of the fact that, in performance, the female personages' fictionality was incorporated within the physicality of the courtly women on the masquing stage. However, the bodies of the masquers, who were recognised by their watching peers and who represented both the virtues and trans-gressions of the courtly noblewoman, carried, perhaps inadvertently, a meaning which did not accord with masculine courtly ideals. As the fictionalised queens of Jonson's transcript were bodied forth by the women who inhabited the costume and scenery of the stage set, those alternative texts of stage, costume and performance inevitably rendered the literary text's elision of physical representation unworkable.

The transgressive nature of the masquers' physicality is one underlying reason for the elision of their bodies from the literary masque text and the surfacing of their presence in the physical texts of costume and scenery. In turn this absence suggests an anxiety over the relationship of the female body to performance and further tensions concerning the interaction of the female body, language and architecture. In *Queens*, the House of Fame provided the main means of structuring the representation (textual, performative and architectural) of aristocratic Jacobean femininity, and it simultaneously constructed and framed the masque's self-referential focus on these representational strategies. The constructs of stage machinery and costume surrounded the masquer with physical restraints, defining the way in which the gendered aristocratic body could perform. These effects can be especially felt within the masque's construction of the literary canon and the presentation of the woman as textualised icon within the multiple texts of *Queens*.

The relationship between extra-literary components and the aristocratic masquing body is nowhere more obvious than in Jones's scenic designs,

12 The House of Fame, from *The Masque of Queens* (1609), by Inigo Jones

where the masquing body itself acted as an expressive text. Contextualising these designs in terms of contemporary scenic and architectural discourses reveals the significance of *Queens*'s particular synthesis of architecture, body and text staged in the spectacle of the House of Fame, and allows for a reading of the conflicting tensions of the performing body of *Queens*, a masque bound up with the representation of queenship and the negotiation of female power. This reading recognises the masquers' often-discussed amazonian transgression as a product of their physical representation and corporeal performance. Through its central positioning of the gendered body in stage architecture, costume and dance, *Queens* interrogated female representation and performance. Furthermore, although the juxtaposition of female masquers and male transvestite actors was a common occurrence in the Jacobean masque, through its treatment in *Queens* Jonson's masque became a self-conscious examination of female representation and the nature of women's masquing itself.[41]

Inigo Jones's initial conception of the female body in this masque was architectural. The women were presented as living statues, signifying parts of the meaningful building of the House of Fame. As the most important components of this, the main piece of the masque's scenery, the communicative female body formed the central focus of *Queens*'s stage vision. At the masquers' appearance their bodies were presented under the auspices of Renaissance Vitruvian architectural theory, which specifically gendered its main tenets of symmetry and proportion:

> From [proportion] result the principles of symmetry. Without symmetry and proportion there can be no principles in the design of any temple; that is, if there is no precise relation between its members, as in the case of those of a well shaped man.[42]

Situating the female body as the imperfect other, the founding principles of this theory were the proportions of the perfected male body. The masquers' imperfect bodies were further reified in the figure of the statue; enthroned within the House, the female masquers were an architectural spectacle serving the statue's function of corporeal display for the audience's gaze. The essence of the living female statue, a trope which figures again prominently in my reading of Campion's *Lords' Masque* in chapter 4, is the masquers' confinement in the static passivity of surface adornment; rather than self-presenting, their representation was as created artefacts.

It is tempting to see this scenic definition of the female body as reflective of the equivalent courtly ideological restrictions upon feminine language and sexuality. The most far-reaching of all of these was, of course, that constraining the masquer to silence. And when considering the relationship of the female performing body to linguistic expression, this injunction becomes particularly allusive. In a performance which centred on issues of text, language and canonicity, the House itself is implicated in an enactment of the bonds between Renaissance architecture, language and the body, with Jones's visual stage text synthesising these concepts into an expressive whole. The scenic text of *Queens*, then, depicted the linguistic canon as a bodily construction fashioned from the corporeal actuality of the female courtly performer. The House, 'whose columns be / Men-making poets', and which, of course, echoes Chaucer's own monument to poetry of the same name, itself becomes a linguistic structure; it is the literary canon, fashioned upon the synthesis of text, architecture and the gendered body.[43] Founded upon the dimensions and imaginative perception of the body, this design, a signifying building which 'bodied forth' the canon ('personating it'), expressed the communion of architectural, bodily and linguistic texts.

Although the female body would seem to have been present in the physical text and absent from the literary one, the relationship between that body and the literary canon was not simplistic. Despite Jonson's elision of the female body from the published transcript, his literary representation of the women reasserted their relationship to the canon, particularly when juxtaposed with the scenic text of the House. The staging of the architectural female body placed it in a direct relationship with language and textuality, since the noble masquers accessed linguistic expression through their threatening physicality. In addition, the architecture which presented and defined the masquers' body in *Queens* also made it the masque's central spectacle in both theme and performance. The term 'spectacle' and the phrase 'making a spectacle' converge in this masque to denote both the masque genre's ocular discourse of courtly magnificence and the type of gendering unpacked by Mary Russo. Russo discusses the 'specifically feminine danger' of the exposure and the loss of boundaries involved in spectacle, positing it as something which happens to women; however, it is clear that in *Queens* the essential volition involved in the act of 'making a spectacle out of herself' reversed this passivity and assigned its female performers an empowering demonstrative quality.[44] The stage architecture of *Queens* clearly shows the convergence of these extremes. A two-tiered continuation of the Banqueting House, distinguished by the proscenium arch and by its height from the floor, the House staged a conceptual continuity between court and visionary ideal.[45] Conceptually and structurally, it sited the female masquing body at the centre of performance; positioned at the convergence of the stage's perspective sightlines, the female body was at the centrepoint of the visionary and actual world of the ritual court. Essentially ocular and literally visionary, then, Queens, as The Vision before it, centred upon the spectacle of the female body exposed to the king's interpretative gaze. However, one of the effects of the female presence inside the House of Fame was that, although attempting to remain exclusively male, the House – the literary canon – was premised around the female body, destabilising the dominant male presence at the conceptual and practical heart of both the symbolic stage architecture and literary creation. Given this, the alignment of the queens with canonical literature is an allusive contrast to the non-courtly knowledge and experience of the transgressive witches, distinguishing between these versions of femininity through their class and canonical status.[46]

The representation of the body within the ideological decorum of the Jacobean court created tensions within Queens, tensions reflected in the masque form's own fractured synthesis of disparate arts and expressive potentialities. Perhaps more importantly, as the central structural component of the masque performance and stage machinery, the female presence in Queens reworked the gendered premises of Renaissance architecture. This is probably best illustrated in the masque's reversal of the model of the Vitruvian caryatid. In the original model the female caryatid bore the building's physical weight while the conceptual weight of that architecture's aesthetic and ideological standard was borne by the male body. Queens reversed the passive weight-bearing of servitude, transforming the caryatid into an embellishing female statue, free to descend from Jones's elaborate pedestal. In contrast, the inanimate, weight-bearing male poet-statues remained static. In a similar vein Jones reworked his source text, the allegorical House of Virtue and Vice of Filarete's Tratatto di Architectura (1461–64), to raise the female masquers to the higher level, rather than consign them to the lower one designated for prostitutes.[47] This both distanced the women from the sexualised figure of the prostitute and emphasised their authoritative position in the Jacobean court. So, in its treatment in Jones's House of Fame, the trope of the female body as architectural construct was both constraining and liberating – the created were given agency while the poets, the creators, remained lifeless. In the same way the description of Artemisia, who ingested her husband's cremated body and was herself monumentalised, 'making herself his tomb', endowed the female body with the agency of architectural commissioning and creation, and with amazonian rule.[48] Designating as male the static supporting function of the House, Jones's design blurred the masque's strict hierarchical distinctions. To be sure, the disturbance of the conventional gender dynamics of Renaissance architecture is accompanied by a mistrust of the feminine within the masque's linguistic text (the women were accepted into the House and into representation itself "gainst all opposite voice').[49] In its architectural presentation of the female body, however, *Queens* staked a claim for that body's significance.

The House of Fame, a patriarchal linguistic construct made material through the created artefact of the female body, is a contradictory structure. Although it constrained feminine self-definition, it also fashioned the masquing body as a signifying force: female masque performance, therefore, became a negotiation of restrictive boundaries. This mode of performance demanded that the masquers' bodies, on display in the House during Heroic Virtue's speech, should be watched and appreciated as spectacle. Wynne-Davies's description of the female masquers as being 'released' from the scenery to perform in danced motion is useful here; the masquers were freed from contained stasis within the House into a different order of physical expression in the dance.[50] A recognition of this pattern of holding and release calls attention to the complex structuring of imaginative space in *Queens*. The masquers withdrew within the House and descended inside it to the masquing stage, emerging through a central doorway suggestive of the building's interior. While the insularity of courtly society allowed women to masque, they are represented here as if on the imaginative exterior of the House; as statues defined by architecture, the women's representation was dictated by the gendered ideologies of the masculine public sphere. Emerging on to the masquing stage, the masquers also moved into the enclosed community of the Banqueting House and, eventually, into a new order of physical expression. This shift into motion was enacted in interiority as the noblewomen emerged into the masquing hall through doors which connect distinct imaginative incarnations of the same space. Defined by the discourses of architectural and public space, the representation of the gendered performing body altered with the shifting perception of the spaces in which it performed.

Crucially, this descent was not made through the masquers' own energies, but was a drawn-out process mediated by scenic items. The masquers emerged on to the stage in chariots, strongly reminiscent of the pageant cars used for Prince Henry's baptism in 1594, with the notable exception that these chariots were pulled by the witches rather than 'a moor'. The amazonian queens (conveyed in the chariots much as Anna herself was 'conveyet' during her Edinburgh coronation) remained static scenic spectacles. Although on one level the image of the hags, who earlier created a vision of hell through their dance rather than any scenery, can be read as spectacularising the self-willed female body harnessed to conformist women (the queens), a more problematic dynamic simultaneously emerges here. Entering from the House, the chariots existed as an extension of Jones's shifting scenery; movement, then, the marker of scenic difference between the masque stage and the non-courtly theatres, and perhaps exploited to the full here by Jones precisely for its novelty, was denied to the masquers. Scenic motion appropriated the female kinetic principle, literally harnessing the energies of the witches to the scenic structures and constraining the masquers to stillness. Both witches and queens were effectively restrained from self-willed movement; though one group was exalted, one humiliated, the experience of confinement was shared. The harnessing of the witches' energies was the domination not simply of women over women but of machinery over the female body.[51]

The queens finally abandoned scenic containment to generate significance through movement in the masquing dance (social and performative) on the floor of the Banqueting House. Despite tensions over the feminine presence, the court masque created the female performing body as text; the creation of a physicalised literary canon around the gendered architectural body granted the noblewomen entrance to textuality. This corporeal textualisation is best illustrated in the dancing of Prince Charles's name, discussed in full in chapter 1. Jonson's description emphasises the bond between the silenced female body, corporeal linguistics and architectural theory: 'the motions were so even and apt and their expression so just, as if mathematicians had lost proportion they might there have found it'.[52] Here the moving female body created proportion: the architectural principle was the foundation for the linguistic expression of the Jacobean female masquer. The female body (fashioned as the literary canon in the architectural construct of the House of Fame which it itself creates) became explicitly textual in the dance of the name, denying women's dislocation from linguistic significance and disrupting the pressure to feminine silence. As in *Blackness*, the physicalisation of the female masquers led not to their exclusion from linguistic expression but instead, in the staging of the architectural and textual female body, to the physicalisation of language itself.

The scenic fashioning of the female body was not unique to *Queens*, but rather was consistent throughout the early Jonesian/Jonsonian masques.

Whilst this spectacular display served much the same purpose as that found in Daniel's *Vision*, it controlled rather than utilised the kinetic impulse of the female body, which meant that it was actually predicated along vastly different lines. The presentation of the female masquers in the scallop shell of *Blackness* (which displayed the women and propelled them to the front of the masquing stage); the three-way motion of the Throne of Beauty in the masque of the same name; the display of the female masquers of *Hymenaei* as a 'discovery' (where they remained during Reason's speech before descending in 'two great clouds'); these moments set a pattern of static female bodily spectacle and the appropriation of female movement by containing scenic items.[53] Under certain circumstances, however, male masquers also became scenic spectacle, a notable example being Prince Henry in the moving chariot of *Oberon*.[54] Within a single-sex masque, therefore, nobles of either sex were static spectacles, often presented in the motif of release from imprisonment by the monarch's active gaze. The distinction between male and female performance, however, lies in the fact that while noblewomen consistently formed passive displays (the female body subjugated to the monarch's will within the discourse of courtly magnificence), aristocratic male performance altered with the nature of the masque genre itself. When noblemen performed alongside female masquers in the double masques *Hymenaei* and Campion's *Lords' Masque*, the dynamics of their performance were substantially altered. In contrast to the static female masquers of *Hymenaei*, the male performers had to 'issue forth' from a globe and went 'dancing out on the stage'.[55] In the presence of female performers, male masquers were represented as increasingly energetic, unable to be contained by the scenery. The exaggeration of gendered characteristics in mixed performance is most clearly shown in *The Lords' Masque*. Here the gendered division of kinetic energies formed the central conceit; the contrast between the encapsulation of the women within the icon of the statue and the semi-divine energy of the male lords who were figured as dancing stars could hardly be more overt.[56] Exclusively male masquing enacted the passivity of erotic power before the monarch examined in chapter 1. However, when male and female masquers shared a stage, masculine performance altered to portray an intensification of gender roles while female performance remained unchanged. The gendered body was a scenic component within these masques, the female body consistently so, the male only so long as it maintained an exclusive relationship of power and subjugation with the monarch's gaze.

As part of this gendered distinction between male and female masquers, scenic motion was a vital tool in the representation of femininity. In each of the scenic transformations which constitute the action of *Queens*, between the fiery hell and the House of Fame, and the *machina versatilis* which revealed the queens and Fama bona, the switch was sudden. Jonson's transcript stresses both speed and surprise: 'Here the throne wherin they sat, being *machina versatilis*, suddenly changed, and in the place of it appeared Fama bona', echoing the description of the hell, which having 'quite vanished [...] in the place of it appeared a glorious and magnificent building figuring the House of Fame'.[57] These descriptions emphasise place and replacement; the stage machinery was a succession of alternating visions of femininity. Insisting on the bond between demonised witches, transgressive queens and the exalted abstraction Fama bona, it in effect presented successive visions of the same, ultimately threatening, femininity. The three types of womanhood ended the masque inextricably bound together within a hierarchical male-authored stage-space; Fama bona watched from the heights of the House while the queens rode their chariots, followed by the physically debased hags. In a move which reveals the masque genre's class-driven agenda, this hierarchical female community was broken only by the further descent of the masquers for the measures and revels. Within a court whose prioritising of class over gender facilitated female performance in the masque form itself, class delineated the performance of femininity.

Within the sustained bond of the three incarnations of womanhood, however, individual female representations were distinguished by their performers. While the extremes of the early modern polarised representation of the feminine were performed by male transvestite actors, the queens, less easily categorised as clearly virtuous or vice-ridden, were performed by women. The self-referentiality of this feminine representation is borne out throughout all the various incarnations of the feminine in *Queens*. The bonds between Queen Anna and the Dame are particularly instructive. Given that male performers could enact female transgression with impunity, Anna's transgressive performance in *Blackness*, resolved only the previous year in the performance of *Beauty*, related suggestively to the transvestite male performers of the witches and specifically to that of the Dame. The Dame herself drew attention to her transgression through her costume, and her demands that her followers should bare their feet and knees evoke the controversy surrounding Anna's own over-revealing costume in 1605.[58] The nascent antimasque, which was formalised at Anna's own request, was a forum which encouraged the performance of the antithesis of the courtly ideal and so was eminently suitable for the representation of the Queen's own gender crime by a cross-dressed male performer. This self-conscious dislocation of the memory of previous court performances, and the self-referentiality of the performance of femininity, is closely tied to the performance of these incarnations of the feminine by male and female performers.

Exposing the amazon:
costume as scenery

When the masquers descended from the stage for the intended social confirmation of the revels of *Queens*, the transgressive reality of the icons which they represented became clear as they took hands and danced with members of the court. In the decorous dance it was costume which signalled the transgression of the courtly codes of feminine physical decorum. Embellishing and defining the physical actuality of the female body in movement, the costumes of *Queens* were extensions of the stage machinery – costume as scenery. In performance, and in the masque form in particular, costume is a means of structuring the signifying space of the gendered body and of informing the imaginative space of the stage; in the case of the masque genre it defined the body for the gaze of a specific audience, working with or against conventions of the corporeal ideal. Yet the women masquers also energised these scenic items. In effect Inigo Jones found an alternative stage in the aristocratic masquing body and was able to create meaning through the alteration of its form. With this in mind it is wholly fitting that Jones should have designed the conceptually unified scenery and costume. This unity of design (embracing costume, scenery and performance space) reached its logical conclusion when in 1619 he designed the third Banqueting House. In order to illuminate the avant-garde nature of the masquing of the court of Anna of Denmark, it might be useful to see the House of Fame as a precursor of that later building, unified with the existing performance structure of the 1606 Banqueting House and gesturing towards a future (as yet unconceived) performance space.

As an integral part of Jones's overall design for the masque, the designs he created, while operating primarily as practical working designs for costume manufacture, were also constructed representations of the courtly masquing body. Heavily influenced by continental mannerism, Jones's designs depicted the courtly body within a specific representative discourse.[59] In his doing so the designs for *Queens* also show themselves as a kind of visual panegyric; they are ideological presentations of the ideals to which the dancers should conform in pose and movement, both flattering and advisory representations of the masquing body.[60] This can be seen in the fact that, although slightly abstracted in facial and bodily features, individuals can be recognised in certain designs, such as that for Anna herself (figure 13). The royal performer would have recognised herself in this design, which would need both to offer her a flattering representation and the manufacturer a workable pattern. The advisory nature of these visual representations of the courtly masquing body can, however, perhaps best be seen in the way in which these texts depict that body in movement or dance. The designs for the queens show a particularly striking active quality, especially in comparison to the 'iconic, even heraldic pose [...] adopted for the communication of nobility' which Leslie identifies in the domestic tradition of the visual representation of the Renaissance courtly body (figures 14 and 15).[61] Jones's designs display 'a conception of the figure in which the bodies of the performers move, have weight and volume, and display the contours of a classical figure'.[62] They are complex representations of the courtly body and served several practical and ideological functions at once.

The recognition of the active nature of the masquing body requires an appreciation of the physical realities of *Queens*'s dances and of the practical demands of costume to accommodate such movement. Writing about the courtly celebrations of Christmas 1603–04, Dudley Carleton commented on the mistakes made in the costumes for the male dancers: 'Their attire was rich but somewhat too heavy and cumbersome for dancers, which put them beside their galliards.'[63] The practicalities of performance, then, demanded that, at the same time as being figurative representations, these designs also had to take account of the actuality of the masquing body, while using the model of the active classical body. Representing both the physical actuality and the idealisation of the courtly body and a fusing of classical, Italianate and domestic influences, these designs are complex representations in their own right.

The representation of feminine movement in these designs continued *Queens*'s strategic appropriation and definition of female kinesis by the stage machinery. Although remaining structured by the scenic definition of costume, the female body was liberated to move through its own powers in dance. The extent of the masquers' corporeal transgression became most apparent as they moved from the masquing stage into the communal space of the dancing floor. What is missing here, of course, is knowledge of the results of the collision between the designer's controlling vision and the variable of the individual courtier's performance

13 Headdress for Queen Anna, from *The Masque of Queens* (1609), by Inigo Jones

14 Candace, from *The Masque of Queens* (1609),
by Inigo Jones

15 Artemisia, from *The Masque of Queens* (1609), by Inigo Jones

of courtly bodily grace in movement and dance in the execution of the masque. Whilst it is tempting to speculate about the individual potential for rule-breaking, there is no evidence to suggest that this was ever taken up by Jacobean courtiers. However, we can be sure that this descent from scenic confinement certainly created transgression, generating significance through the alternative scenic structures of the masquers' martial, amazonian and transgressive costumes. The potential for such disruption existed within the ideal vision of the masque world and within the definition of the bodies of those who appeared to be the personifications of virtue but who in performance interrogated the definition of that ideal.

As part of this courtly ideal, the designs of *Queens* depicted an eroticised female body. Several designs clearly show the masquers' breasts or cover them only with gauzy material. Aristocratic female breasts were often bared in the Jacobean masque, as Jones's designs for the masquers of *Love Freed* and for Tethys show (figures 16 and 17), and the French and Elizabethan court fashion of exposed female breasts continued into the Jacobean reign (in 1617 Busino described Anna herself with her 'bosom bare down to the pit of her stomach, forming, as it were, an oval') and into the court masque.[64] This assertion of a sexualised femininity as consistent with the ideological requirements of the courtly woman is clearly apparent in *Queens*; Artemisia's breasts are barely hidden by a covering of light material and their shape is emphasised by the outlining of the costume (figure 15). This masquer was depicted to the watching court as an erotic spectacle. This pattern is repeated, and even those costumes which do not directly expose the breasts emphasise their presence. The costume for the unidentified queen, for example, displays bare breasts under a gauzy covering supported by a corset above an abdomen which is also scarcely concealed.[65] Although the exposure made possible by the corset is conventional, the garment does have another significance. Although these designs have an undoubted classical influence, this method of exposing the female breasts through the hard lines of corseture stems from an exaggeration of domestic fashion, melding the everyday dress of the court with an elevated classical ideal in much the same way as the masque itself elevated the courtier's everyday identity in its allegorical performance. Furthermore, the soft lines of the material covering the arms, shoulders and chests, and the hard lines of the enclosing bodice which defines the upright courtly torso is also significant. As I have previously noted in the designs for *Oberon*, the striking effeminisation of the male figure is achieved through just this contrast between the hard encasing lines of the bodice and the eroticised soft material swathes which

16 A Daughter of the Morn, from *Love Freed From Ignorance and Folly* (1611), by Inigo Jones

17 Tethys, from Daniel's *Tethys' Festival* (1610), by Inigo Jones

emulate the line of female breasts. The courtly body, male or female, seems, in single-sex performance at least, to have been fashioned along the lines of a similar erotic ideal, based on the spectacle of that courtly body.

The kind of exposure of the female body found in the masque was a courtly phenomenon. Though Chirelstein points out that there are 'no known full-scale portraits from this period that depict truly rounded breasts and nipples' and attributes their 'alluring display' in the masque to its 'idealised and privileged context', she does recognise the currency of a deep décolletage in many Jacobean court portraits. Furthermore, she demonstrates that women's breasts and nipples were fully depicted in 'the most private of art forms', the miniature.[66] To privacy I would add the miniature's elitism; the frank representation of the female body was confined to an art form commissioned and owned by the aristocracy, and to the elite theatricals of the masque. Responses to the public display of the body from beyond the court were, however, more complex. One example might be Patrick Hannay's description of the reaction of the proletariat to the sight of Anna's

> large, low, open breast,
> Full, white, round, swelling, azure-vain'd, increase
> The error, for they thought none liuing would
> Lay out such parts, for all eyes to behold:
> So curious were the colours which were showne,
> As Nature hardly could from Art be knowne.[67]

Hannay's lingering engagement with this description provides a detailed picture of the courtly practice of breast-exposure and vein-painting, and contrasts the reactions of the non-courtly witnesses with those of the knowledgeable elite. Though the dialogue of art and nature flattered Anna, the erotic shock of the non-courtly audience to this exposure also implies censure towards such artifice – Hannay uses the same means to praise Anna as contemporary critics used to attack such practices.[68] Within the insularity of the Banqueting House, however, such eroticism and its consequences formed part of the bodily ideal of the female masquer. Defined by both gender and class, courtly women were required to conform to the demands of female chastity, while simultaneously displaying their bodies in a manner which would have brought condemnation upon the non-courtly. Female aristocrats, therefore, were positioned at the nexus of the discourses of courtly membership and chaste female withdrawal; it seems that the masque often placed contradictory demands upon

the courtly woman, requiring a performance which signalled their conformity to silence, chastity and withdrawal through the erotic display of
the female body.

Certain aspects of the physical display of *Queens* were wholly in line
with the court's expectations, and this is so for the discourse of race. For
example, the design for Candace portrayed the 'renown of Ethiopia'
without black make-up, displaying feminine sexuality without repeating
the damaging transgressions of *Blackness*.[69] In certain ways, however, the
uncovering of the body itself required caution. For example, though
the court allowed its women to display their breasts, other areas of the
female body, such as the arms and shoulders, could not be shown without
breaking with decorum.[70] And here, once again, the masquers' costumes
were conformist. So, although the design for Lucy Russell as Penthesilea
was clearly erotic as her breasts and abdomen were displayed (one breast
perhaps hidden by her amazon sash), this eroticism remained respectable
because her shoulders, the top of her arms and her legs were hidden
from sight (figure 4). Certainly a degree of bodily display was demanded
of the women, but it was kept within strictly defined limits. An instructive
contrast is perhaps that between the non-courtly transvestite Dame, whose
physicality contravenes the court's decorum, and the masquers who, on
the whole, conform to these codes.

Such moments notwithstanding, the designs' martial and amazonian
traits remained *Queens*'s most overt expression of feminine non-conform-
ity. These classically inspired costumes, with their militaristic armour,
buskins and headpieces, transgressed most obviously through their reworking of the amazonian trope.[71] The swathe across the torso, common
to Penthesilea, Atlanta, Berenice and Thomyris, was a further pointer to
the image of the amazon. Referring not only to the female warrior's
bow, but also to the practice of removing one breast to allow easy use
of this weapon, the swathe is a shorthand indication of the way in which
the assumption of masculine traits redefined and reshaped the female
body.[72] The bared breast may be acceptable within the court masque,
however, since, viewed through the defining structure of costume, the
masquers' prominent breasts marked the performing female body as a site
of ideological conflict. The martial, and therefore masculine, erotics of
these costumes transgressed the passively erotic femininity of the court's
ideal. The distance between the two was manifested in the conflicting
signals which arose from the conventional eroticisation of female bodies
which also appropriated more threatening masculine qualities of martial
and political engagement. Strikingly similar in conception to the shift of

gender categories within a martial framework depicted in *Oberon*, these designs are a marker of the tensions surrounding female agency in the Jacobean court.

The amazonian traits expressed within these costumes and in the transcript of *Queens* have been addressed in detail by critics, but bear some brief repetition here.[73] The threat posed by the amazon is signalled in Jonson's description of Penthesilea as 'honoured in her death to have it the act of Achilles'.[74] In the realm of Renaissance male fantasy the figure of the amazon is necessarily complemented by the textual fantasy of her death and reification: the only good amazon is a dead amazon.[75] Though not apparent in performance, such recuperative textual strategies complemented the corporeal constraint of the female body in *Queens*. One aspect of the threat of erotic militarism which such strategies sought to contain lay in the intertextualities between Anna's representation as queen consort and the reign of Elizabeth I. Although, because of the risk attached to the inverted image of patriarchal order, the amazonian trope was not explicitly used to compliment Elizabeth I, it was intimately linked with her reign and became more common following her death. Schwarz describes the use of Elizabethan iconography in *Queens* as 'singularly inappropriate to James' and notes that it took place during a wave of Elizabethan nostalgia.[76] And, indeed, the representation of the female masquers suggests that this masque existed as part of a tradition of female rule rather than to praise the authority of James I. For example, Valasca's husband-murder in the name of true order hints at a restoration of an earlier female rule and threatens the familial construction of gendered Stuart absolutist authority. It is tempting to speculate that echoes of Mary Stuart surfaced in this image; James's mother and Anna's co-religionist, accused of the murder of her husband (Lord Darnley) and of bearing an illegitimate child (James himself), bore a certain similarity to the disruptive figure of Valasca and the threat the latter posed to patriarchal stability.

Criticism of *Queens* has prioritised the court's masculine knowledge; James I's interest in witch trials has largely been privileged over Anna's lived experience.[77] The hags' 'great purpose', the overthrow of courtly festival, maps on to the Berwick witch trials which followed Anna's marriage and arrival in Scotland in 1590.[78] Although the festivals of coronation and entry which began the consort's reign in Scotland were threatened with disruption, Jonson's 1609 masque figured itself as another ritual definition of queenship threatened by the power of disruptive femininity. Significantly, the historical events of the Danish marriage and the witch trials, and their later imaginative reworking in *Queens*, each juxtaposed a virtuous femininity with a threatening opposite from which it apparently could not be separated. However, the intense critical focus on the inclusion of James's interests in this masque should not obscure the importance of Anna's role as the central performer of *Queens* and as the supposed object of the Berwick witches' apparent curse. James himself does not seem to have been the main concern of a masque primarily involved with an examination of queenship and femininity; the King was in fact an almost neglected presence. If the watching James was embodied within the masque, it was in the performance's only non-transvestite actor, the static, verbose but essentially weak Heroic Virtue. As Schwarz says, the 'Jacobean queen's masques detach the display of women's power from the referent of the king' – the threat of the amazon is that of female community and male redundancy.[79]

Such female community also points to the essential similarity of the witches and queens and so helps to collapse the artificial polarisation between the monstrous and virtuous woman in this masque. Emerging together into the social space of the masquing hall at the culmination of the main masque, the simultaneous movement of the witches and queens implied an assimilation and survival of the witches' powers.[80] In its apparent division of conformity and transgression between the queens and witches and in the denial of this by the formers' amazonian qualities, this masque can be read as both supporting and denying the polarisation of female representation within the patriarchal court hegemony. What it certainly does, however, is problematise the representation of the feminine and present the threat of femininity latent within the most virtuous of women. While, for Purkiss, class is the primary division between these alternate representations of femininity, attention should also be paid to the role of gender in effecting this separation.[81] Although the exalted deity of Fama bona and the transgressive and humiliated figures of the witches were performed by male transvestite actors, female performance enacted a far less definable womanhood – the female masquers were representations of a challenging femininity which did not fit easily with contemporary masculine perceptions and which had consequences for the structure and strategies of the masque form itself. Male performers enacted the polarised representations of femininity, but female masquers performed the blurred category of a femininity which, as Sherry Ortner once put it, stood beyond these extremes.[82] Both virtuous and transgressive, the depiction of the queens questioned the very nature of both categories as a means of describing courtly women. On stage the fear that even virtuous women may have stood beyond masculine depiction is translated into that of the empowered, ruling woman – the fear of the amazon.

The court masque's juxtaposition of transvestite male performance and female masquing predated the simultaneous performance of women and men-as-women on the early Restoration stage, but has received little critical attention. Although transvestite male performance had long been established in the public and private theatres, this unprecedented juxtaposition is significant, precisely because it is revealing of the gendered attitudes towards the perception, representation and performance of women in the Jacobean court.[83] Put before an audience versed in transvestite male performance, this juxtaposition could work to highlight the presence of female masquers, emphasising still further the contrast between these distinct forms of female representation – the cross-dressed male body and the 'real' female body. In its treatment of these distinct markers, *Queens* centred upon the representational strategies of femininity available to it: the witches, men acting as transgressive women, were displaced by the queens, women acting as men, in a way which contested the corporeal and literary representation of the feminine.

The empowering specularity of the female body in this masque's scenery and costume highlights the novelty of women's performance in the juxtaposition of female and male-as-female performance. Central to the masque visually in the House of Fame and thematically in that scenery's corporeal and literary representation of different versions of femininity, the body of the masquing woman and the perception of female performance were at the heart of *Queens*. What is more, this scenery was also expressive of the constraints which limited female performance in the masque genre itself; while it restricted the female body, scenery simultaneously created it as a signifying performance medium. That body was expressive despite and because of the physical definition of femininity through the structuring influence of scenery and costume. In its use of the resources of the masquing stage *Queens* became a remarkable interrogation of the structures of female representation and political and social agency within courtly women's performance.

It is inevitable that a reading of the material text of the masque will have a forceful impact on interpretations of the genre. This chapter's readings of *The Vision* and *Queens* clarify the importance of the meaningful building to the performance of the court masque. Whether that building was the masque's playing space, as in the case of the Great Hall at Hampton Court, or whether it was staged within the masque itself as in the House of Fame, the discourses of architecture contributed to the construction of significance in the ephemeral and context-dependent masque form. Such architectural discourses are also integral to the reading of the text of the female body in performance. Through the staging strategies of *The Vision* and *Queens*, the courtly female frame was transformed from the resurrection of a Tudor body to an architectural Stuart corporeality. Despite this shift, however, the aristocratic female body remained central to each of the court masque's performance modes. Though the innovations of raised stage, shifting scenery and centralised perspective radically altered the masque, the design of the House of Fame demonstrates that these transformations did not diminish the centrality of the female aristocratic body. Rather, this body became manifested within architectural discourses of physical confinement, discourses which were distinctly Stuart in their conceptualisation of courtly femininity. Hence *The Masque of Queens* was simultaneously centred on and destabilised by the presence of the very same expressive female body that it sought to contain within the architecture of stage and costume.

CHAPTER FOUR

Disputed marriages:
the female courtier as spectator

On 23 October 1612 Frederick the Elector Palatine arrived at Whitehall to meet his future wife, Princess Elizabeth, daughter of Anna of Denmark and James I. After processing up the Thames, he entered Whitehall with Prince Charles to be greeted by the striking tableau of the royal family, James I, Anna, Elizabeth and Prince Henry, seated on a dais in the Banqueting House. Frederick approached, as numerous diplomats, ambassadors and royal visitors had done before him, and was greeted effusively by the English King. According to contemporary accounts, the Elector then turned to Anna; however, here the welcome seemed distinctly frosty: 'she entertained him with a fixed Countenance; and though her Posture might have seemed (as was judged) to promise him the Honour of a Kiss for his Welcome, his Humillity carried him no higher than her Hand'.[1] The scramble for the proposed marriages of Elizabeth and her brother, Henry Prince of Wales, has been well documented, as has James I's desire, thwarted by the Prince's premature death, to achieve a balance in the unions of his offspring by matching his daughter with a Protestant ruler and marrying Henry to a Catholic princess. It was, of course, inevitable that Anna should oppose the Palatinate match; she had been involved in negotiations for Catholic marriages for her children, and by 1613 was encouraging a Spanish match for Princess Elizabeth.[2] After the Prince of Wales's untimely death in November 1612 placed Elizabeth closer to the throne, her marriage assumed both a greater importance and uncertainty, and there were rumours that the Scots court faction wanted the Princess to marry the Marquis of Hamilton.[3] However, once the Palatinate match had been ratified, the festival which celebrated the marriage was the most extensive Jacobean England had seen, and, indeed, the first English royal wedding since that of Mary Tudor to Philip II in 1554. These extensive festivities, and the positioning of the royal family within them, can be used to access the shifting status of court masque performance in general and female performance in particular. In addition the celebrations are revealing of the marriage networks which operated between the courts of early modern Europe. Certainly, the entertainments for this marriage had an influence upon the dynamics of the engagement of both royal women with a culture of court spectacle.

Anna's disapproval of the Palatinate match clearly informed her display of sternness to Frederick at his arrival, but her presence in the tableau itself is perhaps harder to gauge. Indeed, the Queen's opposition to this marriage would later manifest itself in her withdrawal from court ritual, as when she absented herself from the affiancing in the Banqueting House on 31 December 1612. Chamberlain, in telling parentheses, explains her non-attendance as follows: she was 'troubled (as they say) with the gowte'. However, the King, who 'was not out of his chamber in three or fowre dayes before nor since, having a spice of the same disease', did put in an appearance.[4] Withdrawal, as we have seen, is a strategy which figured prominently in Anna's career, coming to have even greater significance in the second decade of the seventeenth century with the waning of the Queen's political power. The female refusal to perform was a complex gesture which, as suggested in chapter 1, points to the rejection of the norms of a courtly performance which, for its success, was dependent on a female participation. However, as contemporary observers commented, the Queen did later appear to begin to mellow towards the marriage as it and the alliances which it formed became increasingly inevitable.[5]

The roles of both Anna of Denmark and Princess Elizabeth in the entertainments for the latter's marriage emphasise the distinctions which existed between individual royal women in the Jacobean courts. The influence of religion and faction, and the position of both women with regards to their roles as both givers and receivers of the common currency of royal favour, all distinguished Anna from her daughter. Within Jacobean courtly society, aristocratic and royal women were at the nexus of conflicting demands of class and gender; political, factional and familial allegiances overcame any simplistic sense of gender solidarity and also bring into question the validity of looking for an uncomplicated early modern proto-feminism. The relationship between these two royal women was not a simple equation but a fractured and complex alignment; to present an image of a community of women opposed to a single patriarchy would simply replace one monolithic vision with another, equally fraudulent one. And, certainly, the relationship between Anna and Elizabeth within the gender discourses of the Jacobean courts was not one-dimensional, but was deepened and exacerbated by the mother's Catholicism and the daughter's fervent Protestantism.[6] Evidence of the tensions between the two surfaced in the preparations for the Palatinate match, during which there were reports of arguments in which Anna was said to have called her daughter 'Goody Palsgrave' and the latter to have retorted that she 'had rather be the wife of the Palsgrave than the greatest Papist Queen in Christendom'.[7] Clearly, such insults delineate Anna's notions of class status, queenship and religious adherence in obvious distinction to her daughter.

The eventual marriage of Elizabeth and Frederick on 14 February 1613 was celebrated with a set of *magnificences* lasting almost two weeks, comprising ceremonials such as Frederick's investiture as Knight of the Garter, public spectacles such as a firework display and a sea battle on the Thames (intended to be spectacular, but in fact something of a failure), and events intended only for the court itself, including three masques and fourteen plays performed at court by the King's Men.[8] Thomas Campion's *Lords' Masque* (the only one to include female performers) was staged on the evening of the marriage, George Chapman's *Memorable Masque* on the following day and Francis Beaumont's *Masque of the Inner Temple and Gray's Inn* was begun on 16 February and completed on Saturday 20 February.

Conducted along the lines of continental *magnificences*, these entertainments were designed to cement the Protestant alliance between England and the Palatinate. The entertainments were, therefore, closely involved in the networks of international dynastic negotiation and in the domestic representation of marriage in general. Although this festival has been much studied, there remains a hitherto unasked question: what representation were the royal female spectators of this festival and of its masques afforded, and how did Anna and Elizabeth relate to the single instance of female performance included in these celebrations? Furthermore, what might it mean that a marriage to which the Queen (previously the main producer and performer of court masques) was openly opposed should have been celebrated with such an extensive set of entertainments, masques and plays?

The masques which will form the main focus of this chapter quickly demonstrate that the specific circumstances of this moment offered a concept of elite women's engagement with performance distinct from that seen previously in the Jacobean court. Above all, neither Anna nor Elizabeth performed in the Palatinate festival's masques. This prolonged and controversial festival of masques and plays, unprecedented in the Jacobean court, positioned its royal women as the spectators of a predominantly male courtly performance. This shows the extent to which the status of the court masque, always dependent for its definition on the shifting factional politics of the Jacobean courts, had changed since *The Masque of Queens* four years earlier. Of these developments one of the most important was a shift in the involvement in masque performance of women in general and of Anna and her court in particular. *Queens*, the apotheosis of Anna's masquing and a display of her concept of queenship, marked the end of a specific period in the history of Jacobean female performance, and the years following Jonson's masque saw Anna gradually relinquish control of the Whitehall masquing stage to other courts and factions. In a period which was also one of transition for the monarch, with the emergence of masques patronised and staged by the Inns of Court to honour the King and his own re-establishment as a masque patron, James's masques began to dislodge Anna's from centre stage.[9] Between 1604 and 1609, the King's masques, or those commissioned in his honour, had been restricted to marriage entertainments such as *Hymenaei* or *The Lord Hay's Masque*. Indeed, the performances of these years outlined two distinct courts. James's court, devoted to Anglo-Scottish union, figured its authority through the gendered construct of the patriarchal family, best exemplified in *Hymenaei*; in contrast, Anna's court danced an image of female community and of a continuity of queenship in performances such as *The Vision, Blackness* and *Queens*. As I have suggested, many of the tensions of the Jacobean masque really arose from the difficulties of embodying the demands of the different Jacobean courts, and in particular the assertions of gender and political difference which Anna's masques attempted. In addition the politics of the masque form were compromised by the conflicting demands of Anna's position as both queen consort and masque performer in her own right. However, by the time of Jonson's *Golden Age Restored* (1615), the first masque to follow the Palatinate and Somerset marriages, James's masques had effectively replaced Anna's as the court's annual performance. As a consequence these later masques were freed from the necessity of pleasing both king and patron, and, with James fulfilling both roles, achieved a less problematic homage of the watching sovereign.

Anna's withdrawal from performance at Whitehall has often been characterised as a by-product of her son's death in 1612 and the loss of Elizabeth to the continent.[10] Although the general emotional outpouring which followed Henry's death and Anna's deep grief, still demonstrable in her refusal to attend Charles's inauguration as Prince of Wales four years later, certainly contributed to her apparent abandonment of performance, it is too simplistic to see these events as the sole determinants shaping the shift in the trend of Jacobean female performance.[11] Although Anna was undoubtedly a leader of courtly female performance, her withdrawal does not fully account for what has been perceived as a general female retreat from the masque at this time. Even disregarding the gendering of Anna as mother rather than queen, historical evidence contradicts a total abandonment of performance by either Anna or her women. On the contrary, as I discuss in chapter 5, her coterie's retreat from Whitehall masquing in fact accompanied a phase of performance and spectatorship beyond the boundaries of the court; her progress to Bristol and Bath in June 1613 and the dancing of *Cupid's Banishment* (1617) at Greenwich Palace suggest the emergence of a finely nuanced picture of the various sites in which Jacobean power was staged and performance was enacted.[12] And, as chapter 5 demonstrates, if grief kept her from performance, it did not preclude Anna from a continuing engagement with other forms of cultural production.

In early 1613, however, with Henry's death just behind her and Elizabeth's departure imminent, it would be easy to identify such emotional distress as the ruling influence in Anna's involvement with the Palatinate festival. This, though, would be inaccurate, since, prior to his death, Henry had been the pivotal force behind the celebrations, which in turn continued to reflect a political outlook with which his mother was not in tune.[13] Indeed Henry's sudden death in November 1612 exercised a defining influence over his sister's wedding, causing it to be postponed until February 1613 and substantially altering the agenda for the surrounding festival. Among the changes were the cancellation of two masques. Records have survived of one, which David Norbrook has belatedly entitled *The Masque of Truth*, commissioned by Henry; the second, which remains unnamed, was commissioned by Elizabeth herself.[14] Despite the marriage's postponement and the alteration of the festival, the pro-chivalric content of such entertainments as *Prince Henry's Barriers* of 1610 and the evidence of Henry's unperformed masque suggest that the festivities were to have been an unapologetic Protestant polemic which fitted in with Henry's own political and cultural programme. The resulting February marriage was, therefore, a somewhat diluted version of the intended celebration of Protestant ideology, but one which nevertheless figured the Palatinate match as an archetypal marriage and bore the traces of Henry's involvement.

While mourning for Henry may have prompted Anna to distance herself from the February marriage festivities, the process of her marginalisation from the masquing stage predated her son's death. As earlier sections have suggested, the second decade of the Jacobean reign in England saw the Whitehall court masque, previously a stage for female opposition, begin to be reappropriated by male aristocrats. Despite his youth, it was Henry who had initiated this process when he began dancing and commissioning works from Jonson, an artist previously associated primarily with the Queen's masques. Henry had begun to take an interest in his mother's masques in 1609 when he requested an annotated edition of *Queens* from Jonson, and he encroached further in 1610 with *Prince Henry's Barriers*. In fact, Henry's involvement radically altered the nature of the Jacobean masque, bringing a third prototype of royal authority – that of the militant Protestant chivalric hero – to the stage. The Prince's purposeful cultivation of chivalric imagery and a militant Protestantism, evident in his impersonation of Meliadus in the *Barriers*, was associated with what some critics have described as a nostalgic Jacobean perception of the Elizabethan era as a golden age of chivalric achievement.[15] The demands placed upon the masque poet by the existence of these three courts can be clearly seen in Daniel's *Tethys' Festival* (1610). Danced by Anna and her women for Henry's inauguration as Prince of Wales, and praising James as its privileged spectator, this masque delicately balanced the agendas of the courts of King, Queen and heir. Such an act of fine adjudication was also maintained, more or less successfully, in *Oberon*, but in this case between the courts of James and Henry alone.

In 1613, however, after Henry's sudden death and the break-up of his court, this attempt at even-handed dealing seems to have been somewhat destabilised. Rather than performing, the Jacobean female elite, and royal women in particular, seem to have been engaged in spectatorship, and so to have occupied the positions defined immediately before the Prince's death. Furthermore, in the light of the fact that the festival's patrons were James I, Frances Bacon and, as was intended, Henry himself, there was little room for female patronage on this occasion. However, perhaps because of her political affiliations with her brother and her agreement with her father's choice for her husband, Elizabeth was, to some extent at least, also involved in masque patronage for her marriage celebration. In November 1612 the Venetian Ambassador wrote that the Princess was 'preparing a sumptuous ballet of sixteen maidens, of whom she will be one' and referred again to a masque of 'lovely maidens' in a letter of 11 January 1613, only a month before the wedding.[16] Although plans for the marriage were still flexible in late 1612, it is interesting to see Elizabeth's masque mentioned as going ahead after her brother's death.[17] The masque, however, was not performed, and Barbara Lewalski suggests that it was cancelled either because of grief or because of Elizabeth's dependence upon Henry for its success.[18]

Elizabeth's intended patronage and performance in a masque would have been a fitting marker of her own courtly status, and an extension of her own as yet rather undeveloped performance career. Elizabeth had danced in *Tethys' Festival*, and its central conceit, the personification of rivers to depict nations and masquers, was carried over into both Beaumont's *Masque* and the unperformed *Masque of Truth*, perhaps as a compliment to the Princess's personation of the Thames. However, Elizabeth's attempt to commission for her own wedding was unsuccessful, and her undoubted enthusiasm for performance did not find an outlet in the Jacobean court, but, it seems, had to wait until she was established in her own court in Heidelberg.[19] The failure of Elizabeth's attempt at patronage, which had perhaps been inspired by her political and religious proximity to those commissioning and performing in this festival, would seem to mark the Palatinate festivities as a site for male patrons and performers. The Princess's marriage festivities appear, especially when set within the wider context of the development of Jacobean female court performance, primarily to confirm the recuperation of the male masque performer and patron after the female domination of the masquing stage.

Royal women as spectators of the Palatinate masques

What, then, were the dynamics of female spectatorship? What might it have meant for a royal woman to watch such masques, and what distinctions might have existed between Queen Anna's and Princess Elizabeth's positioning in relation to these spectacles? As suggested in the analysis of Anna as a spectator of Scottish court performances, the gender dynamics of the watching female audience could impact strongly upon the nature of the male spectacle. Indeed, in certain moments during the 1613 festival, Anna and Elizabeth adopted positions similar to those which the Queen had taken during her time in Scotland. For example, the day after the wedding both women, accompanied by the courts' female elite, watched from the windows of the Banqueting House as James, Frederick and Charles ran at the ring.[20] Again, as in the tourney for the 1594 baptism of Prince Henry, these spectators contributed to the fashioning of a chivalric masculinity.[21] While the dynamics of the royal women's spectatorship were complicated by a single instance of female performance, examined below, an interesting parallel does exist between Anna's former position as incoming queen consort and her daughter's position as a new queen consort about to leave her homeland. Anna, no longer the object of the marital quest but now its facilitator, watched entertainments reminiscent of those which had surrounded her own marriage and definition as consort, while Elizabeth, a consort as yet not arrived in her marital court, witnessed the celebratory representation of her future role. As far as Elizabeth was concerned, therefore, these masques may have placed specific demands of royal femininity upon their spectator.

One place where such demands are to be found is the Palatinate masques' depiction of national identity. Clearly, events such as a royal marriage raised the profile of the consort and her role in shaping a sense of national identity in her court of origin, and the discursive implications of such practices appear in the masques which celebrated Elizabeth's imminent departure from England. Take, for example, the image of marriage itself and the part it played in the international Protestant union between England and the Palatinate. Both Campion's *Lords' Masque* and Beaumont's *Masque of the Inner Temple* were intrinsically concerned with the nature of marriage and in predicting the future results of the union. Beaumont's antimasque, for example, was predicated on the incompatibility of the sexes, as demonstrated in the argument of Iris and Mercury. This was then replaced in the main masque by a male display of courtly athleticism, itself then transmuted into an act of gender harmony; when the male masquers took watching women from the audience out to dance in the revels, the progression from gendered turmoil to peace, signalled by the display of male grace and the positioning of women as audience and dancing partners, reached its climax.

More significantly, perhaps, these masques also defined an ideal of queenship for Elizabeth to take beyond her local shores, one in which female loyalty and the provision of heirs figured large. Campion in particular presented the need for heirs to cement the political and marital union between England and the Protectorate, an outcome which was imaged as the apotheosis of Protestantism.[22] Certainly *The Lords' Masque* figured the marriage union between England and the Palatinate as a means of reasserting the reformed faith in Europe to the benefit of the Jacobean court. For example, Sibylla's declaration, originally in Latin, presented this union as a triumph of Protestant ascendancy: 'Let the British strength be added to the German: can anything equal it? One mind, one faith, will join two peoples, and one religion, and one simple love.'[23]

Such a religious renewal was made possible through the recreated Protestant perception of the importance of marriage, already discussed in chapter 2, which situated Elizabeth (as its 'British' representative) at the

heart of dynastic, religious, political and international networks and connections. Immediately before this declaration, Sibylla's words are equally
revealing of the role which Elizabeth was to play: 'How the beautiful
bride responds to the handsome husband! How full of power! She expresses
her father in her face, the future mother of male progeny, the mother
of kings, of emperors.'[24] Carefully eliding Anna from Elizabeth's representation, and focusing on the Princess's inheritance from James and the
prospect of her future royal motherhood, this speech also depicts the role
of the new consort as perceived by her court of origin. In fact, the
definition of the queen consort in the performance of her home court
was resolutely colonial, registering her future heirs as a means of colonising
her new court on behalf of England and Protestantism. In this the
entertainments for Elizabeth's departure clearly differ markedly from those
which had welcomed Anna to Scotland.

Certainly the language used by Sibylla centred on the perceived
identity of Elizabeth's homeland. The term 'British' was of especial
significance in the Jacobean period and, in the wake of James's cherished
and by this time thwarted project of Anglo-Scottish union, a particularly
loaded designation. Unsurprisingly, perhaps, all three masques for the
wedding demonstrate a concern with the idea of links between 'Britain'
and courtly Europe, and so by implication with the place of England
within what the plans for *The Masque of Truth* called 'ceste Isle heureuse'
(this happy isle) of 'Britain'.[25] Preoccupations such as these were arguably
'natural' to entertainments which dealt in the networks forged by international marriage negotiations and by the movement of the queen consort
throughout the courts of early modern Europe. Indeed, Chapman's
masque, with its conceit of Virginian masquers, also took pains to
position 'Britain' within a wider fabric of colonial associations. What is
significant here is that such networks circulated around the figure of a
newly created queen consort; the royal woman held a central position
in the marital negotiations which criss-crossed the European continent.
Traces of a discourse of the exchange of the queen consort can be found
in the three masques danced in the English Palatinate festivities and in
the entertainments staged for Elizabeth once she had left England, in her
progress to Heidelberg.

Such resonances of nationhood surfaced in, for example, Beaumont's
conceit of the personified rivers Thames and Rhine. Here Beaumont,
echoing the inaugural masque for Henry as Prince of Wales, reworked
this trope to suit the agenda of the Protestant alliance and its factional
supporters. The image of the rivers forged a link between Elizabeth and

the sea voyage which, for those in seventeenth-century 'Britain', was a defining aspect of the concept and courtly representation of a queen consort and her relationship to the nation. And, indeed, such a trope found a further echo in the wider Palatinate festival in Frederick's river entrance into Whitehall, in the water progress of the masquers of the Inner Temple and Gray's Inn and in the mock Thames sea-battle between the English and the 'Turks', all of which drew attention to the nature of the national boundaries of island 'Britain' and to the departure of a queen consort as in some respects a colonialist enterprise.[26] In Beaumont's *Masque*, however, rather than effecting the delicate balance between the courts of the King, the Queen and the Prince of Wales attempted by Daniel, the trope of the Thames and Rhine was altered to take account of the dedication of the masque to the King's court. While Daniel subjected his rivers to Tethys, the female ruler of the ocean, Beaumont framed Elizabeth as subject to the marital authority of Frederick's Rhine in a significant shift which delineated the new balance of power on the masquing stage. Now the balance of power worked to reinstate James's image of authority through the traditional structures of marriage.

This preoccupation with the representation of nationhood continued in the shared trajectory of several of the Palatinate masques, which depicted the movement of the colonised to the colonisers. Chapman's *Memorable Masque*, much as *Blackness* had done in 1605, figured James himself as the imperial sun, with the distinction that the King's empire was here extended to the Americas, his power personified in the approach of masquers personating Virginians praising the King.[27] Such concerns re-occurred also in the projected *Masque of Truth*. The description of the unperformed masque, published erroneously by Jocquet in Heidelberg in a French pamphlet, outlines a spectacle which was more overtly religious in content than most of its Jacobean predecessors, its main conceit being the union of the world with England through the reformed Protestant faith.[28] First to appear were to have been the Nine Muses. They would then have been followed by Atlas, with a globe reminiscent of that utilised in *Hymenaei*, which he sought to discharge from his care to Alethiea (or Truth) in her chosen home of 'ceste Isle heureuse', 'Britain'.[29] From this globe emerged the queens and princesses of Europe, Asia and Africa and their entourages, who had travelled to the English court to honour James. The spectacle was to have concluded with a Protestant apocalypse, as the globe vanished to be replaced by a paradise. In this vision appeared an angel with a flaming sword and a skull at his feet, who revealed Truth, surrounded by angels and cherubs amid the stars. Of course, in dealing with the plans for the unperformed *Masque of Truth*, I am engaging not with actual female spectatorship but with the intended positioning of women against the performances of the Palatinate festival. To pursue such an argument demonstrates the projected dynamics of that *magnificence* as intended before Henry's death and so demarcates the influence of the Prince in its most extreme and unrealised form. *The Masque of Truth* is a record of the way in which women might have been intended to watch and respond to these performances.

As the conceit of the queens of the three continents reveals, this projected entertainment bore several important similarities to the canon of Jacobean female masquing. In addition to staging female rulers reminiscent of those of Jonson's *Queens*, *The Masque of Truth* also centred on much the same central metaphor as did the *Masque of Blackness*. Restaging the exotic and royal female traveller's quest for James I in his English court, the masque plan which Jocquet recorded extended this trope to encompass not only Africa but also Europe and Asia, perhaps including the European continent in reference to the recently accomplished marriage. However, rather than being bodied forth by transgressive courtly women, the female questers of *The Masque of Truth* were more simplistic female representations of perceived racial and religious error, characters who were to obtain redemption through their approach to James. The queen of Africa, for example, received an especially damning description:

> Sortez, Affrique monstrueuse
> En erreurs plus qu'en animaux,
> Et cerchez en ceste Isle heureuse
> Le repos à tous vos travaux.
> C'est icy que la VERITE
> Veut que son temple soit planté.
>
> (Come out, Africa,
> More monstrous in your errors than your beasts,
> And seek in this happy island
> Rest from all your work.
> It is here that TRUTH
> Wishes its temple to be erected.) [30]

Approaching James's throne with a submission which certainly had not characterised the daughters of Niger, these figures of royal female heresy – pagan in the case of Africa and Asia, specifically Catholic in the case of the European princesses of Spain, Italy and France – reworked the approach of the impenitent masquers of *Blackness*. They sought repentance initially in Alethiea as the representation of Protestantism, and ultimately in James himself. This intertextuality, which centred on the reconfiguration of a courtly femininity acceptable to the King's court, would, if performed, have carried a clear message to Anna, positioned, as she was, as spectator. Furthermore, the conceit of the journey to an island 'Britain', which was so pivotal to *Blackness* and seemingly central to the masque in its Jacobean form, seems to have been interrogated in this masque. The image of the marital quest, here apparently intended to be reclaimed by Henry's court, was a marker of a more pervasive reappropriation of the masquing stage itself from its previous female occupants. In appropriating the defining trope of the queen consort, Henry's court was also rewriting the courtly representation of that figure and her role within the Jacobean court.

The image of the marital quest was not, however, limited to the English festivities but was also to be found, perhaps as part of the pan-European discourse of courtliness, in the lavish entertainments which Elizabeth witnessed on her progress to Heidelberg. Welcomed on her journey with addresses, firework displays, tilts and tournaments, the new Electress also watched representations of her husband as 'le brave IASON'. Such a personation echoed the imagery of the marital quest which, significantly, had characterised the entertainments for her mother as Scottish queen consort.[31] Once again we are dealing with the figuration of a king who crosses the seas to win a bride and the concomitant representation of that bride as dowry and bringer of heirs. When considered alongside the Scottish pageantry of the 1590s, it seems that the arrival of the queen consort in her new environment precipitated concerns over the status of the newcomer which manifested themselves in this dangerously ambiguous imagery of Jason's heroic but ultimately disastrous quest.

In *The Masque of Truth*, however, the queen consort, the counter of marital exchange, was placed at the centre of the masque. This masque's trajectory – the movement of women to James's court – constituted a crucial reversal of Elizabeth's projected journey, but it bodied forth the movement that Anna had previously made and which her daughter would soon undertake. Certainly this reworking of *Blackness* firmly distinguished the Protestant Elizabeth from her Catholic mother, and in figuring the female queens as supplicants to the English throne for the true reformed faith the masque laid an implicit burden of evangelism upon the Princess. There was, of course, an association of the Princess Elizabeth with a tradition of queenship taken from her namesake. Such a connection would support an implicit symbolisation of the princess as the champion of Protestantism. The figure of truth, which had been so central to Elizabeth I's career and an emblem of the reformed religion, was here invoked to forge a bond between the two Elizabeths.[32] In so doing, of course, *The Masque of Truth* carefully figured the Princess as the heir to Elizabeth Tudor rather than to Anna of Denmark.

There are many problems and pitfalls in interpreting a masque which was never produced. For example, while the queen consort and conceptions of queenship formed the conceptual heart of this masque, it is uncertain whether the queens and their entourage were intended to be given a distanced representation by cross-dressed boys or to be danced by women of the court. Certainly it would have been problematic to have noblewomen perform the demeaning roles of pagan queens and, again, the obstacle of representing blackened female performers, although overcome with more or less success in the performance of *Blackness*, would not have alleviated these tensions. At some point the organisers would have had to choose between the blackened faces which had proved to be so controversial in *Blackness* or a less literal representation of Asia and Africa, avoiding blackness in the manner of *Queens* in its depiction of Candace. Despite such issues there are hints in Jocquet's description that the masque may have originally been planned as a double masque; for example, after the emergence of the European princesses from the globe, Atlas called out the princes. A 'grand ballet' with the princesses would then have unfolded, implying that the roles of the princesses and princes were to be performed by the women and men of the court. Furthermore, the appearance of characters on to the stage from a globe is a direct echo of *Hymenaei*, another double marriage masque. It is, therefore, distinctly problematic to assign these roles to either women or transvestite boys. Despite the contradictions inherent in Jocquet's description, however, one conclusion which can be drawn is that the female roles, strongly influenced by discourses of class, religion and gender and circling around the figure of the queen consort, would have been central to its creation of meaning whether performed by cross-dressed female representations or 'actual' women.

Such were the demands which were placed on the newly created queen consort as she left England for the Protectorate; Elizabeth was figured less as a queen who must be assimilated into her new culture than as a queen who must act as an ambassador for the culture and ideologies of the court from which she left. In line with the Scottish entertainments which governed Anna's representation through the image of James VI as involved in the romance quest, however, Elizabeth's representation as bride was to some extent dependent upon that of the bridegroom. The discourses of militant Protestantism which greeted Frederick had their apotheosis in the unperformed *Masque of Truth*, which Henry had commissioned to serve his particular religious and political purposes. In this sense Frederick's representation was a defining influence upon that of the bride.

Female performance in the Palatinate festival: Campion's *Lords' Masque*

Despite the scarcity of female commissioning and patronage in the Palatinate festival, Anna and her daughter did witness one example of female performance. Thomas Campion's *Lords' Masque*, performed on the wedding night itself, was the only one to involve women masquers and as such is particularly important for a consideration of female representation in the Palatinate festivities. Significantly, *The Lords' Masque* was one of only two double masques danced in the Jacobean courts, the other being *Hymenaei*. There were, therefore, mutually reinforcing ties between these two performances, perhaps the most important of which was their shared privileged spectator, James I. These two masques were the only instances of Jacobean courtly female performance which were neither commissioned nor danced by Anna, but were instead aimed at James. When Jacobean women masqued, it was usually under the auspices of the queen consort. However, in the King's court it seems that the unavoidable female masquing presence was legitimated by a double masque and its accompaniment of performing women with male masquers.

The links between these two masques went beyond the mixed sexes of their performers to their iconography and, beyond this, to James's cultural influence. Significantly, in *The Lords' Masque*, Campion invoked the motif of Juno and Jove which, in the performance of *Hymenaei* for the 1606 Essex/Howard marriage, had staged a transvestite Juno as the presiding deity of national and marital union, her presence reflecting on the figure of Jupiter and so back to the watching James as Jove himself. In doing so this masque had advanced the Stuart formulation of authority through the gendered construct of the patriarchal family, set up in opposition to the performance of female authority in the Queen's early Jacobean masques. *Hymenaei*, as the main example of a King's court masque in the first decade of the Stuart court in England, was pivotal to the development of Jacobean female court performance. In this light the figures of Jove and Juno seem to have been employed by Campion to designate *The Lords' Masque* as belonging to the King's court through a familiarly deployed marker of the marital formulation of Stuart authority. In addition the figure of Jove in both masques reflected on James's position as the centrepoint of the masque, the importance of which is clarified by Daniel's careful avoidance of any alignment of Anna and Juno in *The Vision*, which safeguarded her position as masquer independent of her royal spouse. Returning to a trope used only rarely in the first decade of the seventeenth century and which had been avoided in masques commissioned by both Anna and Prince Henry, Campion reasserted James's royal authority by figuring his king as the pre-eminent classical god within a marital framework.

In these ways James's masquing history established him as the patron and controlling force of Campion's masque, but what representative strategies defined those women who danced in *The Lords' Masque*? Against a context of female spectatorship rather than performance or patronage, Campion employed a specific set of images to depict those women who did perform. The conceit of the masque was as follows: Orpheus, the masque presenter, freed Entheus, representative of poetic inspiration, from the cave of Mania, the goddess of madness. Once safe from this apparently baleful female influence, these two figures of male poetic power together invoked Prometheus and precipitated a spectacle of dancing stars which were then transformed into noble male masquers. The scene was split into two levels; the bottom was revealed first and depicted 'a wood in perspective'. This then changed to reveal 'four noble women-statues of silver, standing in several niches, accompanied by ornaments of architecture', over each of which were gold reliefs detailing the Promethean myth.[33] According to the conceit, these women, animated by Prometheus from clay models by stolen divine fire, had been transformed into statues by Jove as a punishment for this theft. It seems, however, that Jove's anger was beginning to lessen, since Entheus declared of the statues,

> Lo, how fix'd they stand;
> So did Jove's wrath too long, but now at last
> It by degrees relents.[34]

Once the women had been transformed, they were taken out to dance by the male masquers and the revels began. However, a further conceit remained: following the revels, the prophetess Sibylla entered towing an illuminated silver obelisk flanked by golden statues of the bride and bridegroom. Once on stage, this figure prophesied the future success of the marriage and the flourishing of Protestantism as the true religion before concluding the masque and the evening's festivities.

It is striking that the only appearance of women in the Palatinate festival, should be figured through the containment and reification of an image such as the statue. However, this imagery was not unique to Campion within the Palatinate *magnificence*, since it was also restaged in the final masque-like moment of *The Winter's Tale*, performed for the court two years after its initial run at the Globe. Such an intertextuality, or at least a shared thematic concern, hints at an interplay between the masques and plays of this festival. An examination of the strict physical confines of the woman-as-statue illuminates the status of the masquing stage in this festival and, in particular, the perception of female performance. Certainly Campion's image of the female statue was a conservative strategy; it relied on the reification of the female performer, establishing a contrast between the static immobility of the courtly female masquer and the celestial dynamism of the masque's male performers in the gendered dynamics of bodily and scenic motion. In particular the containment of the female within the statue image converged on the Marian discourse of the chaste woman as icon. This portrayal of a feminine ideal crafted within the new Protestant discourse of marriage was related to the watching figure of the Princess Elizabeth herself and to her political and religious allegiances.

The figure of the female statue ran through the courtly entertainments of early modern Europe, and its presence was forcefully registered in the first major example of the French *ballet de cour*. In the *Ballet Comique de la Reine* (1581), the enchantress Circe transformed the twelve dancing naiads, performed by Queen Louise and her women, into statues, and, as suggested in chapter 1, their immobilised bodies became the locus of conflict between the opposed forces of the ballet, their stillness a marker of Circe's illegitimate power, their restoration to movement a marker of the restoration of legitimate (or rather, male monarchical) control.[35] Such an impulse of transformation was, of course, a structural component of the masque genre, but the trope of the re-animating power of the monarch's gaze was a common motif of early modern courtly entertainments, appearing for example in *Le Ballet de Monseigneur le Duc de Vandosme* (1610) and again within the Palatinate festival itself – the restoration of the knights at the conclusion of Beaumont's *Masque*.[36] However, *The Lords' Masque* did not quite map on to these other performances. Although the female masquers were transformed from statues into dancing courtiers, their reanimation was less a result of their exposure to the king's gaze than the result of Jove's lessening anger. Indeed, rather than the liberation of idealised courtiers from imprisonment by illicit forces, as in Beaumont's *Masque*, Campion staged Jove's rehabilitation of women masquers who were in fact themselves the representatives of illegitimate power, that of the feminine itself. The revitalisation of the statues in this case reflected the legitimisation of the illicit feminine impulse by divine grace to take part in a male-authored and commissioned masque. Clearly this was rather less positive than the representation afforded to the male masquers of Beaumont's *Masque* and implies a certain ambivalence towards female performance. However, the result of Jove's (and by extension James's) lessening anger was to restore the women necessary to the masque form to legitimate performance within the King's masque and under the restored control imposed by male co-performers.

The image of the statue has clear connotations of reification and the physicalisation of the female. The women masquers personating the statues, robbed of will and verbal expression, were physicalised in their initial appearance on Jones's stage, transformed into created artefacts fashioned from clay by the higher consciousness of the male creator, embodied by Prometheus. In this particular double masque it is possible to assess the impact of the presence of mixed sex masquers through the distinct representative strategies used for masquers of each gender. Campion's conceit represented these women as bodily matter given life by masculine, Promethean fire, a celestial energy found also in the stars which were the original form of the male masquers. This, of course, echoed early modern theories of conception and the association between women, the female masquer and the body, which had further ramifications in this masque. Calling on the Pygmalion myth, Campion's masque embodied a misogynistic impulse of the physicalisation of women and the creation of a controllable feminine ideal.[37] Such a discourse of creation, which circles around the creation of both literature and of life itself, is perhaps the most important impulse in the opening section of *The Lords' Masque*. Campion figured the creative impulse as a masculine quality, a product of the heat associated with the male in early modern conception theories and of the patriarchal God in Judaeo-Christian tradition. Sexual and universal creation converge in a gendered act, and the artists who follow God's lead in this masque, notably Entheus as the masculine figure of poetic inspiration and Prometheus and Jove as the creators of women, were also represented as male. The figure of the artist, therefore, lay at the centre of Campion's conceit, and, associating the noble male masquers with Promethean fire through the celestial energy of the stars, the male principle was established as creator and the female as created artefact in the masque's performance.

By invoking the trope of the creating male and created female, Campion restored a dichotomy which had been successfully challenged in Anna's performance in *The Masque of Queens*. In the House of Fame Jonson had staged the static male figures of poets and historical leaders who remained inanimate on the side of the House while the women masquers descended to dance, taking on themselves the burden of creating meaning usually reserved for the figures of male poets who remained immobile on the side of the House of Fame. Again, such a reversal was clearly connected to the dynamics of masque patronage, since in *Queens* Anna had renegotiated the relationship of courtly women with artistic creation, a balance which Campion then restored to its original, exclusionary, form in *The Lords' Masque*. This vision of literary and world creation was closely related to the heart of the masque genre, since it was the wealth of the patron and the ingenuity of the designer and writer which facilitated the creation of the masque world itself. Princely magnificence was, of course, the *raison d'être* of the masque. As a display of the health and wealth of a nation to both its enemies and allies, the genre's goal of near-perfect illusion also demanded an awareness of the process of creation which lay behind the spectacle. While containing the recognition of the impossibility of a perfect created world, the masque form also contained an implicit assertion of the importance of attempting perfection through financial expenditure and mental ingenuity. In this case both wealth and ingenuity were the preserve of the male patron (James) and the male poet (Campion).

The discourses of masculine creation were similarly mirrored in Inigo Jones's staging techniques for this masque. The transformation of the male masquers from stars occurred in a downwards movement that implied the divinity of the masculine essence which descended to the court, while the unconscious, physical female clay was elevated through its combination with male spirituality. For Campion's masque Jones had used an innovative split-stage presentation, consisting of an upper and a lower stage, which was used also in Beaumont's *Masque*, although there is no evidence that this was designed by Jones.[38] Such an unusual division of stage space brought the dichotomy between antimasque and main masque which structured this performance genre into the visual structure of the masque's performance. This specific structuring of imaginative space was a means of making visible the downwards invocation of blessings into the court by the masque performance, embodied in the progression of the divinely inspired male masquers. Furthermore, this split stage also allowed Jones to experiment with a new means of concealing action and mechanical motion from his audience, a method ideologically distinct from, for example, the rotating *machina versatilis* of *Queens*. And, of course, vertical movement carried a distinct ideological burden in the court masque; in employing this image of communication between the celestial and the sublunary worlds, this vertical reading of space allowed Jones to depart from the spatial dynamics of *Queens* in favour of a more absolutist stage space entirely appropriate for a masque of the King's court.

There are constant allusions to classical and Christian divinity in Campion's masque, and the trope of creation (both classical and biblical) seems to further reinforce its rather conservative representation of the courtly female. For instance, Campion's presentation of the Promethean creation myth points to the importance bestowed upon the marriage of Elizabeth and Frederick, which was presented to its audience as the rebirth of the human race and of Protestantism within a pan-European alliance. But Campion's manipulation of the Promethean creation myth also illuminates the perception of women within this new social order and the amelioration of Protestant marriage. *The Lords' Masque*'s presentation of this narrative did not entirely accord with the received version of the legend. For instance, Hesiod had the creator of Pandora, the first woman, not as Prometheus but as his brother and her future husband, Hephaistos.[39] In addition, in this original version, the theft of the divine fire was carried out before women were created and was not intended for that purpose, but rather to ease the life of mankind. Rather than being created by stolen fire, therefore, Pandora was originally given life by Jove as a punishment for Prometheus's transgression; Hesiod portrays her as a beautiful but baleful object, necessary for the propagation of the human race but causing only pain.[40] Rather ironically, Campion, by not portraying women as a punishment for men's transgression but rather depicting men's punishment as retribution exacted for creating women themselves, bestows women with a degree of limited autonomy. There is little positive about being punished for one's very existence, but women existed in the discourses of this masque in their own right, not as an intrinsically sinful snare for masculine entrapment.

Furthermore, Campion also realigned the familiar biblical hierarchy of creation in a manner which impacted on the representation of his female performers and those of women watching the spectacle. For example, the female clay figures reflected the Genesis narrative, in which God created

Adam from the clay of the earth. The biblical Eve, however, was formed from the flesh of Adam's pre-created body, and this was an important aspect of the reasoning behind supposed feminine inferiority.[41] Though Campion adhered to this sequence of precedence, he departed from convention by figuring women as created from clay and the male as a spiritual force imbuing her with life, giving both sexes a discrete conceptual existence before the supposed moment of creation. Although such a realignment did nothing to affect the hierarchy of gender, the autonomous sources of the sexes did again grant the female a limited degree of equality. The traditional inversion of the procreative process, which subordinated the female through her dependence for creation on the male, was elided, and the perception of women begins to show a shift towards a greater equality that perhaps displays the influence of the increasing Protestant esteem of marriage. This was clearly an incomplete process. After all, each of the myths referred to above imagined the creation of woman as simultaneous with the institution of marriage, as, in another link with *Hymenaei*, Entheus requests that Prometheus, the creating deity, 'In Hymen's place aid us to solemnize / These royal nuptials'.[42] Standing as a marker of the divine disapproval of the feminine, the statue also represents a transitional image, a sign of the alleviation of divine wrath achieved through the union of Elizabeth and Frederick. Their wedding is depicted as a pivotal moment in the conception of marriage itself, the sanctioning of the very existence of women within the newly defined bounds of the Protestant marriage ideal.

Positioning the watching newly married couple at the conceptual heart of his masque, Campion required a specific kind of spectatorship from his elite audience. Such spectatorship was in itself gendered, as the costume designs for this masque reveal. Inigo Jones's designs demonstrate the dynamics of the male and female gaze, the celestial energy and eroticism of the male masquers and the nature of male spectatorship. The costumes of this masque established a clear distinction between the representative strategies used for the male and female masquing courtiers. While the noblemen danced in costumes which, reminiscent of Henry as Oberon, revealed their torsos and legs with close-fitting materials depicting the fiery stars and drew the eye to their bodies (figure 18), those of the noblewomen were far more restrained (figure 19). It would seem that a similar kind of masculine representation took place here as in other major male-performed masques, such as *Oberon* or *Pleasure Reconciled to Virtue*, which crafted a male ideal of eroticism based on an effeminising impulse and granted its male dancers access to the masculine power structures of

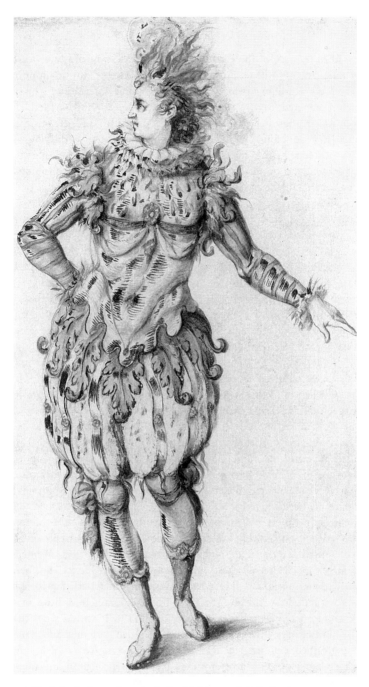

18 A lord, from Campion's *Lords' Masque* (1613), by Inigo Jones

19 A lady, from Campion's *Lords' Masque* (1613), by Inigo Jones

the mainstream court. Witness, for example, the exaggerated waist and hips of the design, the impression of breasts created by the material swathes, and the simulated low-cut neckline below the ruff, which echoed those of earlier female masquers. Certainly the male masquers were erotic centres of attention. In addition, their suggestive and extravagant costumes predicted the same dynamics of masquing power between the dancers and the spectating James and Frederick which were later to be found in *Pleasure Reconciled*. This may perhaps also explain the elision of the female masquers' transformation from Campion's masque description. In contrast to the lengthy description of the transformation of the male masquers, the moment of female transformation has no explicit reference; one can only ascertain that it has occurred through Orpheus's remark: 'See, Jove is pleas'd; statues have life and move.'[43] Such an elision of the motif from the text's central focus cannot deny its operation within the spectacle of performance, but perhaps suggests a tension over its presence within a masque which centred upon its male masquers' physicality.

By way of contrast, the female masquers' costumes are rather more illuminating than their textual representation. In fact these costumes and the way in which they depicted the masquing noblewomen were rather unusual. Featuring a heavy neck ruff not seen in Jones's previous designs for female masquers, and carefully covering the body (in particular the stomach, breasts and neck), they were the rich antitheses of the gauzy and revealing costumes usually worn by women in Jacobean Twelfth Night masques. A comparison between Jones's costumes for *The Lords' Masque* and those he designed for *Love Freed From Ignorance and Folly* two years earlier (figure 16) shows just what a radical difference existed between these two depictions of the feminine. The earlier costume, similar to those of *Queens*, was a combination of domestic corseture and the exposure of the female body under gauzy materials. This formed a stark contrast to the heavy covering of the female body in Campion's Palatinate masque. It would seem that, although some vestige of the previous amazonian sash (now part of a cloak) seems to have survived, the female bodily ideal expressed by Jones in *The Lords' Masque* differed quite markedly from that put forward in the masques which the architect had earlier designed for his Queen's performances. Whilst the feminine ideal of Anna's masques was one of erotic bodily exposure, the female body of the King's Palatinate masque was elaborately and purposefully covered. As no designs by Jones survive from *Hymenaei*, there is no way of knowing whether this was a consistent trait of masques associated with the court of James I. However, the evidence of *The Lords' Masque* does suggest that the feminine bodily ideals of the male and female courts were quite distinct and were predicated on the exposure or concealment of the female body. Furthermore, as my reading of the costumes of *Blackness* makes clear, such an exposure and the threat it posed to the ideologies of the mainstream court was central to the representative strategies of Anna's performances. In contrast, this king's masque, at least, would seem to suggest a distinct strategy of female bodily representation which was concerned to defuse the threat of the female masquer through the decorous representation of her body.

There are, however, further resonances to be drawn from the image of the woman as statue. The early modern conception of sculpture regarded it as containing mysteries or riddles, lending itself naturally, as Leonard Barkan puts it, 'to a sense that it contain[ed] something, an essence or a truth trapped inside'.[44] So, in Campion's usage, the image of the statue purported to offer a defining image of the feminine essence, encapsulating it within the confines of the physical emblem. Furthermore, within *The Lords' Masque*, such feminine reification demanded the monumentalising gaze of a spectator, either James I as privileged spectator or the slightly less elevated Frederick and Elizabeth. What is clear is that Anna, watching a masque to celebrate a marriage she had publicly opposed, and Elizabeth, watching members of her own faith and allegiances, would both have been presented with a constrained rationale for female existence.

Such a constraint existed also in regard to the relationship of the female body to language in this masque. This aspect of female court performance surfaced forcefully in *The Lords' Masque*, and was closely tied to the resonances of the image of the woman as statue. Despite the clear classical influences in Jones's career as a masque designer, early modern English statuary in general was of a complex nature; classical statuary was on the whole known about rather than experienced, and the pre-eminent form of Jacobean sculpture was the theatrical form employed for tombs and monuments, likened by Bruce Smith to 'pageant device[s] or stage mansion[s]'.[45] This theatricality was essentially the dramatisation of the everyday; these monuments depended on their likeness to life, so much so that it caused complaints from certain quarters. John Weever wrote that tomb monuments were a place where a viewer

> may easily discerne the vanity of our mindes, vailed under our fantasticke habits and attires … and so the Temple of God shall become a Schoolhouse of the monstrous habits and attires of our present age, wherein Taylors may finde out new fashions.[46]

Such verisimilitude and the theatricalisation of the everyday were certainly qualities of the costumes of the female masquers for *The Lords' Masque*, which seem to stem from a primarily domestic influence. Rather than the complex allegorical figures of *Blackness* or *Queens*, these designs delineated the identity of extravagant but commonplace courtly women, and in doing so dramatised a courtly rather than an allegorical identity.

Such a dramatisation of the everyday was further complicated by the resonances of idolatry which surrounded the animated figures of the female statues. In a scene so concerned with the visual and with the containment of significance within the physical, the connotations of idolatry are particularly prominent. The masque genre, filled with emblems which were the 'secular counterpart to ... religious images', itself contributed to this dynamic.[47] To a Jacobean court the mere appearance of statues within this masque would perhaps carry connotations of religious worship, idolatry and Catholicism through the association with church sculpture in ways which impacted on the status of female representation in Campion's masque. For, even given the framing of their re-animation by the gaze of James I, the resonances of Catholic worship surrounding the statues are suggestive. Such a connotation would imply that women, too, were to an extent divine, and more importantly, divine within the Catholic scheme of things.

Whatever the connotations of the idolatrous image and its relationship to the Catholicism of the watching Anna, the image of the statue also forged a connection between the female masquers and language or speech. After all, idolatrous statues were statues to be spoken to in prayer and which, on some level, might possess the power to answer back. Though connected to the figure of the speaking statue through their similarity with domestic tomb statuary, which was often upright and in an animated lifelike pose, the statues of *The Lords' Masque* were distinctly silent. However, as we have seen in other Jacobean masques, the bodies of these masquers quite literally gestured towards speech in the decorum and expressivity of the dance. Movement provided the distinction between the animate and inanimate woman performer, and granted access to a discourse of bodily expressivity within the masque. In line with Jacobean masquing convention, the silent *Lords' Masque* accompanied its statues with the pictorial language of narrative friezes of the Promethean myth. These narrations rendered the women of this masque emblematic in nature; the female statue formed the emblem's illustrative heart while the physicalised narrative friezes acted as the explicatory motto. Just as pictorial language had become associated with the masque form, so the depiction of the female masquer as a kind of emblem tied in closely with the nature of a genre which itself seemed to consist of a tripartite emblem.[48] With the emblem of the female statues, however, the main question is one of interpretation and the privileged spectator is given the power to read the emblem, in this case, as so often in the masque, the female body.

The connection between the statue and language was, therefore, close and complex. And, as the nature of the emblem and its proximity to the masque genre suggest, such a bond between statuary and language was not uncommon in the masque form. Campion's emblematic women traced a similar trajectory to those of *Blackness*, who were depicted through the hieroglyphs analysed in the introduction to this book, and Jonson's text on this moment makes clear the perceived mutual link between statues and the sculpted language of hieroglyphs.[49] The Adamic connection of the hieroglyph with the 'reality' behind language correlates with the statue's perceived containment of the essence freed by the sculptor. Both are physicalised significance of a certain kind; indeed, in the case of Campion's masque, this meaning, held and explained by the statue, is the perceived essence of woman herself.

Where Campion's masque differs from *Blackness* is in the nature of the physical language which it presented. Rather than being only emblematic, this particular pictorial language constructed a narrative, one of female creation and punishment which both contained courtly women and sought fully to explain them once and for all. The narrative friezes which were described by Campion as standing over the sculptures during their transformation denote sculpture not only as a physicalised language, but also as a pictorial narrative. This is a further step through the progression of the bodily or physical language staged in the court masque and one which suits the progression from hieroglyph to the more nuanced narrative form of the statue. The linguistic or corporeal expression allowed to the women of this masque was, in comparison to the performances of the Queen's court, conservative in its distancing and control of women in relation to language. And, distanced from the female body in this masque, the friezes of this masque, consisting of architectural detail framing the spectacle of the women's animation, seek to explain and account for the nature of the courtly woman. In contrast to the mobile and signifying female masquers of *Queens*, the women of the aptly named *Lords' Masque* were reduced to adorning statues ruled by Orpheus and Entheus, figures of male literary and poetic authority.

The early modern statue was considered to contain a secret; in *The Lords' Masque* that secret was the female body and expression. The spectacular

miracle of the masque's transformation offered a version of female representation constraining in comparison to those of Anna's earlier
performances. The use of the woman-as-statue offered a definition of the
'essence' of the female nature, depicting a chaste and silent feminine ideal
demanded by the spectatorship of James I, and Elizabeth and Frederick.
Princess Elizabeth would therefore have been the audience for a merely
partial liberation of the female in this rebirth. However, the image of
the statue-as-woman was dependent upon the perspective of James I, the
male linchpin of the masque, whose spectatorship defined and monumentalised female performers, allowing women access to the masquing stage
only under the strictest controls. Through this it is clear that the prevalence
of an image such as the female statue within these marriage celebrations
was related to the changing status of the masquing stage as it was reclaimed
by male performers allied to James I rather than to the female court. In
general the entertainments staged as part of the Palatinate festival reacted
against previous female cultural and political engagement to offer the
royal female spectators a notably conservative vision of femininity in
comparison to that of Anna's own masques.

The Palatinate festival throws light on the nature of royal women's
spectatorship. However, it can point also to the interfaces between court
and city theatre patronage, since it was an interface between court masque
performance and the London city theatres. Many of the actors who danced
in the court masque performed also in the fourteen plays which were
staged in close proximity to them in the court. Such interaction between
city and courtly theatrical practices might also illuminate the active role
which both Anna and Elizabeth took as patrons of the city theatre
companies. Within the Palatinate festival a display of courtly magnificence
and spectacle, masque and drama were brought into juxtaposition, highlighting their sharing of a cultural space and moment. Since Jones
radicalised the masque form's development in 1605 with *The Masque of
Blackness*, rejecting the conventional dispersal of scenic items in favour of
a specific focus and the use of perspective, court masques and playhouse
dramas had coexisted as staged theatrical forms, sharing audience members
and, in the case of the private theatres, a similar spatial layout.[50] Members
of the court could be exposed to both forms in dramatic performances
in Whitehall, and elements of the elite community also frequented city
theatres such as the Blackfriars private playhouse. The Palatinate marriage
festivities were an extension of the Christmas practice of the court, when
a series of plays and a Twelfth Night masque were performed at Whitehall,

but, although not unique in bringing the two disparate forms of masque and play into close contact, the 1613 celebrations were certainly a remarkably extended example of such a partnership. For example, this can be seen in the well-known and much-commented-upon reuse of the morris of the second antimasque of Beaumont's masque by Fletcher and Shakespeare in *Two Noble Kinsmen*, even down to the distinctive baboon.[51] Such intertextualities between city and court theatres may shed light on the positions of both Anna and Elizabeth as theatrical patrons beyond the court.

More importantly for this book, however, the Palatinate festival represented a moment when the masquing stage was realigned with the patronage of James I and with his political and factional agenda. This, the most extensive of Jacobean festivals, staged James I's cherished match through the gender and performance politics of the King's court. In a moment of transition for the masquing stage, it was reclaimed by the male masquer, and the disparate political allegiances of those groups which made up the Jacobean court were reflected and altered by the masques which were performed.

CHAPTER FIVE

The contested masquing stage:
The Somerset Masque,
Cupid's Banishment *and the space*
of the female court

By 1613 and the Palatinate festivities it seemed as if the highpoint of female masquing reached in *The Masque of Queens* had passed and with it the courtly woman's domination of the Whitehall masquing stage. By the staging of the Somerset marriage festivities in December of that year, the profound changes which had developed since Anna's most prominent performance seem to have crystallised. At first glance, indeed, the picture at the end of 1613 seemed rather bleak. The final conventional masque in which Anna danced, Jonson's *Love Freed From Ignorance and Folly*, had been staged in 1611 and Campion's *Lords' Masque* for the marriage of Princess Elizabeth and Frederick, Elector Palatine, marked the final Whitehall appearance of any female masquers during the reign of James I. We have seen that Henry's short-lived prominence as a patron had begun to reinstate male performers on the masque stage, and that this was followed by the reappropriation of that stage by James I's male favourites. Anna's performance career seemed to wane with her political influence and with this shift in the provenance of the masque. However, she did make one final showing: Thomas Campion's *Somerset Masque*, in which Anna participated but did not masque as such, was the last appearance she or any other woman made in a Whitehall masque before the arrival of Henrietta Maria in 1625. Despite appearances, this did not mark the end of her engagement with the genre, but rather signalled a shift in the style and nature of her performances.

Despite the undoubted waning of women's performance in Whitehall, the female aristocrat's apparent retreat from the court masque can be better characterised as a redirection of cultural energies into performance beyond the Whitehall power-centre and into alternative forms of patronage and production. Anna herself remained an active patron, employing Inigo Jones for prominent projects such as the Queen's House at Greenwich, and the architect Soloman de Caus, who had accompanied Elizabeth on the Palatinate progress and dedicated the treatise *Institution Harmonique* (1615) to Anna, designed the Greenwich gardens.[1] Her commission of the treatise of maritime sovereignty *De Domino Maris* (1616) from the Scottish scholar William Welwood was perhaps a more overtly political act. Aimed at securing her the monopoly of inland water fishing rights, this commission also implicated Anna in the later debate over maritime sovereignty between James I and Christian IV.[2] Furthermore, Anna's coterie did not withdraw from patronage. As Lewalski has demonstrated, Lucy Russell remained an important cultural force beyond Whitehall, a garden designer and the centre of a country house coterie of writers.[3] Both she and the Queen were the dedicatees of Aemelia Lanyer's *Salve Deus Rex Judaeorum* (1611), and their involvement as active patrons and the targets of dedications continued in the years after *The Somerset Masque*. Russell remained involved with the masque genre until at least 1617, abandoning performance for the less controversial position of organiser in, for example, Jonson's *Lovers Made Men* (1617), while in a resonant gesture, her queen withdrew from performance to the position of privileged spectator in *Cupid's Banishment*.

This little-known masque offers the best evidence for categorising Anna's removal from Whitehall as a conscious withdrawal rather than as only a forced retreat, and its study allows a reappraisal of the nature of the institution of the court itself through the space and performances of the female court. When the Queen's court is included in the Jacobean court, and that institution itself thought of as disparate and fractured entities, polycentric rather than monolithic, a new picture of the nature of this early modern institution emerges.[4] This distinct model of the early modern court can be seen in the final years of Anna's life and in the performances in which she was involved during the years 1610–17. In shifting the centre of her power and performance beyond Whitehall, Anna removed to an alternative centre of power. *Cupid's Banishment*, in particular, at first glance an obscure out-of-court performance, was not so much out of court as out of Whitehall, and reveals much about the space and nature of the female court and the growing importance of the established gesture of withdrawal from mainstream court ceremony. *The Somerset Masque*, Anna's last performance in Whitehall, and *Cupid's Banishment*, the last with which she was known to be involved before her death, were pivotal performances for this female court and both form an important part of the emergent tradition of Jacobean courtly female performance. Thomas Campion's *Somerset Masque*, danced on 26 December 1613, celebrated the controversial marriage of Robert Carr, Earl of Somerset, and Frances Howard, the recently divorced wife of the Earl of Essex, and stood as a close successor to the Palatinate festivities. The highly unconventional instance of female performance which this masque contained illuminates the development of Anna's career and the changing status of female masquing in the Jacobean courts.

Performing the King's will: court factionalism and Campion's *Somerset Masque*

Thomas Campion's masque for the Somerset marriage celebrations, pivotal in the movement of courtly women away from Whitehall, can be read in ways which confront established assumptions regarding the performance of the elite female community. Campion's masque was a striking reworking of Anna's earlier oppositional performances within the context of her later political failure and marginalisation from the Whitehall masquing stage.

The background to this entertainment is well known: the scandals of the Essex divorce, James I's manipulation of the council in support of Robert Carr, and both Campion's and Jonson's difficult task of synthesising panegyric with reality have been discussed in detail.[5] Less attention, however, has been paid to Anna's role in the collision of court scandal and performance in Campion's entertainment. *The Somerset Masque* has not yet been interpreted in terms of its performance, its intertextualities with Anna's previous masques, the unprecedented nature of what was in fact an enforced performance on her part and the ramifications of such coercion for the development of female masquing. By manipulating the memory of Jacobean courtly ritual, *Somerset* simultaneously called upon and discredited previous female masques within the new courtly climate of female exclusion. As Anna's final masque performance, and one which seems to reject both earlier oppositional performances and the possibility of any such future engagement, it relates disturbingly to the Stuart tradition of female masquing.

The high stakes involved in *Somerset* are evident in the staging, only a few weeks later, of a rival set of celebrations for the marriage of Anna's own favourites. 'All the talk is now of masking and feasting at these towardly marriages [...] The King bears the charge of the first, all saving the apparel, and no doubt the queen will do as much on her side which must be a mask of maids, if they may be found.'[6] These weddings were, respectively, the Somerset match and that between Lord Roxborough and Lady Jean Drummond, Anna's lady-in-waiting and co-religionist, held on 2 February 1614. The queen's 'mask' was in fact Daniel's pastoral *Hymen's Triumph*, commissioned by Anna and performed in Somerset House.[7] While substantiating Anna's ongoing patronage, this scenario also delineates the parallel structures of what now clearly seem to be perceived as distinct court establishments; Chamberlain names Somerset House as the site of the 'Quenes court (as yt must now be called)'.[8] Royal favour, the common currency of each court, was exchanged in the sponsorship of prominent courtiers' marriage celebrations. Anna kept the Earl of Essex close to her during the feast, part of a series of entertainments which formed a parallel to the earlier Palatinate *magnificence*, and in doing so fashioned her own favourite as courtier in a way which mirrored the structures and performances of the King's court.

If masques can be assigned to various of the rival Jacobean courts, then *The Somerset Masque* certainly came from the court of James I. Echoing the theme of re-animation found in Campion's *Lord Hay's Masque* and *The Lords' Masque*, the conceit complimented James's protection of the court by having the King free the masquing lords from the paralysis of false fame which it claimed had surrounded the Carr/Howard marriage. This transformation and the shift from the abstracted land and seascape of the antimasque to the main masque's vision of contemporary London formed the entertainment's pivotal moment. However, this transformation also demanded a remarkable performance from Anna and in doing so placed her at the heart of the representation of the controversial marriage. While the enchanted performers of contemporary French *ballets* upon which Campion drew for his motif of the imprisoned lords were re-animated simply by the monarch's gaze, the rather different method used here was entirely unprecedented in the Jacobean masque. Anna, who, significantly, was not a masquer, was obliged to restore the lords on the King's behalf by plucking a bough from a tree of gold, brought to her as she watched from the royal dais.[9] This was a highly unusual moment: in no other masque was an audience member actively involved in the moment of transformation in this way, and in no other masque did actors leave the stage as its agents. Clearly, one factor in this remarkable performance was the need to praise James under the difficult circumstances of the Somerset marriage; for Campion to position James himself as the explicit transformational force would have corresponded too blatantly to his manipulation of the divorce commission and so Anna provided a necessary and convenient referent.[10] Yet this could have been achieved through more conventional means, such as a spoken compliment or a professional stand-in for the royal spectator. Given that these options were not used, the real question would seem to be why Campion should have chosen to involve his queen in such an unnecessary and unusual performance.

The explanation may lie in Anna's well-documented opposition to the match between Robert Carr and Frances Howard. The former Essex faction, opposed to the Howards despite their shared Catholicism, had by 1613 coalesced around the Queen and, though James's reinstatement of the Essex loyalists in the alliance of Robert Devereux and Frances Howard in 1606 had marked the rise of both families, the original rift between them was exacerbated by the break-down of the very marriage intended to cement their reconciliation. In addition Anna's own opposition to Carr's burgeoning career was soon to lead her to introduce George Villiers to the King's bedchamber. In 1613, however, although the match had incurred Anna's displeasure, Carr had James's full support for his marriage and the celebrations went ahead.

An association with controversial marriages seems to have been a feature of Thomas Campion's masque career. He was the author of the *Lord Hay's Masque* for the marriage of Honora Denny and James Hay, *The Lords' Masque* for the Palatinate wedding and, most controversially of all, *Somerset* itself. Importantly, Campion's employment as masque writer for the Somerset union extended an association between himself, the King and the Howard faction initiated in 1607 with the *Lord Hay's Masque*.[11] Performed by several Howard supporters, *Somerset* clearly indicates the extent to which the court masque was the tool of faction and a marker of favour; this masque came from and spoke for the King's coterie.[12] Although *The Lords' Masque* celebrated James's policy of pan-European religious appeasement, and Campion's other entertainments pursued a concept of Anglo-Scottish dynastic union reminiscent of Jonson's *Hymenaei*, all three served James's manipulation of the dynastic and factional balance of the court, nation and Europe. Such factionality was, however, a feature of the masque form and is clearly demonstrable also in Anna's own career; the Queen danced as a conventional masquer only in her own commissions from Daniel or Jonson. *Somerset*, her first performance in a masque staged by a rival faction, is the exception which proves the wisdom of her earlier policy. Obliged to participate in an entertainment directed towards a rival court faction, Anna became involved in a performance of support for a marriage which she had openly opposed.

David Lindley has pointed out that Anna's eventual acquiescence to the Somerset match facilitated the performance of *Somerset* itself, since her capitulation allowed the wedding to be celebrated in Whitehall. He also suggests that the Queen's high-profile role as catalyst for the masque's transformation was intended to offer 'a Royal guarantee' of the couple's virtue in the face of scandalous rumour.[13] Yet, given Anna's open opposition to the match, what does it mean that she was invited (or rather obliged) to enact her approval in such an unprecedented manner? A closer examination of the detail of Anna's performance on this occasion points to the ambiguities of her role in both masque and court. Given court society's knowledge of the Queen's objections, the implications of her performance undermined rather than exalted her – though the masque hailed her as the 'Sacred hand' of queenship, Anna's performance was in reality a forceful reminder of her necessary dependence upon the King.[14]

The bizarre nature of Anna's performance can be illuminated through her oppositional masques, which her participation in *Somerset* seemed to defuse. Sponsored by James and his favourites, *Somerset* used imagery reminiscent of the gendered model of power constructed in *Hymenaei*, in the invocation of Hymen and Jove.[15] In doing so *Somerset* emphasised marital relationships, female chastity and the rule of the husband; Anna, who in masques such as *Queens* had opposed the marital construction of Stuart political and temporal authority, was now obliged to enact a ritual blessing of the union of members of a rival faction which simultaneously condoned the patriarchal construction of royal authority.

This remarkable moment, during which the Queen bore the weight of the masque's conceit, had a profound effect upon *Somerset*'s structure and meaning. Lindley remarks that the transformation of the masquers is 'rather perfunctory' and 'merely endorses what has already been achieved' in Anna's banishment of the antimasque. Although he attributes this failure to the 'difficult circumstances of its composition', I would add that the extreme emphasis upon Anna's performance also helped to distort *Somerset*'s structure.[16] In a masque danced by noblemen, the pivotal transformation between antimasque and main masque depended upon female engagement and raised the profile of female performance itself. What is more, in a heightened instance of the general conventions of the masque form, Anna's necessary performance was carefully constrained in order to ensure its conformity and the entertainment's success. The reversal of the romance conceit in the Chorus's declaration, 'Since Knights by valour rescue Dames distrest, / Let them be by the Queene of Dames releast', at first appears to empower female performance.[17] Yet the cost of facilitating male masquing through the release of the men by their queen was Anna's real political capitulation in front of the watching court. Such an undue emphasis upon coerced female performance within *Somerset* placed an unbearable pressure upon the structure of this masque.

In addition to straining the masque's structure, this conceit also drew the imaginative status of the Whitehall masquing stage itself into question, offering the royal dais as its overt rival. This becomes clear in the movement of the Golden Tree through the masquing hall; the transvestite Destinies 'set the Tree of Golde before the Queene', by whom it was then given to a nobleman, who then passed it to a squire.[18] In moving the tree from the masquing stage, across the dancing floor, to the dais and back again, the visual performance of the bond between stage, hall and dais intensified the status of the Banqueting House, and the state in particular, as symbolic social spaces of performance. The royal and courtly audience of *Somerset* were explicitly identified with their aristocratic co-performers upon the raised stage; such a link between performance and the contemporary political situation was emphasised by the masquing hall itself, the fourth wall of which was transformed into a vision of the city beyond. The relationship between performance and courtly actuality was further intensified in Anna's own problematic positioning in this masque. As she watched from the King's state, dressed for dancing in the revels rather than for masquing, the ambiguity of whether the Queen was a masquer or an audience-member was signalled primarily by Eternitie's use of the name 'Bel-Anna'.[19] This Jonsonian name, last applied to Anna in *Queens*, implicated her in the masque's conceit even as she watched from what was technically off-stage, and heightened the integral relationship between the masquer's assumed persona and courtly identity. Instead of an allegorical costume and a place on the masquing stage, on this occasion Anna's performance was signalled only by a name; the layer of theatrical artifice was stripped to a minimum, and Bel-Anna stood for Queen Anna in court ritual and court life. By simply naming Anna after her previous personation, Campion brought her policies and loyalties inside his masque in the performance of the Queen as queen.

Although unusual in the form it took on this occasion, the potential for such performance lay within every masque. James had himself indulged in several impromptu interjections from the dais, demanding that a dance should be repeated (Beaumont's *Masque of the Inner Temple*, and Jonson's *Beauty*) or exploding with displeasure (*Pleasure Reconciled*), and his participation demonstrates the ambiguous nature of the dais itself.[20] However, what distances *Somerset* from the spontaneous outbursts of the King is that the Queen's participation was pre-ordained. In a reversal of the situation of the previous decade, when James watched as Anna performed opposition, in this masque non-performance became a position of power and performance a marker of submission.

Yet while the masque should have demonstrated the monarch's power in the reanimation of the masquers under his gaze, the need to ensure Anna's public performance of the King's will also demanded that James's authority was to some extent displaced on to his consort. In what is almost a paradigm for Jacobean courtly female performance Anna's necessary engagement had to operate within the strict limitations imposed by the King's agenda. However, conformity to such regulations was not a foregone conclusion and the possibility of female refusal was not unprecedented; after all, *Somerset* followed Frances Howard's refusal to dance in *Love Restored* (1612) and Anna's own rejection of the Protestant sacrament in the English coronation. Anna's compliance in 1613 suggests, therefore, that she was no longer in a position to refuse. Excluded from the main masque and restricted to a brief but politically loaded mode of performance, Anna's participation freed the male masquers to dance, and heralded the retreat of the courtly woman from the Whitehall stage. The very detail of the performance in which she was involved contributed to this effect, since, while her performance did reinstate Anna in a central position, it simultaneously reworked the iconography of her previous performances to enact female submission through the medium of performance itself. Despite the stock nature of much of the iconography and conceits of the Jacobean masques, *Somerset* was unusual in the extent to which such intertextualities clustered around the Queen and her previous performances. By creating an intimate relationship between *Somerset* and previous female masques, Campion invoked women's performance in a way which discredited both its practice and its opposition to the mainstream court.

The most suggestive relationships between this and earlier masques exist between *Somerset* and Jonson's masques of *Blackness* and *Beauty*, themselves central texts in the development of female masquing. Predicated around maritime imagery, all these masques depict the arrest of an overseas journey of homage by the power of non-courtly forces, Jonson in the journey of the Daughters of Niger, and Campion in that of the knights from 'every quarter of the earth'.[21] In *Somerset* this maritime imagery finds its clearest expression in the descriptions of its scenery, for which no designs survive.[22] Furthermore, in invoking the conceit of the enchanted storm, both *Somerset* and *Beauty* drew upon Anna's journey from Denmark as a representative trope of alien femininity, much as did earlier Scottish performances. Such maritime imagery and the conceit of Britain as the island-centre of the known world were constants throughout Anna's performance career, and were given particular emphasis by her own difference. This image was at the centre of Daniel's *Tethys' Festival*, which figured the Queen as a sea-goddess and her ladies as British rivers.[23] Daniel depicted Anna in a liminal relationship to island Britain; she does not inhabit the land but is instead associated with the waters which, both native and other, defensive and threatening, simultaneously protect and isolate Britain. The image of water itself is both gendered, associated with the open fluidity of the female body, and political, connected with Anna's engagement in disputed maritime sovereignty. In turn *Somerset* used this imagery and reworked a motif closely linked to the depiction and self-representation of the queen consort, calling upon memories of her performances in this public display of her apparent defeat.

In addition the visual images of Anna's performance in *Somerset* also came directly from her earlier career and contrast her about-turn on the Somerset match with her previous political influence and opposition. The most striking example of a shared image is the prominent emblem of the golden tree. The Savoy agent Giovanni Battista Gabaleoni's description of *Somerset*, although unclear over the timing of the plucking of the bough, identifies the golden tree as an olive, the Biblical emblem of the fruitful wife.[24] The olive is an emblem of marital fertility and the rule of the husband. Prefigured by Henry Peacham's choice of the olive tree as Anna's emblem in *Minerva Britanna* (1612) and dedicated to Prince Henry, the image had close associations also with the Queen herself (figure 20).[25] Although it was a common masque motif, the golden tree cropped up also with remarkable frequency in the careers of both Anna and Campion, and was associated throughout with enchantment, transformation and sovereign power. Yet while this imagery predicated Anna's authority upon that of her husband, the golden tree was also an image offering multiple interpretations. In addition to its marital significance, St Paul had compared the Jewish nation to the lopped branches of the olive tree in an image which was admonitory and punitive: 'because of unbelief [the branches] were broken off, and thou [the gentiles] standest by faith. Be not high-minded, but fear.'[26] It seems, therefore, that in Campion's masque Anna's association with the golden tree was fashioned from her personal icono-graphy and that of early modern femininity and it can be read as a warning to concur with the King's wishes. In this sense the removal of the golden

13 TO THE THRICE-VERTVOVS, AND FAIREST OF QVEENES, ANNE QVEENE OF GREAT BRITAINE.

Anagramma D:
Gul: Pouleri.

In ANNA regnantium arbor.
ANNA *Britannorum Regina*.

A N Oliue lo, with braunches faire difpred,
Whofe top doth reach vnto the azure skie,
Much feeming to difdaine, with loftie head
The Cedar, and thofe Pines of THESSALIE,

* Non claffes,
non Legiones,
| eriade firma im-
perii munimenta
quam numerum
liberorum. Ta-
citus. 4. Hift:

Faireft of Queenes, thou art thy felfe the Tree,
The fruite * thy children, hopefull Princes three.

Which thus I gheffe, fhall with their outftretcht armes,
In time o'refpread Europa's continent,

* parcere fubiec-
tis. &c.

* To fhield and fhade, the innocent from harmes,
But overtop the proud and infolent :
Remaining, raigning, in their glories greene,
While man on earth, or Moone in heauen is feene.

Fatum

20 Emblem for Queen Anna, from Henry Peacham, *Minerva Britanna*
(London, Wa: Dight, 1612)

branch is as much the punishment of Anna's failure to concur with James's will as it is the freeing of the enchanted masquers. Simultaneously, however, the associations of the image of royal trees in both Stuart and

Medici iconography render it equally interpretable as a compliment to Anna. Mary Stuart's embroidery of the *impresa* of the lopped tree and Lorenzo de Medici's Virgilian-inspired *impresa* of the golden bough, 'If one is torn away another will not be lacking', are statements of the perpetuity of the royal line through the gift of the heir.[27] This image might have been read by the emblematically sophisticated in the audience as a statement both of Anna's power as queen consort and of her dependency upon the authority of her husband. What is clear is that the golden tree was a debatable and open-ended image for an early modern audience, susceptible to various and apparently conflicting interpretations and that this ambiguity echoes the consort's dualistic, liminal position within the power structures of the court.

Though the image of the golden tree occurs in *Tethys' Festival* and in multiple form in the masquers' transformation in the *Lord Hay's Masque*, it first appeared in Anna's masquing in *Blackness*. As outlined in the introduction, D. J. Gordon identified the image of Anna and Lucy Russell dancing as Euphoris and Aglaia carrying the painted emblem of the 'golden tree laden with fruit' as an expression of royal and spiritual fertility.[28] Furthermore, the fruit on the tree of *Blackness*, which prefigured Peacham's representation of the royal heirs as the fruit of Anna's tree and 'fruitful vine', was positioned in a masque which used the trope of the consort's gift of the heir to present a radical refiguration of the sexuality of the royal woman. Finally, the image of the fruit-laden tree is found also in the emblems of the chateau of Dompierre-sur-Boutonne, where with the motto 'Tu ne cede malis' and the motif of women sowing seeds, it expresses perseverance and survival.[29] All in all, it was from this 'Tree of Grace and Bountie' that Anna had to pluck the branch in order to facilitate the Somerset match which she had so strongly opposed.[30] Campion's masque, centring upon the construction of marital authority and aristocratic female fertility, and emphatically referring to Anna's performance career, staged an emblematic iconography which both celebrated and denied the transgressive representation of female sexuality of her own earlier masques. Royal female fertility, the source of the queen consort's power, was here depicted in an image susceptible to interpretation as both a celebration of its survival and female refiguring and as expressive of the male control of these impulses.

The pattern of referral to earlier Jacobean female masques can be found also in emphatic verbal echoes of *Blackness* and *Beauty*. For instance, the opening speech of the First Squire reworked prominent images from the Jonsonian performances. Whilst Jonson had opposed the blackening

Ethiopian sun to the cleansing power of James's imperial light, the Squire's speech immediately presented the Syrian sun as a force of disruption, threatening the 'fruite of Peace and Joy' and by implication the fruit of dynastic heirs.[31] Such interconnections continue with the reference to 'churlish Boreas', which Welsford identifies with the 1608 Florentine *Ballet of the Winds*, but which also cropped up in the same year as the aggressive nascent antimasquer of *Beauty*.[32] The similarities between the 'grisled skin coate, with haire and wings' of *Somerset*'s pantomimic antimasquer and Jones's design of the russet and white robe, grey wings, and 'rough and horrid' hair and beard extends this intertextuality back into the visual.[33] The difference between Campion's and Jonson's figurations, however, lies in the fact that the former's antimasque of the four winds presents fully fledged figures of discord. Indeed Campion transforms Jonson's imagery to make it more powerfully negative; both the sun which so controversially blackened Anna's skin in *Blackness* and the North Wind which heralded her return to the masquing stage with bleached skin in *Beauty* are now presented in their more conventional negativity to honour James through his consort's submission.

A further instance of such intertextuality demonstrates the impact of Campion's imagery in contrast to its previous manifestations. The figure of 'Africa, like a Queene of the Moores, with a crown', who entered in the antimasque of 'the foure parts of the earth' is a composite image of Anna's personation of a 'blackamore' in *Blackness* and a female ruler in *Queens*.[34] Yet the representational strategies of the female within these masques differ drastically, with Campion's use having more in common with the damning depiction of the pagan Queen of Africa 'monstreuse / En erreurs plus qu'en animaux' (more monstrous in your errors than your beasts) in the unperformed *Masque of Truth* (1613).[35] Within the imperialist discourse of *Somerset* which exalts Europe as 'Empresse' and aligns the female body with territory, the alien female monarch of the Jonsonian masques reverts from self-performance to Campion's passive symbol of territorial possession performed through the body of the male actor. Structural differences are also significant; transferred from main masque to antimasque, the figure of the black queen is aligned with the forces which were to be dispelled by the power of the King. The transgressive courtly femininity of the daughters of Niger and the exalted queens is refigured in the antimasque figure of *Somerset*, banished from the main masque and from female self-performance. Anna, the only woman allowed to perform on this occasion, is represented as the conformist supporter of royal policy in her everyday self.

In addition to the use of the Jonsonian name 'Bel-Anna', *Somerset* has other important similarities to *Queens*. Fame, 'Great Honors Herrald', is at the heart of both masques.[36] Although Fama bona's representation in *Queens* was not unproblematic, it was the central conceit of Jonson's masque, whilst, in contrast, Lindley identifies *Somerset*'s basic conceit as false fame.[37] The dual aspects of fame – malicious rumour and virtuous reputation – are divided between *Somerset*'s antimasque and main masque. Both Fame and Anna stand at the pivotal point of transformation between these two components and are therefore strongly identified with both. While Fama bona is represented by a transvestite actor, Campion uses the various figures of the antimasque (paralleling the Jonsonian witches, Ignorance, Suspicion, Credulity, Falsehood, Murmur, Malice 'whetting of her forkèd tongue', Impudence, Slander, Execration, Bitterness, Rage and Mischief) to create a composite presentation of malignant fame. Jonson's figures of gossip and slander – the sins of the tongue – create a composite image which Purkiss characterises as non-courtly female knowledge.[38] These figures are themselves most clearly echoed in Campion's male-performed female personification of Credulitie, who was a witch in *Queens* and an 'Enchanteress' in *Somerset*.[39] The negative duality which Purkiss identifies in Fama bona is connected explicitly with perceived feminine duality and anxieties surrounding female admission into the patriarchal construction of language and authority. Such an opposition between the courtly and non-courtly, common scandal and female sexual reputation, maps on to *Somerset*'s reworking of fame as false and disruptive.

Since the division between witch and queen in *Queens* is far from clear-cut, Anna's pivotal position in that performance identified her to some extent with the forces both of the court and of the antimasque. Equally, the moment when Anna took the branch from the golden tree in *Somerset* and effected the transformation to the main masque was also the moment when she was obliged to enact the loss of her own authority in the face of the King; she was identified with both James's power and the dispelled antimasque, and both were internalised in her performance. In founding *Somerset* upon the conceit of false fame, Campion reversed the dynamics of Anna's previous performance: Fama bona became false fame, masque became antimasque. Illegitimate (non-courtly) power in *Somerset* was encapsulated in the obscured presence of the female enchantress. Although Credulitie is identified as an enchantress, a more specific correlation between female and enchantress can be found in the Queen herself. Anna, the woman who 'Can all Knotted spels unty' is, as in *Queens*, also the woman who would rid the court of oppositional enchantment.[40] Yet as the alien queen consort, the royal female versed in magic, Anna was implicated also in just that illegitimate knowledge and power which her performance banished.[41] The recycled figures of previous antimasques – Boreas, Credulitie and the black queen – are a disparate force without a leader; but both the French *ballets* which influenced Campion and the domestic masque tradition identify a single powerful figure as responsible for such enchantment. The missing figure-head was supplied by Anna herself. As the woman of illegitimate knowledge whose humiliation transformed antimasque to main masque, the Queen was Dame to this antimasque's scattered hags. Such an identification demanded that *Somerset*'s audience should construct an explicit parallel between their Queen's performance and the actuality of the courts of Anna and James. Performing with the minimum of thea-tricality, Anna explicitly acted as herself and as the referent for the figurehead of the antimasque forces of enchantment. The statement of female community and authority made in *Queens* was here diverted towards propagating the power of the male court.

The figuration of Anna as *Somerset*'s hidden female enchantress is further illuminated by the accusations of magic in the Essex divorce court proceedings. The decision to shift the representation of witchcraft away from the bride and on to the Queen was risky, yet wholly in line with the discourse of Jacobean courtly female performance and, as Purkiss demonstrates, early modern cultural production itself.[42] Furthermore, there are contemporary parallels between Anna's enforced performance and the defeat of illegitimate female power in French court entertainments. Campion's use of Tasso as a precedent to validate the contemporary reworking of classicism highlights the intertextuality between this masque and the 1617 *Ballet de Renaud* which took Tasso's epic *Jerusalem Delivered* as its source.[43] Both this *ballet* and its influential predecessor, the *Ballet Comique de la Reine* (1581), ritually enacted the defeat of female enchan-tresses – Alcine and Circe respectively – in homage to the power of the monarch. Phallocentric power was figured in the *ballets*' wands (Circe's was presented to the royal dais by Minerva) and the branch of *Somerset*. In the latter masque, therefore, Anna was aligned with such oppositional women as Circe, Alcine and the Dame, and depicted as securely con-strained within the discourse of the alien queen consort and the witch – discourses which negotiate female authority and the threatening em-powered woman in the Renaissance. It is worth expanding on Lindley's and McGowan's observations to point out that the *ballets* which influenced Campion were staged during the regency of Marie de Medici; images of

the conquest of illicit female enchantresses expressed French courtly
society's tensions over female rule and the 1617 *Ballet de Renaud* employed
these images as a near-explicit warning from Louis XIII to the Queen
Mother.[44] Campion's departure from this model merely intensified the
implication of the transgressive nature of female political involvement.
Evidence that courtly entertainments were already and would continue
to be an accepted forum for the enactment of the submission of the royal
female to the will of the male monarch can be seen in the completeness
with which *Somerset* maps on to the submission of Catherine de Bourbon
to Henri IV in the *ballets* composed for her by Catherine de Parthenay
in 1592–93.[45]

Somerset was unmistakably opposed to the policies and performances
of Anna and her court; it drew its most exalted female spectator into an
enactment of submission which was itself an attack upon the emergent
practice of women's performance in the Jacobean court. Anna's identification with the witches of the antimasque of *Queens* was entirely
disempowering. Binding the Queen to the performance of an authority
which she had opposed, *Somerset* constructed her shared humiliation with
the witches bound to the chariots of the virtuous queens. In this way
the tradition of Jacobean female performance was mined to create a new
balance of power within the factional masque of the Somerset wedding,
and political opposition was worked through in a performance which
was itself a sought-after means of altering the balance of factional power.
It would also seem inevitable that Anna's capitulation within *Somerset*
should damage her status as queen consort, but, contrary to the earlier
performance of *Blackness*, often read as disregarding Anna's queenship but
in fact representing notions of female authority in a way unpalatable to
Jacobean court ideology, there are no recorded concerns over the damage
done to Anna's royal status within this later masque.[46] *Somerset* could
publicly demean the Queen's status precisely because this was done in
the service of the patriarchy offended by her earlier transgression.

One further important fact emerges from Anna's apparent humiliation
in 1613. *The Somerset Masque* again clearly demonstrates the disparate
nature of the Jacobean courtly female community, and recalls the differences that lay between Anna and her daughter. There were, after all,
differences between women like Anna and Howard who may otherwise
seem to have been united in transgression against the unspecified other
of the 'rest' of the court. Beyond the construction of an opposition
between 'conformist' and 'transgressive' women, there are important
distinctions within these categories, usefully illuminated through the roles

of the Queen and her subject. The two women performed together in *Queens*, while Howard's mother, relatives and their factional supporters were involved in *Blackness*; their careers share an element of transgression against the courtly feminine ideal and of marginalisation within much previous analysis.[47] Despite their shared nonconformity, however, Anna and Howard were polarised by their involvement in the Jacobean court's power structures. Furthermore, the approaches of these women to performance also demonstrate significant variations. Although Frances Howard was involved in courtly performance, she was not a cultural agent in the same sense as her queen. Anna's self-conscious use of patronage, performance and commissioning far outstripped Howard's, and her masques performed a redefinition of female courtly authority.

It is clear also that Anna of Denmark's masquing career was not a steady progression towards an increasingly unfettered female performance, but should be read rather as a series of negotiations, accommodations, successes and defeats. The court masque was a factional tool, and *Somerset* demonstrates the Queen's marginalisation from mainstream court performance at the moment of its enactment. The claim staked so strongly for female performance in *Queens* seems to have been lost in Anna's enforced participation in *Somerset*. Yet Anna's engagement with the court masque did not end when she plucked the golden bough, and withdrawal from the Whitehall masque did not put an end to courtly female cultural engagement. In fact I would argue that it was precisely this strategy of withdrawal which offered itself as a means of handling disempowerment in Whitehall, and facilitated the development of further female performance and self-representation. The movement of the female court beyond Whitehall and into new arenas of performance was indicated as early as 1613 in Anna's progresses to Bristol and Bath, but an especially important example can be found in the performance of Robert White's masque *Cupid's Banishment* in Anna's own court at Greenwich, through which the implications of the marginalisation of the courtly female from performance in Whitehall and the strength of the gesture of withdrawal can be fully explored.

'We can no more express than we already have': memory, speech and silence in Robert White's *Cupid's Banishment*

One of the few certain facts about *Cupid's Banishment* is its performance on 4 May 1617 in Anna of Denmark's court at Greenwich Palace. Little direct documentation survives of this masque beyond the single manuscript copy preserved by one of its performers, Richard Browne who played the role of Diana.[48] There are no eyewitness descriptions, no detail of audience composition, no account references such as fill the gaps in our knowledge of other masque performances. Yet, not withstanding this scarcity and the masque's elision from cultural criticism, *Cupid's Banishment* is a document of immense importance for the assessment of female performance. Robert White's masque, though insubstantial and derivative, was also a statement of intent. Staged for Anna of Denmark, inspired and organised by Lucy Harington Russell, and performed by members of the first recorded English girls' school (the Ladies Hall at Deptford), White's text also recorded what may be the unique instance of female speech in the Jacobean court masque.

As a performative document, *Cupid's Banishment* can be read as a statement of Anna's marginalisation and her withdrawal from performance in an out-of-court production. Equally it can be taken as evidence of the shift in the locus of courtly power away from its Whitehall centre at a time when performance within the court had been appropriated by James's male favourites. The production of a masque danced by female masquers before their Queen in her court at Greenwich altered the agenda of praise, deflecting it from James (absent on progress to Scotland between March and September 1617) and towards his consort. Anna's withdrawal from performance and her unprecedented assumption of the coveted centre-point of power at the head of the hierarchy of the masquing hall can be read as a sophisticated performative compensation for her failed bid for the regency in James's absence. The rejection of Anna's bid in favour of Bacon, who was placed at the head of the Council, only highlights the issues of eligibility to rule and the delegation of the absent monarch's authority, those issues which had also surrounded George Keith's Danish performance as James's proxy in 1589.[49] The lengthy absence of the monarch whose body was the symbol of Stuart absolute authority left a vacuum at the geographical and symbolic centre of power, and Anna's appropriation of the position of privileged spectator, in all other masques reserved uniquely for the monarch, was the symbolic enactment of the political engagement which she attempted within Jacobean society.

Despite low expectations of Anna's dealings with the Council, when she removed to Greenwich Palace during James's progress all the evidence suggests that most influential courtiers followed her there. On 24 May 1617 Chamberlain reported that 'Most of the counsaile kepe there [at

Greenwich] about ... [the Queen], saving such as have necessarie attendance at the terme, and those come still on Saterday night and tary Sonday. The rest are only absent on Star-chamber dayes, which have ben few or none this terme.'[50] Supporting this is George Gerrard's report, on 9 May 1617, that Anna 'stays at Greenwich and never missed one Lent sermon. The Prince and Council came to them also.'[51] Greenwich itself might provide some answers to the question of why the court should cluster around Anna in this way. Positioned beyond the boundaries of London but within easy reach, it was both a liminal site and one which had a long tradition of the fostering of court culture. Indeed the most likely venue for White's masque, the semi-permanent Disguising Theatre at the palace, was built by Henry VIII for the 1527 French embassy.[52] Equipped with such a theatrical space, which was flanked on three walls by tiers of seats, Greenwich provided Anna with the means to stage the entertainments of a rival court.[53] What is more, Greenwich Palace was also the site of the Queen's House, Inigo Jones's innovative classical commission from Anna, which was halted at her death and completed for Henrietta Maria. The delay to its completion has masked the fact that the cubic design of the great hall was a significant anticipation of the Whitehall Banqueting House of 1619 and so a forerunner of the central site of state ritual in early modern England.[54] As a space of female cultural agency, and of a well-established court culture, Greenwich was an ideal site for the location and performances of the Queen's court, whose flourishing presence at Greenwich challenges the perception of Whitehall as the sole site of courtly power.

To this site came many of the elite of the court and, as Gerrard suggests, perhaps also Prince Charles, whose whereabouts during the absence of the monarch and whose possible proximity to his mother impact on the meaning of this masque occasion.[55] It is more certain, however, that Lucy Harrington Russell, dedicatee of the masque text and organiser of the performance, was in attendance. Russell, Anna's most prominent female courtier since 1603, was here involved in the appropriation of masculine state ritual. Her position as masque patron echoed that of Bacon in relation to the Inns of Court in the Palatinate festivities; what is more, the progress of the masquers from the Ladies Hall into Greenwich to dance for their queen mirrored that of these male students in 1613.[56] In echoing the practices of such institutions, the journey of the masquers to Anna's Greenwich court deflected mainstream Whitehall-centred court ceremonial to honour Anna within her own structures of authority. However, the move which most resonantly fashioned this female performance and its surroundings as a counterpart to the King's court was Anna's withdrawal from performance to the position of privileged spectator.

At this point the position of Bacon, head of the Council and himself a masque patron, is worth further consideration. Bacon's own ceremonials, particularly his entry in state as new Lord Keeper to Westminster attended by the followers of the Queen and Prince only a few days after the staging of *Cupid's Banishment*, are an interesting commentary on those dedicated to Anna.[57] Although Anthony Weldon's account of Bacon's unofficial regency is clearly coloured, the description of these ceremonies as the usurpation of sovereign pageantry identifies Bacon's entry as the appropriation of state ritual.[58] In such a context Anna's own appropriation of the position occupied by the monarch in the state ritual of the masque carried great political significance. While James was regaled by progress entertainments on his way to Edinburgh, Anna was the focus of the court ritual of *Cupid's Banishment* and Bacon appropriated state ceremonial in London.[59] It would seem that the theatre of statecraft in the early seventeenth century was multi-focused, centring not only on the monarch but also on other, lesser figures of authority. In the light of this knowledge, *Cupid's Banishment* was at once both an out-of-court performance and a deflected court ceremonial, a realignment of court performance to centre upon an alternative authority figure.

In *Cupid's Banishment* Anna and her coterie of culturally engaged women also interrogated the very notion of the masque as *court* masque. Although the students of the Ladies Hall were admitted to courtly performance, they differed from earlier female masquers in being peripheral to the centre of power, and so their performance allows us to question the definition of court membership.[60] The masque's positioning in Anna's Greenwich court and the participation of the schoolgirls challenged the nature of a genre that could be staged within the confines of the court, and confronted the nature of the court itself.

Staging the female voice:
4 May 1617

My starting point for a detailed discussion of the performance of *Cupid's Banishment* is the assertion in the list of performers, 'Mistress Ann Watkins acted Fortune', the only use of the term 'acted' for a female participant.[61] This is followed within the masque text itself by a unique instance of female masquing speech, which the manuscript credits to 'Fortune':

We are engaged to Time for this occasion
That meets our wishes with such good success.
For this great courtesy I'll create
Some unexpected joy to crown thy hours,
Thy minutes, I'll so turn upon this wheel of mine
That men hereafter shall call thee happy Time.
Hymen, Mercury, how welcome you are hither.
We can no more express than we already have.[62]

Ann Watkins was, therefore, perhaps the first woman to act in a masque. Invoking Mercury's eloquence, the final line of this short speech is a modest but confident assertion of the power of female expression.

Such a speech relates interestingly not only to the traditions of female performance but also to the male court entertainments in the years surrounding White's masque. Performed as part of the Somerset marriage festivities in 1613, Jonson's *Challenge at Tilt* had also centred on the figuration of Cupid as a means of defining a courtly sexuality. The *Challenge* consisted of two warring Cupids, each claiming to be genuine, and each representing the courtly sexes' apparent notion of love, which were finally reconciled in marital harmony in the choreographed tilt and by the appearance of Hymen. The representation of male courtliness in this earlier entertainment is of particular interest when juxtaposed with Fortune's speech. Love itself was depicted by the Cupid representing the male courtiers as 'the true issue of valour and beauty, [...] no love can come near either truth or perfection but what is manly'.[63] Perhaps more importantly when considering the links between this performance and the later staging of *Cupid's Banishment*, this Cupid went on to claim that he would counter female Persuasion with 'Mercury here to charm against her, who gives all lovers their true and masculine eloquence'.[64] This, standing in direct contrast to Fortune's invocation of Mercury as a marker of and inspiration for female eloquence, establishes a firm contrast between the representations of courtly sexuality and love between the two entertainments and the position of women in each.

The recycling of the conceit of Cupid figured large in *Cupid's Banishment*, the basic conceit of which was, as the title suggests, a succession of attempts by female characters to remove Cupid from the masque stage and the chaste court of Diana. This court, contrasted with 'some amorous court' where Cupid truly belonged, was the scene of a chaste marriage, organised by Diana, Fortune and Occasion, and of the

crowning of the King and Queen of the Bean.[65] Cupid was here a raging
but impotent figure of fun, whose constant declarations of power over
courtly women were denied in his banishment from both the chaste court
and its chaste marriage. The opening of the masque made a clear
declaration of female independence and of the rights of women to perform,
as Occasion entered and addressed Anna, armed with 'confidence and
royal resolution / Of female worth' to introduce both the Ladies Hall
and the conceit of the King and Queen 'Of Fortune's choice'.[66] One
male intruder, however, was suffered to stay: Bacchus, intent on recon-
ciling Diana with Cupid, entered in a displaced antimasque of drunken
revellers in the centre of the masque, and was granted leave to remain
on the grounds that such behaviour be tempered. The masque concluded
with dances and presentations to Anna and a laudatory speech from
Occasion to the Queen. In the light of the intertextualities between
White's masque and *A Challenge at Tilt*, it would seem that the rejection
of Cupid was in itself a rejection of the paradigm of marital authority
predicated and staged in the court of James I.

The obscurity of *Cupid's Banishment* also hides Ann Watkins's identity.
Very little can be unearthed about this woman, except the possibility that
she is the sister of Alice, another masquer, and the daughter of David
Watkins, the Controller of Works at Windsor Castle from 1618.[67] We
can, however, relate her social position to that of other Ladies Hall
performers. This school was pivotally positioned between the home-based
education of the daughters of the Tudor elite in high humanistic learning
and the later dame schools which educated the daughters of the citizenry
in dance, needlework and etiquette. The school's existence is recorded
solely within White's transcript, demonstrating the bond between female
performance and a more general feminine cultural and social agency.
Indeed the ideologies of early modern female education existed in a
mutual relationship to the masque: *Cupid's Banishment* both expressed and
validated elite models of female education.

At first glance Ann Watkin's speech may seem to be an incongruous
step beyond the bounds placed upon courtly women's masquing, and
one which, as part of the final masque in which Anna of Denmark was
involved, was quickly retracted. This, however, was not the case. Fortune's
speech is an integral part of the tradition of Jacobean female masquing;
this speech and the masque which contains it formed the logical endpoint
of the ongoing destabilising of the confines of female silence within the
masque genre. The outcome of approaching *Cupid's Banishment* in this
way is a reading which deals less with the content of Fortune's speech

itself than with the factors, processes and conditions which made this speech possible in its particular cultural moment.

This unprecedented moment of female speech needs to be understood within the context both of White's masque itself and of the progression towards linguistic expression by female masquers that had been taking place throughout the seventeenth century. In addition the ground was laid for female speech (performatively, politically and socially) in the physical and kinetic texts of figured dance and embroidery. Rather than an incongruous outburst, therefore, this speech was instead the result of a dual process, both within *Cupid's Banishment* itself and within the performance tradition of female masquing in the court of Anna of Denmark. *Cupid's Banishment*, the final masque of Anna's court, memorialised that court's masquing tradition in the performance of figured dance and embroidery and motifs of gift-giving, remembrance, speech and silence.

Unprecedented as it was in the Jacobean masque, Fortune's speech formed part of a frail tradition of the female voice on stage in Scottish and Tudor progress entertainments, and preceded the performances of the court of Henrietta Maria. In 1592 the noblewomen Anne and Elizabeth Russell spoke in the *Speeches to the Queen at Bisham*, produced for Elizabeth I. This entertainment had thematic similarities with *Cupid's Banishment*, dealing with ideas of speech, writing, embroidery and chastity. The Bisham progress, prefiguring White's masque, presented needlework as a quasi-linguistic medium, predicated through gender: 'Men's tongues, wrought all with double stitch, but not one true ... / Roses, egletine, harts-ease, wrought with Queenes stitch, and all right.' [68] *Bisham*'s incorporation of female speech pressed upon generic boundaries in the same way that it affected those of the masque in *Cupid's Banishment*. Importantly, Ann Watkins's speech also predated the song of Madame Coniack, the professional singer of Townshend's *Tempe Restored*, by fifteen years.[69] Such later performances of the female masquing voice can, however, illuminate that of Watkins. One moment of comparison is found in Milton's *Comus* (1634), in which Lady Alice Egerton, then fifteen, and her two brothers sang and spoke extensively.[70] In terms of their performers' age and the status of an out-of-court occasion, *Comus* and *Cupid's Banishment* are remarkably similar. Following *Tempe Restored*, Alice Egerton broke new ground as the first noblewoman to sing within a public entertainment (masque or drama), and one of the first to speak within a masque. *Cupid's Banishment* itself had both female speech and song, the masquers playing the wood nymphs 'sing in joy' and, in the development of female masquing, song operated as an intermediary step between female silence and speech.[71] The similarity in the ages of Watkins and Egerton suggests that youth was a factor in this once transgressive performance. Though little is known of the age or background of the professionals (Madame Coniack and her companion Mistress Shepherd), the first non-professional women involved in performative speech and song were adolescent and operated under the protection of aristocratic figures, in these cases Queen Anna, Lucy Russell and the Earl of Bridgewater. It is possible that the youthfulness of Ann Watkins and Alice Egerton granted a degree of impunity similar to that exploited by the earlier children's theatre companies, an impunity less available to those who no longer stood beneath the control of a father, a family or a school.

Cupid's Banishment presents a very specific kind of speech. Watkins's vocal performance stands at the mid-point between the silence of Jacobean female masquing and the dramatic speech seen in the later pastorals of the female Caroline court.[72] Watkins's position was itself ambiguous, and she was capable of speech precisely because of her liminal existence on the boundaries between court and citizenry. This is reflected within *Cupid's Banishment*: as Fortune, Watkins was aligned with her silent masquing companions, leading the other girls out in the figured dance, identified with that group through age, sex and class, yet irrevocably distanced from them by her unique vocality. Watkins's performance also bears the hallmarks of continental or French influence: as neither a professional performer nor a conventionally silent female masquer, her position had more in common with the aristocratic Mademoiselle de Sainte Mesme, who played the speaking role of Circe in the *Ballet Comique* (1581), than with that of other English performances. The possibility of a French influence upon Anna's court culture is confirmed by the *ballet de cour* danced in Anna's chambers in 1617.[73]

Despite the specific nature of this speech, however, in speaking at all Watkins forfeited the masquer's guarantee of recognition – she was acting. This identifies her strongly with the male performers of *Cupid's Banishment*, some of whom, the speakers of the main masque rather than the professional performers of the antimasque, occupied an ambiguous position. Some of those involved in the main masque, such as Charles Coleman who played Hymen, were professionals. Richard Browne, however, was one of a group who, like the girls of the Ladies Hall, were the children of local dignitaries performing for prestige. This displacement of the previously rigid distinction between actor and masquer perhaps facilitated female vocality: in the wake of shifting class distinctions, it appears that conditions were also ripe for a degree of gender equality.

The choice of the conventional abstraction of Fortune, a non-individualised image of women's authority, to stage the female voice is also revealing. Though its reliance on fickleness conforms to the early modern discourse of femininity, this personification also has strong positive associations. Fortune, the embodiment of the power of chance, was explicitly associated with the role of ruler. 'Fortune's doom' was the force behind the masque's major conceit, the selection of the player king and queen.[74] As the actual and symbolic power within the masque, Fortune, alongside Diana, was the performative analogue of the watching Anna, her authority shown in the stage picture in her elevation to the head of the mount, above the King and Queen of the Bean. These figures of seasonal celebration stem from a tradition of carnivalesque misrule which had a strong influence on the development of female performance. White's dedicatory letter also establishes an atmosphere of seasonal celebration which justified his pupils' performance and recognised both the liminality of *Cupid's Banishment* and the proximity of the masque genre to the non-courtly: 'The ground of our plot is, choosing of a king and queen by Fortune's doom, which is a sport our little ladies can use on Candelmas night.'[75] Although White was careful to distance the non-courtly and grotesque elements of the masque form from his pupils (the rejection of Cupid, the chaste marriage and the service of Diana perhaps countered the promiscuous associations of female speech), the unusual positioning of the bacchanalian antimasque and the permission which this structure granted these figures to remain within the court was a recognition of the need for licence and of marginalised performance.

The debate between the chaste and the physical was, however, complicated in the representation of the female performers. The masquers were represented in line with the court's erotic bodily ideal. Though predictably there are no extant costume designs, the wood nymphs are described as having 'their arms half naked with bracelets of berries about them'.[76] This display of female flesh links to Fortune's speech itself through the physical indecorum which resonates through the Jacobean tradition of female masquing, from Anna's performance as Pallas in *The Vision*, through the seminal moment of *Blackness* and its echoes in *Beauty* and *Queens*, to *Cupid's Banishment* itself. White's masquers, although possessed of both speech and song, were constrained to operate within representative strategies similar to those of the earlier silent masques. The marginalisation of the female masquer in this decade is a reminder of the constant danger of losing recently gained ground.

The importance of Fortune was further asserted when Watkins led her silent co-performers out to dance the Queen's name; the juxtaposition of dance and speech was heightened by the presence of the woman who performed both in quick succession. As I suggest below, Watkins's direct approach to language was then consolidated in the more acceptable female activity of the dance, its 'whispering measure' initiated by a woman engaged in a more radical linguistic expression.[77] Through the strategies of song and speech *Cupid's Banishment* was an all-round assault on the constraints of female silence. The attainment of speech was here accompanied by similar representative strategies which had been used throughout the female masques of the Jacobean courts to push upon the prohibition on female speech. In doing so, *Cupid's Banishment* drew upon the tradition of Jacobean court performance, in particular the physical media of dance and embroidery, to support and validate Fortune's speech within that canon.

Embroidery and dance: staging the physical text

> This speech being ended, the GODDAUGHTERS presenting their needlework gifts – one, an acorn; the other rosemary – beginning with the first letters of the QUEEN´s name. They retire all, two by two.[78]

As the performance of *Cupid's Banishment* neared its climax, the audience were offered a moment of insight into the dynamics of the masque form, the offering of a gift from the masquers to the Queen. This was quickly followed by another such moment, when Anna was honoured with the dance of her name by the masquers:

> They pace with majesty toward the presence and, after the first strain of the violins, they dance, [forming] Anna Regina in letters; [in] their second masquing dance [forming] Jacobus Rex; [in] their departing dance is [the formation of] Carolus P with many excellent figures falling off, by Master Onslo, tutor to the Ladies Hall.[79]

The giving of the emblems and the writing-in-dance of the names of the royal family were separated by the presentation of Anna's two god-daughters to the Queen. In this threefold presentation was an emotional climax in which the masque itself, always an offering of state to the monarch, was formally given to Anna. The audience was here presented with two acts of the female creation and performance of text, separated only by a speech from the male actor playing Diana. These emblems represented Anna's initials in pictorial form while the dance drew out her name in the masquers' bodies; all in all, the presentation of these emblems constituted a staged act of memorialisation, the presentation to the Queen of a concrete reminder of her place as privileged spectator. Dance and embroidery, prime aspects of female education and of the performance of *Cupid's Banishment*, were bound together within these emblems: the embroidered text mirrored the earlier danced text and both were physical representations of language. Each of these female textual creations, pictorial embodiments of the linguistic, were centred firmly on Anna. While Fortune's speech attained a forbidden vocality for at least one performing woman, the female-authored texts of dance and needlework supported this innovation.

The apparently uncomplicated presentation from god-daughters to godmother is in fact one of very few instances when the gift-giving common in the masque genre was recorded within the text. Its duality is striking. Embodied within this masque, the personal moment became the public act of presentation to the state. Just as a monarch's actions could never be interpreted solely as personal (witness the caresses James bestowed upon Villiers during *Pleasure Reconciled to Virtue*), so the presentation and acceptance of a gift carried political weight. These moments are at the centre of *Cupid's Banishment*, giving insight into the social and historical context of this masque's creation, and a glimpse into the lives of those performing and spectating.

Approaching Anna, the two girls (tentatively identified as Anne Chalenor and Anne Sandeland) presented her with the embroidered emblems.[80] These gifts were complex cultural constructs and, following Rozsika Parker's re-evaluation of the relation of needlework to the artistic canon, they are central to an analysis of *Cupid's Banishment*.[81] White's description implies that the pieces were embroidered by the performers themselves, something both likely and appropriate. No pictorial record survives of the emblems; we have only the masque transcript's statement that they were embroidered representations of rosemary and an acorn. This in turn is interpreted in White's account as representing 'A' and 'R' (the initials of 'Anna Regina'), a truncated version of the danced text. This conjunction is significant. After a lengthy period of subjugation to the primacy of the written text, cultural critics have recently reassessed both dance and needlework as means of textual creation. As the two girls approached the royal dais carrying the pictorial texts which they themselves perhaps had manufactured, they staged both the texts and process of textual creation. Although their authorship of these embroidered texts can never be ascertained beyond doubt, this is a significant example of the performance of a feminine text, ratifying the liberation of the female voice.

The presentation of the gifts of dance and embroidery to Anna is an example of female masquers engaging in textualised expression. Relating to the means of pressuring female silence present in almost all the masques of Anna's court, and analysed in earlier chapters, dance and embroidery here established a further context for Fortune's ground-breaking speech, now revealed as neither incongruous nor unanticipated, while staging the education of the Ladies Hall. One of the most revealing aspects of *Cupid's Banishment* is the close interaction of education, needlework and dance within the social codes operating upon the elite woman in daily life and the performance of these codes within the masque genre. What role did such accomplishments play in women's society and what possibilities did such texts offer to the female masquer of *Cupid's Banishment*?

Addressing Anna, the male actor playing Diana refers to the masquers' embroidered emblems as 'the timely fruits of their chaste labours', revealing needlework's close links with the feminine and with female education.[82] Embroidery was a necessary accomplishment of the elite woman, and, according to Parker, was considered an appropriate way to inculcate an ideal femininity.[83] While the act of embroidering was itself thought to conform to the silent, obedient and domestic model of the perfect woman, 'Women themselves employed subjects to declare their conformity to the feminine identity they were designated' and biblical subjects were particularly favoured.[84] Both textual and pictorial, both apparently conformist in their physicality, dance and embroidery were open to women for precisely the same reasons, and the desirability of each as necessary feminine accomplishments facilitated their inclusion in *Cupid's Banishment*. In this light Diana's assertion that the embroideries reflect the chastity of the masquers was entirely in keeping with their contemporary perception.

Despite the appropriateness of dance and embroidery to the female masquer, the act of performance involved in the presentation of these emblems to Anna clearly overstepped established norms of domesticity and female containment. After all, although the silent female masquing common in the early seventeenth century did not transgress Jacobean social norms, it hardly constituted the withdrawal from the public gaze which was desired of women, and such silent performance can be seen as a validating strategy for female textual creativity and (given Watkins's speech) textual performance. Women were not expected to perform, but in the case of the courtly woman class overrode gender concerns to propel her on to the masquing stage. The students of the Ladies Hall were not themselves members of the court in a strict sense, but their performance and the education it enacted shows an appropriation of the ideology of the courtly woman. Ever-aware of an audience in her daily life, the courtly noblewoman was trained to perform in the masque, if only in the revels, through the rigorous physical discipline of the dance. Yet while the performative nature of the courtly identity forced both men and women to perform, this was in direct opposition to the gendered discourse of women's retreat from the public arena, which was perhaps manifested in the masque form's prohibition of female speech. On the occasion of *Cupid's Banishment*, however, the ideology of retreat was comprehensively defeated.

Embroidery itself also contained some of these contradictions. Although embroidery was intended as a marker of feminine conformity to the desired ideal, a necessary result of its creation, intensified by its inclusion in White's masque, was its display. Although worked in the partial privacy of the domestic sphere, the status of embroidery, especially tapestries, wall hangings or bed hangings, was paradoxical; it 'ensured that women spent long hours at home, retired in private, yet it made a public statement about the household's position and economic standing'.[85] In addition, although intended to isolate women, the containment embroidery required could instead create a communal female space, like the Ladies Hall. An appropriate example is the bedding in Holyrood Palace for the lying-in of Mary Stuart, created for the female ritual of lying-in and childbirth: its remarkable richness was a political statement of wealth and of the procreation of heirs, itself an act combining intimacy and statecraft.[86] In the overlap of the private and public, the creation of a political work within a feminine space is intensely suggestive for the analysis of *Cupid's Banishment*.

Embroidery, especially that made by aristocratic women, operated upon similar ideological foundations as the court masque itself. Created by the women of the house to mark the patriarch's status, embroidery needed a spectator to fulfil its function. In the same way the Jacobean masque was created to praise James I (whose authority was predicated through a gendered familial structure) and enacted his wealth and power before an audience of subjects and foreign ambassadors. What is more, as the New Year gifts of embroidery to Elizabeth I from both male and female courtiers demonstrate, certain kinds of embroidery were, like the masque, rich gifts of state.[87] The audience who witnessed the embroidery also had an important effect upon its status; for example, the Queen's presence at this masque meant that these embroideries could not be read as wholly personal. Furthermore, the women presenting these needlework texts were themselves involved in this balance of the personal and political, since they were in a sense themselves gifts to the Queen. Named for Anna, they were presented to her to honour her queenship and in the hope of advancement for themselves.

It is becoming clear that the embroideries of *Cupid's Banishment* were themselves theatricalised, that embroidery could be a form of performance and an opportunity for the female creation and enactment of text. The act of embroidery was inherently contradictory; the need for women to confirm their femininity by embroidering assigned them a degree of expressive potentiality.[88] And just as all masques were not monarchical panegyrics, all embroideries were not conformist representations of the feminine ideal, but could embody potentially subversive significances. Needlework's potential to express political meaning within a double code of emblems and embroidery was exploited by Mary Stuart in her panel of the knife pruning a vine with the Latin motto 'Virtue flourishes by wounding'. Embroidered during her exile at Hardwick Hall, it was sent to her intended husband the Duke of Norfolk to convey Mary's resolution in the face of her suffering under Elizabeth.[89] Given such an expressive potentiality, I now want to turn to a reading of the possible meanings of the emblems of Anna's embroideries.

What relevance do rosemary and oak have to the occasion and meaning of *Cupid's Banishment*? Connected with ritual (Herrick's *Rosemarie Branch* states 'Grow for two ends, it matters not at all, / Be't for my Bridall, or my Buriall'), rosemary was an apt choice for this performance.[90] However, the fact that neither acorns nor rosemary figure prominently in contemporary pattern books suggests that they were not an obvious choice. Although one might expect emblems (compact layered physical presentations of meaning closely akin to the masque genre itself) to have influenced the choice of embroidered design, and although there is evidence that humanist emblems were occasionally used as embroidery patterns, there does not seem to be any instance of either rosemary or acorns in any emblem in the domestic or continental humanistic emblem books of the early modern period, although the oak tree does figure in various emblem texts.[91] In fact, given that one of the few contemporary visual representations of rosemary and the acorn is found in an illustrated botanical manuscript (figures 21 and 22), this suggests that the choice of these images sites these particular embroideries not within the discourse of the humanist emblem books but within that of the signifying plants and flowers of herbals and botanical manuals which were produced fairly consistently through the sixteenth and early seventeenth centuries. Indeed John Parkinson, James I's apothecary and the father of the Ladies Hall masquer Katherine Parkinson, himself published two such texts between 1629 and 1640, the first of which was dedicated to Henrietta Maria.[92] Given the involvement of both Anna and Lucy Russell in the commissioning of organic garden texts, and the masquers' personal links to those creating herbals, a genre with a primarily female target audience, it is possible that the women of the Ladies Hall were exposed to this genre and that this was the inspiration for Anna's embroideries.[93]

There are further nuances of the meaning conveyed by these emblems. A simplistic initial reading of the acorn in terms of 'strength and steadfastness' can be augmented by implications of prelapsarian innocence, since the acorn was the nourishment of the Golden Age before the intrusion of husbandry.[94] Rosemary, however, carried a more various burden of meaning. An association between rosemary and the female body can be traced back at least as far as medieval gynaecological handbooks, where it was repeatedly recommended as a regulator of menstruation.[95] Furthermore, Gerard's *Herbal* (1597) states that 'Arabians and other Physitians succeeding, do write, that Rosemarie [...] restoreth speech unto them that are possessed with the dumb palsie'.[96] The restoration of previously restricted speech through a plant associated with the female body has clear connections with a masque which itself staged female speech, and which expressed this restoration through a physical, feminine visual text.

Strongly linked with the Virgin Mary, rosemary may have gestured also towards Anna's Catholicism. Associations with rosemary, the Virgin, and celebratory ritual circulated also around the festival of Candlemas, which was the controversial basis for *Cupid's Banishment*'s performance. The obscure displacement of the 2 February festivities to 4 May might be explained as the invocation of a tradition of seasonal, religious and popular performances to validate female masquing. Furthermore, there was perhaps also a covert reference for the initiated to the Jacobean tradition of female performance, since Candlemas was the occasion of the staging of *Queens* in 1609 and of the 1614 Roxborough marriage entertainments. Further female performances may also have been gestured to, since the masquing of the Ladies Hall was in many ways reminiscent of those of Italian Renaissance convents and English continental Catholic girls' schools, to which *Cupid's Banishment* forms an interesting domestic counterpart.[97] Regardless, the shifting of the celebration of the purification

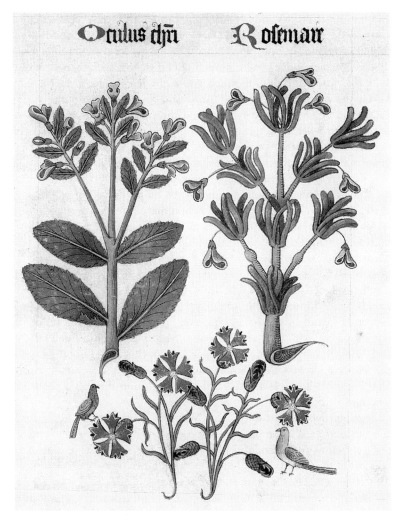

21 Rosemary, Ashmole MS 1504, fol. 16r

of the Virgin to the Marian month of May was a striking use of Catholic ceremonial within the court performance of a Protestant nation.

In this performance rosemary was surrounded by a web of meaning which included the duality of the twice-flowering plant, marriage and funeral rites, dissident Catholicism and the ceremonies of Candlemas,

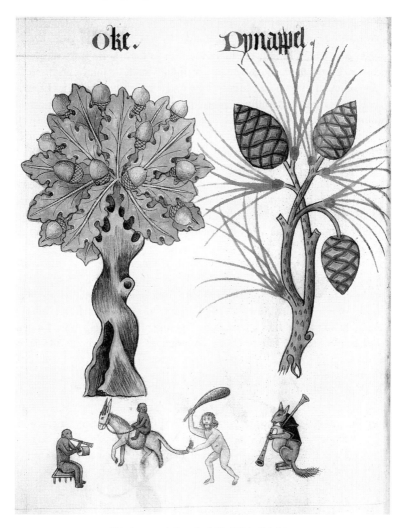

22 Acorn, Ashmole MS 1504, fol. 23v

festive celebration and the expression of loyalty to the monarch. When combined with the encapsulated potential of the oak (Jove's tree) within the acorn, these emblems emerge as a dualistic but essentially supportive offering to Anna; offering hope in the performance of female speech, there was perhaps also consolation for previous silences. What can be said is that these emblems staged a feminised experience; they evaded the mainstream humanism of emblem books to privilege an alternative dis course, one which skirted the literary canon in herbals and pattern books and the courtly in the involvement of figures such as John Parkinson.

In conjunction with female masquing speech, these embroideries express a desire for a greater feminine engagement with the structures of power. Embroidery, like dance, was a necessary feminine attribute, but both display the same tensions inherent in female participation in the masque genre. Furthermore, both can be appropriated to destabilise the courtly feminine ideal and to provide evidence for the rejection of a simplistic interpretation of this masque. There are many important similarities between embroidery and dance which further illuminate their presence within this masque; figured dance and embroidery are bound together in *Cupid's Banishment* by their shared physicality and by their status as necessary attributes of the courtly woman.

The relationship between dance and embroidery in this particular performance is extremely close. Both are physical representations of the Queen's name and title, and the emblems are in fact a shortened pictorial version of the danced text. Created before the ephemeral fact of the dance and surviving after the masque's completion (though how long is uncertain), the embroideries both commented upon and memorialised the danced text. Once the performance was over, however, all that remained were the textual versions of the figured dance in the masque transcript or the more marginalised text of embroidery. This is itself revealing, since embroidered text stands for danced text as masque transcript stands for masque performance. Both embroidery and dance had a dual existence within the official text and as a text-in-performance. Although there is a decidedly different performative impact in the pres- entation of a pre-created artefact such as needlework in comparison to the creation of text in the performance of the figured dance, the dance did perhaps look back to the hidden creation of the embroidered text. As my earlier discussion of Jonson's *Hymenaei* suggests, authorship of dance itself is a complex issue, with claims being staked for both the choreographer (identified as the school's elusive dancing master, Mr Onslo, about whom no more information is available) and the female performers. As a concrete artefact, embroidery is clearly more closely related to a conventional written text, but it shared the fate of the transient dance text; despite its preservational function, neither the embroideries nor any records of them seem to have survived. For present-day readers, therefore, the embroideries are as ephemeral as the dance and both are memorialised only by the masque transcript: just as 'all that remains from the spectacle dances in the printed text of *Cupid's Banishment* [...] is their philological "meaning"', so all that remains of the embroidered texts is their legible significance – Anna's name.[98]

Replicated threefold in dance, embroidery and literary text, Anna's name was of supreme importance within this masque. In *Cupid's Banishment* we find multiple offerings of the monarch's name as tribute, and the group of dancing bodies which assumed that form was the most allusive and elusive of these many performances. The Queen's name, embodied in the person of Anna herself, in the dancers, and in the embroideries, became both body and text in the corporeal approach of the female masquer to language in dance and embroidery. Despite the silence of the majority of the Greenwich masquers, in common with so many other female masquers they achieved expression through constraint. In remaining conformist while pressing on the limitations of the masque genre and the place of women within it, the dances and embroideries of these women complemented and ratified the more radical transgression found in Ann Watkins's speech.

But what of the nature and meaning of the dances themselves? *Cupid's Banishment* was an important moment in the development of the English masque, the first recorded example of the writing-in-dance of a female name. As discussed in chapter 1, Jacobean figured dance was rare enough (descriptions of the dancing of figures are found only in Daniel's *Vision*, and Jonson's *Beauty* and *Hymenaei*), and writing-in-dance, an intensification of the approach to language made in the figured dance, was equally unusual. In fact, writing-in-dance also occurred only three times, in *Hymenaei*, *Queens* and *Cupid's Banishment*. It is striking, given the limited number of Jacobean female masques, that all of these performances involved female dancers, and, when placed in the politicised context of *Cupid's Banishment*, this apparent association between women and writing-in-dance begins to look particularly suggestive.

Francis Bacon's bald comment that 'Turning dances into figures is a childish curiosity' clarifies both the youth of White's masquers and the gender dynamics of the motif of writing-in-dance.[99] Though his remarks suggest that the few occasions on which the figured dance was used had a substantial impact, it is also clear that Bacon's terminology is gendered. The term 'childish' implies an effeminacy that reflects the feminine appropriation of the figured dance. The early modern's conceptual links between women and adolescent or young boys are clear enough in the performance of boy actors in female roles, and passive and silent femininity implies a childlike lack of force and strength. In addition, however, the term 'childish' had connotations of the effeminate through the root, 'child', one meaning of which was 'a female infant'.[100] It seems that, in Bacon's usage, to be associated with the feminine is to be infantilised and emasculated, and his contemptuous use of the term trivialises female performance and demeans male participation. The dance, a courtly ideal, was characterised as trivial and emasculating when it became feminised, and correspondingly the feminine creation of text in dance was held in low esteem.

This gendering is validated by contrasts between domestic and continental performances. Jacobean gender delineations are not matched by those of the French *ballet de cour*. For instance, although female dancers danced the name of Alcine, the enchantress of the *Ballet de Vandosme*, it is an unwilling dance by women who are really knights, undergoing the last in a series of grotesque shape-changes, and demonstrates Alcine's illicit control over the dancers.[101] Her unauthorised power is countered in the pseudo-Druidic language of the concluding *grand bal* with which the knights, restored to masculinity, honour their king. This suggests that the 'official' French court view considered male writing-in-dance as legitimate in comparison with its dangerous female counterpart. It seems that the *ballet de cour* gendered the act of writing-in-dance differently than did the Jacobean masque, where dance was a means of expression for its women. In contrast, in the French *ballets*, which permitted noble speech for both sexes, legitimate access to the corporeal expression of writing-in-dance was a privilege apparently reserved for the male performer.

The figured dances of *Cupid's Banishment* can, of course, be read also through the words they created. The dance of Anna's name and title in advance of that of James and his heir was a small assertion of her authority, although it was tempered by the necessary expression of loyalty to James and Charles. In the context of the interplay of textual and performative expression, this apparently superficial shift in fact altered the normally rigid hierarchies of the Renaissance court, exalting the queen consort over the absent monarch. However, in the wake of Fortune's speech, and the constant vocal praise for Anna in song and verse, it is ironic that James should have been honoured in the silence of the female dancers, outwardly conformist to the demands of the hegemony of which he was the figurehead. Prince Charles also held an interesting position in this masque; his was the name represented in *Queens*, and the only one to be danced twice in Jacobean court entertainments. Although *Queens* had staged a feminine opposition to the mainstream court, the name danced was that of the Prince and it is revealing that *Cupid's Banishment*, performed within the female court, shifted its emphasis to the female guest of honour.

The sheer extent of the motif of the danced name (three names where previously there had been only one) calls the background of its inclusion within this masque into question. Cerasano and Wynne-Davies challenge White's familiarity with the masque form, and this can be extended to consider how and why Onslo, the choreographer, should have placed such emphasis on a motif used so infrequently within the Jacobean court.[102] However, such speculation only emphasises the lack of information about the interaction of masque-writer and choreographer in general and about Onslo's background in particular; the dynamics of this particular working relationship remain relatively unclear, as does the extent to which the choreographer (here credited with the invention of the dance) can be considered an autonomous author. Yet one available fact is of particular relevance. The texts of *Hymenaei* and *Queens* both credit their figured dances to the choreographer Thomas Giles; the writing of names in dance seems to have been his professional specialism and this strongly implies that Onslo had been exposed to Giles's work, either in performance or publication.[103]

The temporal gap between *Cupid's Banishment* and the earlier instances of writing-in-dance is also suggestive. The figured dance, linguistic or otherwise, seems to have been a short-lived phenomenon, discarded after 1609 until White's masque. Dating from the period of Anna's most intense masquing involvement, for initiates such as Lucy Russell and the Queen herself, *Cupid's Banishment* was reminiscent of the earlier age of female masquing; it was a positive use of nostalgia evoking earlier female performances from prior to the marginalisation of female masquers through the extensive recycling of an apparently discarded motif. Yet while Anna was honoured as the privileged spectator of the masque, the dancing of her name was validated by that of those more commonly honoured. This need for legitimisation emphasises the limitations of the strategy of writing-in-dance as a mode of female expression; while Anna's name could be danced under the cover of those of her husband and son, the enactment of their names went a long way towards re-establishing masculine authority and evoking the contemporary marginalised status of the female performer for those present.

Standing at the end of Anna of Denmark's masquing career and at the end of her life, *Cupid's Banishment* was the expression of royal femininity within the power structures of the Jacobean court. Perhaps the first masque

to involve a speaking female performer, it was also a memorialisation of
the masquing tradition of Anna's court, documenting her involvement
with the masque genre before her marginalisation from what might be
considered its mainstream. Performing memories of earlier masques,
White's production drew upon the court community's collective performative consciousness to make a statement for female performative and
political authority in the face of its marginalisation. The methods employed
in this process were themselves taken from the canon of female masquing;
the corporeal representative strategies of dance and the bodily text which
pushed upon the constraints of female speech in the masques of the first
decade of the seventeenth century were used again in the second to
facilitate its attainment in the speech of Ann Watkins. Dance and the
performance of the gender and class inflected body are major aspects of
this, the names of the figured dance granted the female masquers entry
into a corporeal linguistic expression which was ratified by the parallel
physicality of the feminine-authored text of the embroidered emblems.
Both dance and the physicalised art of the embroideries were also powerful
expressions of the memory of movement and significance which resided
in the masquing body and which was memorialised in the text. Dance
is performance but it is also memory. Memory and memorialisation,
alongside the offering and acceptance of the gift, offer a dual meaning
of hope for the future and the preservation of the acts of the past. The
restaging of the masque genre's performative and political past prepares
the way for the voicing of female speech, performing both speech and
memory through the medium of the female body.

Moving out from the disputed factional Whitehall masquing stage after
her marginalisation in *Somerset*, Anna and her coterie of culturally engaged
women interrogated the very notion of the masque as court masque
through the performance of *Cupid's Banishment*. In staging this masque
beyond the boundaries of both the conventional court and the city, the
threat of female speech was apparently defused (or rather disguised) within
an apparently marginal performance. It is this liminality that gives *Cupid's
Banishment* its significance: Anna's presence transformed an apparently
unimportant school production into a performance of the greatest significance. In the absence of James I, Anna's assumption of the role of
monarch within the masque and the shift of the focus of authority from
Whitehall to her own palace at Greenwich was the assumption and
creation in performance of the power denied her in the political life of
the court. On this occasion, therefore, female cultural agency and engagement were a means of rewriting elite power structures through the

masque form's specific mode of political performance. The deflection of state ritual away from the monarch and towards the queen consort was the appropriation of masculine state ritual for the performative definition of the autonomy of the Queen's court and countered the process of marginalisation apparently instigated in *The Somerset Masque*; the analysis of the political tool of court performance reveals the disparate centres of Jacobean power and the fractured nature of the court institution. Distanced from Whitehall geographically, but populated by much the same figures, the female court was a space in which Ann Watkins could make the ultimate vocal approach to performative participation.

Anna's enthronement as privileged spectator in her last masque was simultaneously a withdrawal from active performance and the assumption of James I's position as a complementary spectacle to the masque itself. The sparse records that surround *Cupid's Banishment* communicate no controversy at this occupation of the patriarchal seat of power. Perhaps this lack of comment, alongside her failure to become regent, signals a lessening in the impact of Anna's masquing and of her political influence. However, the evidence makes this unlikely, as she was surrounded at Greenwich by the most powerful of the court. Given the progressive marginalisation of female performance in favour of masculine state ritual in the second decade of the seventeenth century, it is possible that *Cupid's Banishment* was simply a temporary upturn in Anna's masquing fortunes. Yet the lack of scandal surrounding this performance perhaps more positively demonstrates the passing of the most controversial moment of female masquing: there was none of the uproar that surrounded *Blackness*, and the recriminations that would surround Henrietta Maria's acting remained in the future. What is clear, though, is that however scantily, both *Cupid's Banishment* and *Somerset* record suggestive historical moments, ones which tell of the shifting relationship of Jacobean courtly women to authority, the court institution and the performance of power.

The legacy of Anna of Denmark: female performance in the Caroline court and beyond

On 2 March 1619, almost two years after the performance of *Cupid's Banishment*, Queen Anna died at Hampton Court, the scene of her first English masquing performance. In these final years she was marginalised from political and cultural authority; describing her last days, the Venetian ambassador wrote that

> of late her Majesty had to bear a change of fortune [...] She lost her health and fell out of favour with the king, while her following of courtiers and her royal adornments fell away from her. Thus at the end of her days, at the age of 44, she had nothing but to lament her sins and to show herself, as she was always believed to be, very religious and sincere in the worship of the true God.
>
> Her Majesty's death does not make the slightest difference in the government of these Kingdoms, except the falling in of 200,000 crowns a year to the king with a quantity of rich and precious belongings and the dismissal of a countless throng of servants and officials. But this loss should grieve your Serenity owing to the love which the queen bore for the republic and for the confidential way with which she dealt with our ambassadors.[1]

Anna's distance from the courtly mainstream is confirmed by her funeral, delayed by financial crisis for a month longer than tradition dictated. It is perhaps worth noting, however, that this period of apparent royal penury was also that of the ongoing negotiations for the costly construction of Inigo Jones's third Whitehall Banqueting House; it seems that, for James I, the house of state performance was a more eloquent and significant marker of magnificence than a consort's funeral.[2]

As my analysis of *The Somerset Masque* and *Cupid's Banishment* has shown, the advancing years of the seventeenth century's second decade also saw the Queen and the courtly female aristocrats of Whitehall marginalised from performance. Yet I would contend that this process does not negate the importance of Anna's previous influence, but instead demonstrates the fluctuations of individual status within an unstable court structure. Anna's loss of power came at the end of a career of oppositional political engagement, cultural agency and dissident performance, the extent of which was shown in ambassadorial struggles for precedence at her masques and in the use of her apartments as a debating forum for the policy of a Spanish match for Prince Henry.[3] And nor does her past seem to have been wholly forgotten by her contemporaries: Donato's appeal for Anna's memory was founded on her previous opposition to the 'official' court culture of James's Protestant pacifism and her own sustained Catholicism. Though in the second decade of the Stuart reign in England Anna could secure neither the regency nor her own position at court, such exclusion is mitigated by her status in her own court at Greenwich and, in any case, does not negate the agency of her lengthy career.

Although at first glance the circumstances of Anna's death and its aftermath seem only to confirm her loss of power, they do provide further instances of the representation of the royal female within state ritual. Her funeral took place on 13 May 1619, and the ceremony offers a final opportunity to identify her agency and representation. Donato's appeal to Anna's Catholicism as a reason to secure her memory relates suggestively to the impact of her more or less covert faith on her representation in Jacobean death rituals. There was some contemporary uncertainty over the actual process of the Queen's death and specifically over her ultimate religious affiliation; some reports described her last moments as 'free from all Popery', while Donato asserted her ongoing Catholicism.[4] Certainly Protestant representatives were present; Anna died in the presence of Prince Charles and members of the privy council, and Chamberlain commented that 'She was earnestly moved by the archbishop of Canterbury, the Lord Privie Seale and the bishop of London to prepare herself and set all things in order, but she could not be perswaded that her end was so neere'.[5] Yet this report of Anna's seeming unawareness of her impending death contradicts Sir Edward Harwood's account that 'Mayerne [her surgeon] told her, as she had requested him to do, when she was within twenty-four hours of her end'.[6] Might these inconsistencies in fact conceal a hidden space for Catholic death rites? If so, it would conform to the pattern of private freedom concealed by public conformity so favoured by James I and a feature of so much of Anna's career.

There is relatively little evidence concerning Anna's death; it seems, for example, that she did not compose a written will. Though there are inconsistencies, there are accounts of an oral will which consistently assert that the bulk of Anna's estate was bequeathed to Prince Charles and which pointedly ignore James.[7] Even in death such a ratification of the queen consort's authority through the heir threatened James's sovereignty. Its discursive impact is perhaps best exemplified in the comments of the Venetian ambassador, who stressed Anna's status as queen consort and figured her as the heir to Elizabeth I:

> before dying, she [Anna] had time to embrace the prince, her son, and had this satisfaction as mother of the succeeding king. [...] She was daughter and sister of the King of Denmark, went to Scotland as the wife of a king, succeeded to the greatness, [...] and the royal condition of the renowned Elizabeth.[8]

However, Harwood wrote that Anna 'verbally left all to the Prince, but the King thinks he himself ought to be heir, as nearest to her'.[9] What is clear is that James disregarded Anna's desires and broke up the estate to pay for her funeral, his summer progress and gifts for his favourites.[10] In the absence, or perhaps erasure, of female writing, the Queen's voice was marginalised and the female will (in both senses) elided. James's appropriation of the role of heir deflected the relationship between the Queen and her son and reasserted Anna's dependency upon his sovereign power even after death.

Turning to the funeral itself, where the evidence is of a more tangible nature, the representation of female royalty showed signs of tensions between Anna's self-representation, and the strategies imposed upon her after her death. In this, the first funeral for an English consort since that of Jane Seymour, the ritual apparatus of the official funeral ceremonial itself marked the distinction between queen consort and regnant, omitting the helmet and gauntlets of the monarch.[11] James himself was not present at the funeral and, although the absence of the king was traditional, the bond between consort and heir was further reinforced as, unusually, Charles processed in front of his mother's hearse in the absence of his father.[12] Anna's funeral seems to have been the locus of both factional and representational conflict, and such tensions can be seen in the details of the ceremonies. The King's household organised Anna's funeral procession which, in contrast to the increasing popularity of torch-lit nocturnal funerals (resonant with Catholic connotations), was conducted in daylight under Protestant rites.[13] The result was not a success, and Chamberlain provides an eloquent description of the 'drawling, tedious sight'.[14] Although the procession was more costly than either Elizabeth I's or Prince Henry's funerals, its lack of courtly magnificence and the squabbles of the Countesses of Arundel and Nottingham for precedence as chief mourner are potent images of Anna's marginalisation and the ongoing struggles of court faction over her dead body.[15]

Despite the divisive nature of the 'official' ritual and its attempts both to marginalise Anna and to appropriate her as a Protestant, signs of her previous oppositional identity can still be discerned. For example, Chamberlain documented the refusal of certain unidentified Catholic women to 'staine their profession with going to our church or service upon any shew of solemnitie, a straunge boldnes and such as would not have bene so easilie digested in some times'.[16] Both the assertion and the toleration of religious difference strike me as significant; once more, as in Anna's 1603 coronation, the ritual definition of a certain mode of queenship was disrupted by the public assertion of female religious difference. The ceremony of Anna's funeral itself, however, presented even more direct assertions of dissidence, highly suggestive both of an oppositional agency within Anna's court and of an accommodation of such difference by James himself.

On 5 March 1619, after her disembowelling and embalming, Anna's viscera were taken down the Thames under cover of darkness and given a clandestine separate burial in the Henry VII chapel of Westminster Abbey. This covert burial, with little accompanying ceremony or heraldry, was the locus for a pronounced expression of difference and factionality; as part of a system of multiple burial ceremonies granted to Anna which stemmed from a Catholic tradition, this rite strongly implies that the direction of at least some part of Anna's funeral ceremony was under the control of her own household rather than that of the King.[17] Counterbalancing the strong Catholic connotations of this torch-lit ritual, however, is the fact that such multiple ceremonies were the growing practice also of the Protestant court elite, as the separate interment of the Earl of Buckingham's bowels in Portsmouth in 1628 demonstrates.[18] Capable of multiple interpretations, this ritual can be read as a ceremonial assertion of Anna's oppositional Catholicism, fitting the established accommodation (and manipulation) of private difference behind a public display of conformity.

Such multiplicity of meaning continues throughout the detail of Anna's funeral rites. One of the most striking features of the mainstream Protestant funeral procession was its hearse. There are two possible designs for Anna's catafalque, one designed by Inigo Jones in what was truly his last architectural and scenic commission for the Queen.[19] Though it is not certain that Jones's design was actually used, the hearse has been identified (not uncontroversially) with a surviving design (figure 23). However, the King's Works' description of the hearse built in the chapel at Somerset House does not fit Jones's surviving plan, implying that his was not the design which was eventually carried out.[20] Despite this uncertainty, Jones's designs for the potential catafalque gesture importantly towards significant aspects of Anna's earlier career.

Jones's hearse reworked one of the most prominent images of Anna's masque performances, the fruit-laden golden tree. This emblem of royal female fertility reconfigured the representation of the queen consort's consummated sexuality in *Blackness*, a process substantially reversed in its manipulation as both a compliment to Anna and a symbol of the punishment of the disobedient woman in Campion's *Somerset Masque*. Particularly resonant in view of James I's recent appropriation of the role of heir, Jones's design had the tree standing above Anna's effigy and so it would have marked the further appropriation of the royal woman's ceremonial representation. The emblem of the golden tree has emerged as a site of conflict in Anna's ritual representation throughout her career, and its restaging in her funeral rendered it an even more complex symbol of contested significance. In combining the iconography of Anna's masquing career with an architectural and statuesque representation of female community in the caryatids which surrounded Anna's effigy, Jones's projected hearse powerfully restated the multiple meanings and representative strategies which had surrounded the Queen and which she had manipulated throughout her life.

A further feature of Jones's design is worthy of comment; his upright effigy of the Queen, intended to represent the body in the coffin, revisits all the issues of statuary and the iconic representation of women which had been such a feature of her performances and of Jacobean female masquing more generally. This unusual upright effigy was a departure from the recumbent figures of Prince Henry and Elizabeth I, and was in the end replaced by a recumbent one in the executed hearse design. Reminiscent of the 'dramatic' upright posture of early modern English tomb sculpture, the effigy expresses the duality of the hearse-as-tomb.[21] An effigy of some kind was a traditional feature of the queen consort's funeral, and Anna's effigy held the coronation regalia of orb and sceptre, defining her queenship and invoking the legacy of female authority which she had inherited from Elizabeth I.[22] Anna's statue, reminiscent of the reification of her body as the passive site of ritual definition during her Edinburgh coronation, was redolent of female monumentalisation. In

23 Projected design for Anna's catafalque (1619), by Inigo Jones

Anna's funeral the passive female body of Edinburgh, itself the locus of conflict between king and clergy, became the hearse's wooden effigy and the icon of the female statue. Defined by the surgeon and the embalmer, the royal body itself literally became the passive corporeal component of Jonson's dichotomy between 'carcass' and 'spirit'.[23] However, as I have established, this polarised conceptualisation of the masque form cannot adequately represent its female performers. The female community of caryatids around the Queen's effigy recalled the architectural representation of the masquers and the caryatids who surrounded Anna in *Queens*, where such dichotomies were effectively complicated; the image of the reanimated female statue, so prominent in *The Lords' Masque*, was here taken to its endpoint as the female masquing community truly became statues. Within this community, the effigy was reminiscent also of the London coronation and of Anna's rejection of reification through self-imposed stasis. When put into the context of Anna's self-representation, therefore, the figure that stood for her in her funeral can be seen as both the culmination of the reification of the female body within religio-political state ritual and a muted re-staging of a destabilising and controversial female performance.

It is tempting to suggest that this dualistic iconographical interpretability was precisely the reason why Jones's hearse was not built, but such a suggestion cannot be more than speculative. What can be said is that this hearse, expressive of both female authority and marginalisation, presented a complex and debated set of images. Furthermore, the juxtaposition of the hearse and the clandestine Catholic funeral implies the performance of an alternative representation of royal femininity alongside and within the mainstream court's 'official' Protestant rites. It is perhaps more significant, though, and more representative of Anna's final relationship to the King's court, that the true beneficiary of the consort's intercessionary position near the King was Villiers, to whom James gave Somerset House after Anna's death.[24]

The hearse was Jones's last architectural design for Anna: it interrupted his commission for the Queen's House at Greenwich which he would later complete for Henrietta Maria. This particular overlap pinpoints an important interaction between the reigns of these two women; just as the new queen consort would take up the material legacy of the Queen's House, Henrietta Maria's cultural agency also showed traces of her predecessor's influence. In much the same way as Anna reworked the legacy of Elizabeth I, so Henrietta Maria had to negotiate the inheritance

of Anna's own cultural self-fashioning and the aristocratic female performance of political and cultural difference.[25] Though for both women the
role of queen consort was heightened by its recent rarity, Henrietta
Maria's status as Anna's successor was itself emphasised by the novelty of
the most unproblematic and direct succession of consorts in over a century.
Furthermore, connected by their shared difference from mainstream Stuart
court culture, both Anna and Henrietta Maria used performance as a
medium for the exploration of difference.

This difference itself stemmed from certain significant similarities in
their cultural positioning in relation to the English court. Both foreign,
both Catholic, the queen consorts brought with them the disparate
influences of European court culture, and distinct European courtly
traditions of performance and femininity. Performance took a major role
in this, and perhaps the best example can be seen in the reflection of
French court customs, such as the *ballet*'s commonplace of female vocal
performance, in English court performance. The importation of alien
cultural practice and Henrietta Maria's unfamiliarity with English ritual
conventions might also explain her subsequent tangles with both courtly
and non-courtly critics, the most notorious among the latter being William
Prynne. It is perhaps obvious that the French model of performance,
identified by John Peacock as current throughout Anna's engagement
with the masque form, should be heightened under Henrietta Maria.[26] I
would suggest, however, that Anna's court performances stood as a
significant precedent for the development of courtly and professional
female performance in the Caroline court, and, in influencing women's
performance in the Caroline court, also affected that of women in the
later professional Restoration theatres. So, with an eye to the continuities
and breaks between the court cultures of the two Stuart queens, is it
possible to identify the main ways in which Anna's cultural legacy was
sustained and moved forward?

Female performance was significantly developed by Henrietta Maria's
acting. The first of her three pastoral plays, Racan's *Artenice* (1626), was
controversial; the Queen's speech and the transvestite performance of
some of her women shocked even the select court audience.[27] However,
the most famous scandal surrounded Prynne's outburst against female
performance in *Histrio-Mastix* and its reference to 'women-actors –
notorious whores'.[28] Published in 1633 and linked with Henrietta Maria's
performance in Montagu's *Shepherds' Paradise*, the repercussions of this attack
for Prynne and the court's clear support for the Queen clearly demonstrate
that the association between the female voice and a transgressive sexuality,

though strong in Puritan quarters, was not insuperable inside the court. The progression to female acting was not unimaginable to a court which had, after all, been exposed to a tradition of female masque performance which had pushed upon constraints of genre and convention quite so powerfully as did Anna's performance in a masque such as *Blackness*.

The discourses of cultural and gender difference which caused so many of the controversies of Anna's performances impacted also upon those of Henrietta Maria. Both Stuart queens were the heads of powerful court groupings, and the Caroline court's disparate centres of power were in many ways similar to the factionality of its Jacobean predecessor. Although critical opinion differs over the extent of Henrietta Maria's agency, recent investigations have shown her to be a clear force in both political and performed court life, and her court coterie, political engagement and performance have recently emerged as the subject of revisionary criticism.[29] Her political involvement was explicit in the civil war, when she stood at the head of the royalist army, and her open Catholicism and anti-Spanish sentiments made her the figurehead of opposition to what Martin Butler has termed the 'official' Caroline court culture.[30] There were, of course, important distinctions between the Jacobean and Caroline court masque, the primary difference being that, in contrast to his father, Charles I was himself a masquer; he and his consort had occasion to perform together and his presence on stage transformed the dynamics of court performance in ways not available to the Jacobean court.[31] However, the fact remains that a tradition of female performance of sorts was established in both of these courts and that this was a powerful influence on the more widespread emergence of women on to the early modern English stage.

In her seminal analysis of the Caroline female court actor, Sophie Tomlinson applies Katherine Maus's argument that the introduction of the Restoration female actor was a non-issue 'precisely because the cultural event provoked by women's acting had already taken place'.[32] This astute observation can, I suggest, be further back-dated and the influence of the female masquers of the court of Anna of Denmark properly recognised. Though the progression from female masquing to acting is a significant distinction between the Jacobean and Caroline female courts, clear connections existed between these modes of performance. The liberation of the aristocratic female voice in performance which flourished in Henrietta Maria's performance was in fact firmly grounded in the court of Anna of Denmark, where the female masquing voice was first heard in White's 1617 *Cupid's Banishment*. This innovation predated Henrietta Maria's acting, the infamous 'pippin-pelted' performance of French female actors at the Blackfriars (1629), and the professional female singers of Town-shend's masque *Tempe Restored* (1632).[33] The female voice was not imported, or rather perhaps not only imported, into English court performance by the French Queen, but instead also developed through Anna's performances and culminated in Ann Watkins's speech.

Perhaps one of the reasons why Anna's performances have taken quite so long to be given a rigorous critical treatment, however, is the preconception that masquing was somehow less than acting and certainly far less generous in the opportunities for expression it offered to its courtly participants. For example, Tomlinson comments:

> It is important [...] to register the distinction between the silent and emblematic participation of women in the Jacobean masque, and the far more dynamic potential for projecting female personality allowed by the declamation, action, singing, and dancing which made up [Henrietta Maria's] theatrical diversions.[34]

Although it is clear that speech allowed women actors certain opportunities, and acting offered more than masquing, it is also clear that an overly rigid application of this distinction has contributed to the marginalisation of Anna's performances and the underestimation of the possibilities of such stagings. This book has sought to demonstrate the powerful expressivity of the Jacobean female masquer, and to reconsider the often-unexamined opposition between female vocality and silence. Rich in political and gendered significance, the aesthetics of Anna's performances offered a greater female expressivity than has previously been realised, and although they were perhaps less expressive than Henrietta Maria's pastorals, these masques are of great significance both as political statements and as a constituent part of the progression of the early modern woman towards a less restricted stage performance.

One conclusion of this book is that the Jacobean female masquer's relationship to linguistic expression was far more complex than has been previously assumed. Within the threatening association of the female body with language and sexuality, the female masquers' performance cannot be clearly distanced from linguistic expression. The pictorialisation of language and the expressivity of the emblematic female body in *Blackness*, for example, demonstrate that the female masquer's physicalisation does not exclude her from linguistic expression but instead results in the physicalisation of language itself. The use of the physical texts of dance and embroidery in masques such as *Cupid's Banishment*, in conjunction with the staging of female speech, further pushes back the boundaries of female expression. Though a single and unrepeated instance of female speech, *Cupid's Banishment* does demonstrate that certain factions of the Jacobean court were already susceptible to such developments. From the moment when women stepped on to the stage which Jones brought into the masque genre in *Blackness*, female performance assumed a greater theatricality. Henrietta Maria, it now seems, forwarded a process in which her predecessor played a pivotal part.

Anna of Denmark's masquing career is fertile ground for the analysis of the gendered aesthetics of early modern performance. While recent criticism has recognised the significance of courtly female cultural agency, the embodiment of this agency within the detail of masque performance and its contribution to the development of female performance has not hitherto been taken into account. This book has attempted to show the way in which the textualised female body achieved expression precisely through the masque's constraints, pushing on generic conventions and exploiting the space of necessary female performance. The signifying gendered body became a self-willed spectacle when the female masquer placed herself at the centre of the stage picture. The masque's disparate performance texts of the female body in dance, costume and movement, the scenic text and the theatricalised social space of performance combined with non-verbal female-authored texts such as embroidery to contribute towards the expressivity of the performing Jacobean female aristocrat. The performance of these non-verbal texts aided the approach to greater female expressivity, and culminated in the performance of the female voice in *Cupid's Banishment*. When read as performance rather than as published text, the masque genre's potential for performative expressivity and for the interpretation and analysis of the feminine creation of meaning becomes far greater.

A further significance of Anna's masquing was its prefiguration, almost sixty years earlier, of the short-lived appearance of transvestite male actors and female performers on the Restoration stage.[35] Suzanne Gossett's analysis of the explicit confrontation of the male transvestite and female performance of femininity in *Tempe Restored* demonstrates the Caroline masque's shifting casting conventions, but my reading of *The Masque of Queens* shows that an awareness of such a juxtaposition was a feature also of Jacobean courtly entertainments. I would not, however, wish to imply that the emergence of the female performer and playwright was an unobstructed linear progression towards the Restoration; a quick glance at the fluctuations in Anna's own status in court politics and performance shows otherwise. With this in mind, however, it does seem that the continuing female involvement in aristocratic house stagings of entertainments and 'dramatic opera' during the closure of the public theatres aided the emergence of the female actor on to the Restoration stage.[36] One clear result of this book is that the idea that there was no domestic precedent for the performances of the Restoration stage must be rejected, since the conditions of the early Restoration theatres were in fact prefigured in the most elite of Stuart performance arenas.

The constitution of a tradition of female performance is an integral aspect of its development, providing a context for masque analysis and addressing female performance itself as a meaningful activity. The final masque of Anna's career, *Cupids Banishment*, was predicated on this tradition and the performance of memory within the masquing body. Forwarding female performance in the staging of the female voice, this itself was achieved through the memorialisation of previous female performances. A complex negotiation of centrality and marginalisation, White's masque demonstrates the non-linear development of female performance, itself a series of negotiations, accommodations and defeats within the history of the female Stuart courts.

Anna of Denmark's masque commissions and performances and her active political and cultural engagement contributed to the emergence of seventeenth-century female performance. Much remains as yet unstudied, but I hope that the re-evaluation of this neglected figure's engagement with the performance of the court masque goes at least some way towards delineating such projects and redressing the balance of critical neglect. One thing is clear: the relatively small number of masques which Anna performed, commissioned or simply witnessed had a substantial impact upon the emergence of female performance both within and beyond the early modern English court.

Notes

INTRODUCTION

1 Sir Dudley Carleton to Sir Ralph Winwood, 1605, in C. H. Herford, Percy and Evelyn Simpson (eds), *Ben Jonson*, 11 vols (Oxford: Clarendon Press, 1925–52), X, p. 448.

2 See in particular Hardin Aasand, '"To Blanch an Ethiop, and Revive a Corse": Queen Anne and *The Masque of Blackness*', *Studies in English Literature, 1500–1900*, 32 (1992), 271–85; Kim F. Hall, *Things of Darkness: Economies of Race and Gender in Early Modern England* (London and Ithaca: Cornell University Press, 1995); Marion Wynne-Davies, 'The Queen's Masque: Renaissance Women and the Seventeenth-Century Court Masque', in S. P. Cerasano and Marion Wynne-Davies (eds), *Gloriana's Face: Women, Public and Private, in the English Renaissance* (New York and London: Harvester Wheatsheaf, 1992), pp. 79–104.

3 Barbara Kiefer Lewalski, *Writing Women in Jacobean England* (London and Cambridge, MA: Harvard University Press, 1993); J. Leeds Barroll, 'The Court of the First Stuart Queen', in Linda Levy Peck (ed.), *The Mental World of the Jacobean Court* (Cambridge: Cambridge University Press, 1991), pp. 191–208; Aasand, '"To Blanch an Ethiop"'; Hall, *Things of Darkness*; Wynne-Davies, 'The Queen's Masque'. Unfortunately, Barroll's recent monograph on Anna of Denmark appeared too late to be taken into account here, but is a valuable step in the revision of critical perceptions of the English queen; J. Leeds Barroll, *Anna of Denmark, Queen of England: A Cultural Biography* (Philadelphia: University of Pennsylvania Press, 2001).

4 Ben Jonson, *The Masque of Blackness*, in *Ben Jonson: The Complete Masques*, ed. by Stephen Orgel (London and New Haven: Yale University Press, 1975), pp. 47–60, p. 48, l. 18.

5 *The Receiving of King James the Sixth and His Queene, at Lyeth*, in J. T. Gibson Craig (ed.), *Papers Relative to the Marriage of James the Sixth of Scotland, with the Princess Anna of Denmark: A.D. M.D.LXXXIX and the Form and Manner of Her Majesty's Coronation at Holyrood House* (Edinburgh: The Bannatyne Club, 1823), pp. 38–42, p. 40.

6 Cited in Peter Stallybrass, 'Patriarchal Territories: The Body Enclosed', in Margaret W. Ferguson, Maureen Quilligan and Nancy J. Vickers (eds), *Rewriting the Renaissance: The Discourses of Sexual Difference in Early Modern*

Europe (Chicago and London: University of Chicago Press, 1986), pp. 123–42, p. 127.

7 Orgel, *Complete Masques*, p. 5.

8 A letter to the Rev. Joseph Mead, 3 December 1626, in Stephen Orgel and Roy Strong (eds), *Inigo Jones and the Theatre of the Stuart Court* (London: Sotheby Parke Bernet, 1973), I, p. 389.

9 Andrew J. Sabol, *Four Hundred Songs and Dances from the Stuart Court Masque* (London: University Press of New England for Brown University Press, 1982), p. 21. Cf. Stephen Orgel, 'Review of *Four Hundred Songs and Dances from the Stuart Court Masque*, ed. by Andrew Sabol', *Criticism, a Quarterly for Literature and the Arts*, 21 (1979), 362–5, p. 365.

10 Orgel, *Complete Masques*, p. 5.

11 Mark Franko, 'Renaissance Conduct Literature and the Basse Danse: The Kinesis of *Bonne Grace*', in Richard C. Trexler (ed.), *Persons in Groups: Social Behaviour as Identity Formation in Medieval and Renaissance Europe* (Binghamton, NY: Medieval and Renaissance Texts and Studies, 1985), pp. 55–66, p. 55.

12 Mark Franko, *The Dancing Body in Renaissance Choreography (c. 1416–1589)* (Birmingham, AL: Summa Publications, 1986), p. 38.

13 Jonson, *Blackness*, p. 47, l. 7.

14 Jonson, *Hymenaei*, in *Ben Jonson: The Complete Masques*, ed. by Stephen Orgel (London and New Haven: Yale University Press, 1975), pp. 75–106, p. 75, ll. 4–5.

15 Jonson, *Blackness*, p. 51, ll. 101–2.

16 Jonathan Sawday, *The Body Emblazoned: Dissection and the Human Body in Renaissance Culture* (London and New York: Routledge, 1995), p. 189.

17 Jonson, *Blackness*, pp. 56–7, ll. 236–42.

18 Peter M. Daly, *Literature in the Light of the Emblem: Structural Parallels between the Emblem and Literature in the Sixteenth and Seventeenth Centuries* (Toronto and London: University of Toronto Press, 1979), p. 21, citing Mario Praz, *Studies in Seventeenth-century Imagery* (Rome: Edizioni di Stori e Letteratura, 1964), p. 58.

19 Francis Bacon, *The Advancement of Learning*, II, xvi, 3, cited in Michael Bath, *Speaking Pictures: Emblem Books and Renaissance Culture* (London: Longman, 1994), p. 51.

20 Bath, p. 52.

21 Emblem 59 in Peter Daly and Simon Cutter (eds), *Andreas Alciati 2: Emblems in Translation* (London: University of Toronto Press, 1985). Geoffrey Whitney, *A Choice of Emblems*, intro. by John Manning (Aldershot: Scolar Press, 1989), p. 57.

22 Jonson, *Blackness*, p. 57, ll. 245.

23 D. J. Gordon, 'The Imagery of Ben Jonson's *The Masque of Blackness* and *The Masque of Beautie*', *Journal of the Warburg and Courtauld Institutes*, 6 (1943), 122–41.

CHAPTER ONE

1 Sir John Chamberlain to Dudley Carleton, 15 January 1612, in Norman
  Egbert McClure (ed.), *Letters of John Chamberlain* (Philadelphia: American
  Philosophical Society, 1939), I, p. 328. Jonson, *Love Restored*, in *Ben Jonson:
  The Complete Masques*, ed. by Stephen Orgel (London and New Haven: Yale
  University Press, 1975), pp. 186–97.
2 La Boderie's comments on the *Masque of Queens* reveals these pre-arrange-
  ments. He states that the Queen had wanted to dance with him 'mais comme
  c'est un métier auquel je n'entens guère [. . .] je la fis prier des le matin par
  une Dame de mes amies qui devoit danser avec elle, de ne m'y point obliger'
  (but as it is a profession about which I know scarcely anything, the following
  morning I had one of my lady friends, who was to dance with her, ask her
  not to oblige me to do it) (Herford and Simpson, X, p. 498).
3 Margaret Maurer, 'Reading Ben Jonson's *Queens*', in Sheila Fisher and Janet
  E. Halley (eds), *Seeking the Woman in Late Medieval and Renaissance Writings*
  (Knoxville: University of Tennessee Press, 1989), pp. 233–64, p. 256. Recent
  works which redress this balance include Skiles Howard, *The Politics of Courtly
  Dancing in Early Modern England* (Amherst, MA: University of Massachusetts
  Press, 1998), and Barbara Ravelhofer, '"Virgin Wax" and "Hairy Men-monsters": Unstable Movement Codes in the Stuart Masque', in David Bevington
  and Peter Holbrook (eds), *The Politics of the Stuart Court Masque* (Cambridge:
  Cambridge University Press, 1998), pp. 244–72.
4 Jonson, *Hymenaei*, p. 76, ll. 17–27.
5 Jonson, *The Masque of Beauty*, in *Ben Jonson: The Complete Masques*, ed. by
  Stephen Orgel (London and New Haven: Yale University Press, 1975),
  pp. 61–74, p. 72, ll. 274–6.
6 Aurelian Townshend, *Tempe Restored*, in *Inigo Jones and the Theatre of the Stuart
  Court*, ed. by Stephen Orgel and Roy Strong (London: Sotheby Parke Bernet,
  1973), II, pp. 479–504, p. 479. William Davenant, *The Siege of Rhodes*, ed.
  by Ann-Mari Hedback (Uppsala: Almqvist & Wiksell, 1973).
7 Margaret McGowan, 'Le Corps Dansant: Source d'Inspiration Esthétique', in
  Jean Cèard, Marie Madeleine Fontaine and Jean-Claude Margolin (eds), *Le
  Corps à la Renaissance* (Paris: Amateurs de Livres, 1987), pp. 229–41, p. 237.
8 Pamela Jones, 'Spectacle in Milan: Cesare Negri's Torch Dances', *Early Music*,
  14 (1986), 182–96. Cesare Negri, *Le Gratie d'Amore: A Facsimile of the Milan
  1602 Edition* (New York: Broude Brothers Ltd, 1969).
9 Fabritio Caroso, *Nobiltà di Dame*, trans. by Julia Sutton (Oxford: Oxford
  University Press, 1986). Caroso's *Il Ballarino* was updated slightly to form his
  second published book, *Nobiltà di Dame*. Thoinot Arbeau, *Orchesography*, trans.
  by Mary Stewart Evans with notes by Julia Sutton (New York: Dover
  Publications, 1967). Robert Coplande, *The Maner of Bace Daunsing*, in *Materials
  for the Study of the Basse Dance*, ed. by Frederick Crane (New York: Institute

of Medieval Music, 1968); Bodleian Library, MS Rawl. Poet. 108, fols 10–11; MS Rawl. d.864. fol. 199, Elias Ashmole, *c.* 1630; MS Douce 280, John Ramsay.

10 Mabel Dolmetsch, *Dances of England and France 1450–1600* (London: Routledge and Kegan Paul, 1959), p. 49.

11 Judy Smith and Ian Gatiss, 'What did Prince Henry do with his Feet on Sunday 19 August 1604?', *Early Music*, 14 (1986), 198–207, pp. 201–2, 204–7.

12 Erasmus, *De Civilitate Morum Puerilium (On Good Manners for Boys)*, trans. by Brian McGregor in *The Collected Works of Erasmus*, ed. by J. K. Sowards (Toronto: University of Toronto Press, 1985), pp. 269–89, p. 274.

13 Carleton to Sir Ralph Winwood, in Herford and Simpson, X, p. 448.

14 Herford and Simpson, X, p. 498. My translation.

15 Juan Fernandez de Velasco, *Relacion de la Iornada del Excmo Condestable de Castilla* (Antwerp, 1604), trans. in W. B. Rye (ed.), *England as Seen by Foreigners in the Days of Elizabeth and James I* (London: John Russell Smith, 1865), pp. 117–24. Smith and Gatiss, p. 205.

16 Jonson, *Masque of Queens*, in *Ben Jonson: The Complete Masques*, ed. by Stephen Orgel (London and New Haven: Yale University Press, 1975), pp. 122–41, pp. 123, l. 21, 134, ll. 327–32.

17 Jonson, *Queens*, p. 125, ll. 87–8.

18 Franko, *The Dancing Body*, pp. 25–41, 47. The use of courtesy manuals must take into account what Franko describes as the potentially utopian nature of dance treatises; Franko, *The Dancing Body*, p. 7.

19 Sir Thomas Elyot, *The Book Named the Governor*, ed. by S. E. Lehmberg (London: Everyman, 1962), pp. 79–80. Franko, *The Dancing Body*, p. 37.

20 Elyot, pp. 78–85.

21 Philip Stubbs, *The Anatomy of Abuses (1583)*, ed. by Peter Davison (New York: Johnson Reprint Company, 1972), no page numbers.

22 Sir John Davies, *Orchestra or a Poem of Dancing*, ed. by E. M. W. Tillyard (London: Chatto &Windus, 1947), p. 24, stanza 37.

23 Franko, *The Dancing Body*, p. 9.

24 Sutton, 'Introduction', in Caroso, p. 25.

25 See Caroso's account of the *grave broken sequence* in the *tordiglione*; Caroso, p. 106.

26 Caroso, p. 107.

27 Cited in Franko, *The Dancing Body*, pp. 45–6, from Claude de Calviac, *La Civile Honestete pour les Enfants avec la Maniere d'Apprendre a Bien Lire …* (Paris, 1560). My translation.

28 Pamela Jones, 'Spectacle in Milan', p. 185.

29 Francis Beaumont, *The Masque of the Inner Temple and Gray's Inn*, ed. by Philip Edwards, *A Book of Masques in Honour of Allardyce Nicoll*, ed. by T. J. B. Spencer and Stanley Wells (Cambridge: Cambridge University Press, 1967), pp. 125–47.

30 Stubbs, *The Anatomy of Abuses*, no page numbers.
31 Mark Franko, *Dance as Text: Ideologies of the Baroque Body*, Cambridge, Cambridge University Press, 1993, pp. 21–6.
32 Pamela Jones, 'Spectacle in Milan', p. 191, figure 5.
33 Jonson, *Beauty*, p. 70, ll. 221–2.
34 Pamela Jones, 'Spectacle in Milan', p. 186.
35 Elyot, pp. 77–8.
36 Elyot, p. 77.
37 Caroso, pp. 266–9.
38 Ibid., p. 163.
39 Ibid., p. 163.
40 Ramsay, MS Douce 280.
41 Franko, *The Dancing Body*, pp. 44.
42 Arbeau, p. 55.
43 Arbeau, pp. 55, 59.
44 Caroso, p. 144.
45 Initially in the 1595 *Masque of Proteus* and with greater effect in 1605, in the *Masque of Blackness*; Orgel, *The Jonsonian Masque* (New York: Columbia University Press, 1967), pp. 8–9.
46 Jonson, *Hymenaei*, p. 86, ll. 279–85.
47 Ibid., pp. 75–6, ll. 1–31.
48 Jonson, *Blackness*, p. 47, l. 7.
49 Montaigne, *Apology for Raymond Sebond*, in *The Complete Essays of Montaigne*, trans. by Donald M. Frame (Stanford: Stanford University Press, 1986), p. 332.
50 Elyot, p. 72.
51 Arbeau, p. 84. See also Davies, p. 32, stanza 69; Caroso, pp. 129–31, 244.
52 Davies, p. 21, stanza 25.
53 Ibid., p. 25, stanza 44.
54 Arbeau, p. 16.
55 Franko, *The Dancing Body*, pp. 14–17.
56 Jonson, *Hymenaei*, p. 86, l. 286.
57 Franko, *Dance as Text*, pp. 15–31.
58 Samuel Daniel, *The Vision of the Twelve Goddesses*, in *A Book of Masques in Honour of Allardyce Nicoll*, ed. by T. J. B. Spencer and Stanley Wells (Cambridge: Cambridge University Press, 1967), pp. 17–42, p. 32, ll. 262–5.
59 *Ballet de Monseigneur le Duc de Vandosme*, in *Ballets et Mascarades de Cour de Henri II à Louis XIV*, ed. by Paul Lacroix (Genève: Chez J. Gay et fils, 1868), I, pp. 237–69, p. 265. My translation.
60 (Powerful love, ambitious desire, vertuous intentions, immortal renown, greatness of courage, pleasurable sorrow, steadfast constancy, known sincerity, happy destiny, loved by all, crown of glory, supreme power); *Ballet de Vandosme*, pp. 265–8. My translation.

61 Francis Bacon, 'Of Masques and Triumphs', in *Essays* (London: Everyman, J. M. Dent, 1994), pp. 99–100, p. 99.

62 Jonson, *Queens*, p. 140, l. 507.

63 Robert White, *Cupid's Banishment*, in *Renaissance Drama by Women: Texts and Documents*, ed. by S. P. Cerasano and Marion Wynne-Davies (London and New York: Routledge, 1996), pp. 76–90, p. 88.

64 A. M. Nagler, *Theatre Festivals of the Medici 1539–1637* (New Haven and London: Yale University Press, 1964), p. 117.

65 Jonson, *Hymenaei*, p. 86, ll. 281–3.

66 Jonson, *Blackness*, p. 56, ll. 228–31

67 Jonson, *Beauty*, pp. 72–3, ll. 276–7, l. 303.

68 Trumbull's account of *Oberon* mentions that 'The new hall of the palace was furnished as usual with [...] a green carpet on the floor', which might deaden the sound of the dancers' feet, further negating a practical explanation for this disjunction; Orgel and Strong, I, p. 206. Daniel, *The Vision*, p. 35; Jonson, *Queens*, p. 139, ll. 478–87.

69 Campion, *Lord Hay's Masque*, in *Inigo Jones and the Theatre of the Stuart Court*, ed. by Stephen Orgel and Roy Strong (London: Sotheby Parke Bernet, 1973), I, pp. 115–21, p. 118, ll. 295–302.

70 Jonson, *Beauty*, p. 71, ll. 261–3.

71 Campion, *The Lords' Masque*, ed. by I. A. Shapiro, in *A Book of Masques in Honour of Allardyce Nicoll*, ed. by T. J. B. Spencer and Stanley Wells (Cambridge: Cambridge University Press, 1967), pp. 95–123. Balthasar Beaujoyeulx, *Le Ballet Comique de la Reine (1581)*, ed. by Margaret McGowan (Binghamton, NY: Medieval and Renaissance Texts and Studies, 1985). Beaumont, *The Masque of the Inner Temple and Gray's Inn*, pp. 125–47.

72 Elyot, pp. 88, 91.

73 Jonson, *Hymenaei*, p. 79, ll. 98–104. The dress code of the social dance demands that the sword be worn throughout – it is removed only for the vigorous galliard; Julia Sutton, 'Introduction', in Caroso, p. 117. Franko, *The Dancing Body*, p. 3.

74 Caroso, p. 119.

75 Arbeau, p. 55.

76 William Trumbull, in Orgel and Strong, I, p. 206.

77 Jonson, *Hymenaei*, p. 95, ll. 544–5.

78 Translated in Orgel and Strong, I, p. 283.

79 Orgel, *Complete Masques*, p. 1.

80 Naunton accused Hatton of entering the court 'by the galliard'; Paul Johnson, *Elizabeth I: A Study in Power and Intellect* (London: Weidenfeld and Nicolson, 1974), p. 214.

81 James Knowles, 'Toys and Boys: The (Homo)erotics of the Jacobean Masque'; conference paper, *Disputing Manliness in Early Modern Britain*, Birkbeck College, University of London, 10 July 1997.

82 Alan Bray, 'Homosexuality and the Signs of Male Friendship in Elizabethan England', *History Workshop*, 29 (1990), 1–19.

83 Stephen Orgel, 'To Please the King: A Review of Mark Franko, *Dance as Text*', *Times Literary Supplement*, 4 February 1994, p. 24.

84 Barbara Ravelhofer has revealed the extent to which this moment may also have been steeped in discourses of national identity, via the French influence on Villiers's dancing; Ravelhofer, 'Unstable Movement Codes', pp. 247–50.

85 Davies, *Orchestra*, stanzas 82–3.

86 Carleton attacked the appearance of Anna as Pallas in *The Vision* for the short length of her skirt; Dudley Carleton to Sir John Chamberlain, 15 January 1604, in Maurice Lee Jr (ed.), *Dudley Carleton to John Chamberlain 1603–1624: Jacobean Letters* (New Brunswick, NJ: Rutgers University Press, 1972), p. 55.

87 Thomas Beard, *The Theatre of God's Judgement* (London, 1612), cited in David Lindley, *The Trials of Frances Howard: Fact and Fiction at the Court of King James* (London: Routledge, 1993), p. 58. The rape of Antonio's wife takes place at a masque; Thomas Middleton and Cyril Tourneur, *The Revenger's Tragedy*, ed. by Reginald A. Foakes (Manchester: Manchester University Press, 1996).

88 Carleton to Chamberlain, Herford and Simpson, X, p. 449.

89 Arbeau, p. 80.

90 Caroso, pp. 140–50.

91 Margaret McGowan, 'Le Corps Dansant', pp. 229–41. Her analysis is based on the sonnet, 'Le Soir qu'Amour vous Fist en la Salle Decendre ...', XLVIII, *Sonnets pour Hélène*, Livre II, in Ronsard, *Oeuvres*, ed. by Isidore Silver (Chicago: University of Chicago Press, 1966), p. 290.

92 Edmund Spenser, *The Faerie Queene*, ed. by A. C. Hamilton (New York: Longman, 1977), Book VI, canto x, stanzas 11–28, pp. 690–3. Hesiod, *Theogony*, in *The Poems of Hesiod*, trans. by R. M. Frazer (Norman: University of Oklahoma Press, 1983), pp. 23–8, ll. 1–115.

93 Davies, *Orchestra*, p. 45, stanza 122.

94 Ibid., p. 46, stanza 125.

95 Ibid., p. 46, stanza 127.

96 Ibid., p. 47.

CHAPTER TWO

1 David Stevenson with Peter Graves (trans.), *Scotland's Last Royal Wedding* (Edinburgh: John Donald Publishers, 1996), pp. 85–6. Several descriptions of the ceremonies and of James's Norwegian voyage exist, including Gibson Craig (ed.), *Papers Relative to the Marriage of King James*, and David Moysie, *Memoirs of the Affairs of Scotland*, ed. by J. Dennistoun (Edinburgh: Bannatyne Club, 1830), pp. 70–84.

2 A. H. Miller, 'The wedding-tour of James VI in Norway', *Scottish Review*, 21 (1893), 142–61, pp. 157–8; Ethel Carleton Williams, *Anne of Denmark: Wife of James VI of Scotland: James I of England* (London: Longman, 1970), p. 23.

According to the dates laid out in the Danish account, it is possible that such a ceremony took place; Stevenson, p. 99.

3 David Norbrook, 'The Reformation of the Masque', in David Lindley (ed.), *The Court Masque* (Manchester: Manchester University Press, 1984), pp. 94–110, p. 97.

4 Louise O. Fradenburg, *City, Marriage, Tournament: Arts of Rule in Late Medieval Scotland* (Madison, WI: University of Wisconsin Press, 1991), p. 76.

5 Gibson Craig, p. vii.

6 Arthur Golding, *Shakespeare's Ovid Being Arthur Golding's Translation of the Metamorphoses*, ed. by W. H. D. Rouse (London: De la More Press, 1904), Book VI, p. 136.

7 *The Kingis Majesteis Declaratioun upoun the Causis of His Depairtur*, in Gibson Craig, pp. 12–16, p. 13.

8 James VI and I, *The Beginning of his Mties Jurnei to Denmarke; Neuer Ended*, in *The Poems of James VI of Scotland*, ed. by James Craigie (Edinburgh and London: William Blackwood and Sons for the Scottish Text Society, 1958), II, pp. 144–9, p. 144.

9 *Amatoria*, in ed. by Craigie, II, p. 74. R. D. S. Jack (ed.), *A Choice of Scottish Verse 1560–1660* (London: Hodder & Stoughton, 1978), p. 173, note 1.

10 Stevenson, pp. 15, 4.

11 Mary Beth Rose, *The Expense of Spirit: Love and Sexuality in English Renaissance Drama* (Ithaca and London: Cornell University Press, 1988), p. 121; citing Alexander Niccholes, *A Discourse of Marriage and Wiving* (London, 1615), in *Harleian Miscellany*, ed. by William Oldys, II (1808–13), p. 162.

12 Rose, pp. 124–5, 121 (citing Niccholes, p. 164).

13 Moysie, p. 80.

14 Ibid., p. 80. Stevenson, p. 35.

15 Stevenson, p. 35.

16 Fradenburg, p. 190.

17 Thomas Riis, *Should Auld Acquaintance Be Forgot . . .: Scottish–Danish Relations c. 1450–1707* (Odense: Odense University Press, 1988), 2 vols, I, pp. 269–70; Mary Margaret Bartley, 'A Preliminary Study of the Scottish Royal Entries of Mary Stuart, James VI and Anne of Denmark, 1558–1603' (unpublished doctoral dissertation, University of Michigan, 1981), p. 180.

18 Stevenson, p. 20; Riis, I, p. 269. Barroll, 'The Court of the First Stuart Queen', p. 195.

19 Riis, I, p. 270.

20 Barroll, 'The Court of the First Stuart Queen', p. 193; Stevenson, p. 79.

21 Victor G. Thoren (with contributions by John R. Christianson), *The Lord of Uraniborg: A Biography of Tycho Brahe* (Cambridge: Cambridge University Press, 1990), p. 1.

22 'Letter from Queen Sophia, Queen Dowager of Denmark, to King James VI. 26 Nov. 1589', in Gibson Craig, p. 19.

23 Riis, I, pp. 137, 269. National Library of Scotland, Denmilne papers, XXVIII, 33.1.11, no. 8: 12 July 1595. Stevenson, pp. 37, 94.

24 Mara R. Wade, 'Festival Books as Historical Literature: The Reign of Christian IV of Denmark (1596–1648)', *Seventeenth Century*, 7 (1992), 1–14; *Triumphus Nuptialis Danicus: German Court Culture and Denmark, the 'Great Wedding' of 1634* (Wiesbaden: Harrassowitz Verlag, 1996). Stevenson, p. 89.

25 Stevenson, pp. 99–100.

26 Ibid., pp. 103, 107.

27 Ibid., p. 58.

28 Michael Lynch, 'Queen Mary's Triumph: The Baptismal Celebrations at Stirling in December 1556', *Scottish Historical Review*, LXIX (1990), 1–21, p. 2. James VI, 'An Epithalamion vpon the Marques of Huntlies Mariage', in ed. by Craigie, II, pp. 134–44. The primary record of Scottish performance is Anna Jean Mill, *Medieval Plays in Scotland* (Edinburgh and London: William Blackwood and Sons, 1927).

29 Sarah M. Dunnigan, 'Scottish Women Writers *c.* 1560–1650', in Douglas Gifford and Dorothy McMillan (eds), *A History of Scottish Women's Writing* (Edinburgh: Edinburgh University Press, 1997), pp. 15–43; and 'The Creation and Self-creation of Mary Queen of Scots: Literature, Politics and Female Controversies in Sixteenth-Century Scottish Poetry', *Scotlands*, 5 (1998), 65–88.

30 *Accounts of the Lord High Treasurer of Scotland*, ed. by Sir James Balfour (Edinburgh, 1900), II, p. 126; cited in Mill, *Medieval Plays*, p. 317, and note 6.

31 Mill, *Medieval Plays*, p. 39.

32 *A Diurnal of Remarkable Occurents That Have Passed in the Country of Scotland Since the Death of King James the Fourth in the Year MDLXX*, ed. by Thomas Thomson (Edinburgh: Bannatyne Club, 1833), 43, p. 87, cited in Mill, *Medieval Plays*, pp. 48, 337, and note 3.

33 Stevenson, p. 104.

34 Ibid., p. 59; *The Forme and Maner of the Quenis Majesties Coronation at the Kirk of Halyrudhous*, in Gibson Craig, pp. 52–3.

35 *Forme and Maner*, in Gibson Craig, pp. 52–3.

36 Ibid., p. 53.

37 *Forme and Maner*, in Gibson Craig, p. 53.

38 Scaramelli, *CSP, Venetian, 1603–7*, X, p. 75; *The Ceremonies, Form of Prayer, and Services used in Westminster Abby at the Coronation of King James the First and Queen Ann his Consort. Performed by Dr. Whitgift, Arch-Bishop of Canterbury, &c. With the Coronation of King Charles the First in Scotland* (London: Randal Taylor, 1685), p. 12. Tessa Rose, *The Coronation Ceremony of the Kings and Queens of England and the Crown Jewels* (London: Her Majesty's Stationery Office, 1992), pp. 105–6.

39 Lewalski, *Writing Women*, p. 43.

40 *Forme and Maner*, in Gibson Craig, p. 53.
41 Ibid., pp. 52, 55.
42 Ibid., p. 54.
43 Gibson Craig, p. 54.
44 See Bartley, 'The Scottish Royal Entries'; *The Receiving of James the Sixt*, and *The Forme and Manner of the Coronatione of Anna, the Quenis Majestie of Scotland, Efter hir Arryving within this Countrie 1590 from Denmark*, in Gibson Craig, pp. 37–42, 47–56.
45 Bartley, 'The Scottish Royal Entries', p. 167.
46 Stevenson, p. 108.
47 Ibid., p. 111.
48 Ibid., pp. 109–10, 111–14.
49 Stevenson, p. 110.
50 Johnston, p. 598r.
51 Stevenson, pp. 110–11.
52 Ibid., p. 145, note 20, citing Calderwood, V, p. 97.
53 Ibid., pp. 108, 144, note 6.
54 *Receiving*, in Gibson Craig, p. 40.
55 Johnston, p. 598r. Johnston's description is ratified by Calderwood, p. 97.
56 Stevenson, p. 114.
57 Ibid., pp. 110, 115.
58 Fradenburg, pp. 244–63.
59 The city accounts mention seventeen masks and payments for the blackening of an unknown number of young men: Bartley, 'The Scottish Royal Entries', p. 137, citing Sir James David Warwick (ed.), *Extracts from the Records of the Burgh of Edinburgh, A.D. 1573–1589* (Edinburgh: Scottish Burgh Record Society, 1875).
60 'The Estate of the King and Quenis Majesties Houshald Reformit', Gibson Craig, Appendix III, pp. 28, 36.
61 Stevenson, p. 109.
62 Williams, p. 21.
63 Hall, *Things of Darkness*, p. 128.
64 J. A. Gade, *Christian IV: King of Denmark and Norway* (London: George Allen & Unwin, 1927), pp. 39–40.
65 Bartley, 'The Scottish Royal Entries', pp. 35, 66.
66 As described in the legend of St Brendan, in *Scotichronicon by Walter Bower, in Latin and English*, ed. by John and Winifred MacQueen (Aberdeen: Aberdeen University Press, 1993), p. 27.
67 I am grateful to Louise Yeoman of the National Library of Scotland for bringing the figure of Scota to my attention.
68 Moysie, p. 84. Stevenson, p. 109.
69 John Burel, *The Discription of the Qveenis Maiesties Maist Honourable Entry into the Tovn of Edinbuvrgh, vpon the 19 Day of Maii, 1590*, in Gibson Craig,

pp. i–vii, p. v; and in *To the Richt High, Lodowick Duke of Lenox, Earl Darnlie, Lord Tarbolton, Methuen and Aubigné, &c. Gret Chamberlaine of Scotland, Iohn Bvrel, Wisheth Lang Life, with Happy Succes in all your Attempts, and Efter Daith, the Ioyes Euerlasting* (Edinburgh: R. Waldegrave, 1595).

70 William Fowler, *A True Reportarie of the Baptisme of the Prince of Scotland*, ed. by Meikle, II, pp. 165–95, p. 184. This edition contains both the Warrender Manuscript account and Waldegrave's anglicised printed text.

71 Fowler, in ed. by Meikle, II, p. 180.

72 Ibid., p. 182.

73 Robert Bowes to Burghley, 31 August 1594, *Calendar of State Papers Relating to Scotland and Mary, Queen of Scots, 1547–1603*, ed. by Annie I. Cameron (Edinburgh: His Majesty's General Register House, 1936), XI, pp. 422–3; the Earl of Sussex to Sir Robert Cecil, 31 August 1594, ibid., p. 423. 'Ordering of the chapel for the baptism', *c.* 10 August 1594, ibid., pp. 411–13 (reprinted from a Scots original, Harleian MS 4637, C. fol. 140). Confirming that the banquet was held on the evening of the baptism, the plan only then refers to 'their Majesties', pp. 411–13.

74 For example, Orazio Busino uses the phrase 'the Queen not being present because of some indisposition' in his description of *Pleasure Reconciled to Virtue* in 1618, Orgel and Strong, I, p. 282.

75 Edward Shorter, *The Making of the Modern Family* (London: Collins, 1976), p. 213.

76 Pauline Gregg, *King Charles I* (London: J. M. Dent & Sons, 1981), pp. 3–5. It is not clear whether Anna attended Princess Elizabeth's christening (28 November 1596, in Holyrood), but she did invite the Catholic Countess of Huntly; Mary Anne Everett Green, *Elizabeth, Electress Palatine and Queen of Bohemia* (London: Methuen, 1909), revised by S. C. Lomas, p. 2.

77 Stevenson, p. 104.

78 For one example among many, see Barroll, 'The Court of the First Stuart Queen', pp. 196–9.

79 This is clearly a second-hand description, recounted by the Venetian Secretary in England; Barroll, 'The Court of the First Stuart Queen', p. 199.

80 Riis, I, p. 278.

81 Barroll, 'The Court of the First Stuart Queen', p. 196.

82 Lewalski, *Writing Women*, cited from a report of their quarrel sent to England on May 25, 1595, printed in Agnes Strickland, *Lives of the Queens of England* (London: Henry Colburn, 1884), VII, pp. 363–4.

83 Gregg, p. 7.

84 Fowler, ed. by Meikle, II, p. 190.

85 Peter Fryer, *Staying Power: The History of Black People in Britain* (London: Pluto Press, 1984), p. 4; Fradenburg, p. 72; Hall, *Things of Darkness*, pp. 23–4.

86 Fryer, p. 2, p. 459, note 3. William Dunbar, *Ane Black Moir*, in James Kinsley (ed.), *The Poems of William Dunbar* (Oxford: Clarendon Press, 1979), p. 106,

l. 5. Robert Lindsay of Pitscottie, *The Historie and Chronicles of Scotland from the Slauchter of King James the First to the Ane Thousande Fyve Hundreith Thrie Scoir Fyftein Zeir*, ed. by Æ. J. G. Mackay (Edinburgh: Scottish Text Society, 1899, 1911), pp. 242–4.

87 Fradenburg, pp. 215–16. Lindsay of Pitscottie and Fryer refer to James IV's role as that of the Black Knight; Fradenburg names him the Wild Knight, which is consistent with the name used by the *Accounts of the Lord High Treasurer*, Mill, *Medieval Plays*, p. 326.

88 Dunbar, in Kinsley, pp. 106, l. 23; 309.

89 Mill, *Medieval Plays*, p. 53, citing Randolphe to Cecil, 7 December 1561.

90 Fowler, ed. by Meikle, II, p. 174.

91 Olav Lausund, 'Splendour at the Danish Court: The Coronation of Christian IV', in J. R. Mulryne and Margaret Shewring (eds), *Italian Renaissance Festivals and their European Influence* (Lampeter: Edwin Mellen Press, 1992), pp. 289–310.

92 Fradenburg, p. 212.

93 Fowler, ed. by Meikle, II, p. 188.

94 Ibid., p. 188.

95 Ibid., pp. 188–90.

96 Fowler, in ed. by Meikle, II, p. 193.

97 Golding, Book VII, p. 141.

98 Fradenburg, pp. 75–9.

99 Fradenburg, p. 79.

100 Diane Purkiss, *The Witch in History: Early Modern and Twentieth-Century Representations* (London and New York: Routledge, 1996), pp. 203–6.

101 For details of Fowler's life and his sometimes strained relationship with Anna, see Henry W. Meikle, James Craigie and John Purves (eds), *The Works of William Fowler: Secretary to Queen Anne, Wife of James VI* (Edinburgh: Scottish Text Society, 1914–40), III, pp. ix–xlii.

102 Fradenburg comments that the trajectory of *Blackness* and *Beauty* is that of an epithalamion; p. 76

103 Riis, I, pp. 272–6, 278–9, 279.

104 Barroll, 'The Court of the First Stuart Queen', p. 199.

105 Duke of Sully, *Memoirs of Maximilian de Béthune, Duke of Sully* (London, 1756), III, pp. 134–5; cited in Karen Lee Middaugh, 'The Golden Tree: The Court Masques of Queen Anna of Denmark' (unpublished doctoral dissertation, Case Western Reserve University, 1994), p. 66.

106 Sir Thomas Edmonds to the Earl of Shrewsbury, 16 June 1603; Lewalski, *Writing Women*, p. 22.

107 John Nichols (ed.), *The Progresses of James I* (New York: AMS Press, undated), I, pp. 168–87.

108 Scaramelli to the Doge and Senate, 6 August 1603, *CSP, Venetian, 1603–7*, X, pp. 77.

109 Peter Davidson and Thomas M. McCoog, SJ, 'Father Robert's Convert: The Private Catholicism of Anne of Denmark', *Times Literary Supplement*, 24 November 2000, pp. 16–17. A select list of earlier discussions includes Alphons Bellesheim, *History of the Catholic Church of Scotland* (Edinburgh: William Blackwood, 1889); William Forbes Leith, SJ (ed.), *Narratives of Scottish Catholics under Mary Stuart and James VI* (Edinburgh: William Paterson, 1885).

110 Scaramelli, 30 July 1603, *CSP, Venetian, 1603–7*, X, p. 72; Nicolo Molin, Venetian Ambassador, *Report on England Presented to the Government of Venice in the year 1607*, in *CSP, Venetian, 1603–7*, X, p. 513.

111 Leith, pp. 361–5. See also Maurice Lee Jr, 'King James' Popish Chancellor', in Ian B. Cowan and Duncan Shaw (eds), *The Renaissance and Reformation in Scotland: Essays in Honour of Gordon Donaldson* (Edinburgh: Scottish Academic Press, 1983), pp. 170–82, p. 174. Conflicting dates for Anna's conversion are given by Fr McQuhirrie, 'The State of Scotland in 1601', in Leith, pp. 272 ff. and by the Rev. Robert Abercromby, in Leith, pp. 263–6. This uncertainty is greatly resolved and a date of either 1598 or 1599 established by Davidson and McCoog, p. 16.

112 Robert Abercromby (English translation) in Leith, pp. 263–6, in Latin in Bellesheim, III, pp. 451–4. Anna's letter is in the British Library, Add. MS 37021, f 25. For correspondence between Clement and Anna and Clement and James VI and I: Arnold Oscar Meyer, *Clemens VIII und Jakob I von England* (Rome: Loesther & Co., 1904), pp. 38–41. Bellesheim, pp. 473–5, p. 473. J. D. Mackie, 'The Secret Diplomacy of King James VI in Italy Prior to his Accession to the English Throne', *Scottish Historical Review*, 21 (1924), 267–82.

113 Leo Hicks, SJ, 'The Embassy of Sir Anthony Standen in 1603' (parts I–IV), *Recusant History*, Part I, 5 (1959–60), 91–128; Part II, 5 (1959–60), 184–222; Part III, 6 (1961–62), 163–94; Part IV, 7 (1963–64), 50–81. Standen to the Jesuit Robert Persons, 17/27 December 1603, *CSP, Domestic, Addenda, 1580–1625*, XII, pp. 433–5, p. 433. Everett Green describes a letter from 'the Queen's spiritual attendant' which details Anna's attendance at the sacrament in the Spanish ambassador's house, and James's knowledge; Everett Green, p. 27, note 5; also Colbert MS 6051, Paris.

114 Lee Jr, 'King James' Popish Chancellor', pp. 172–3.

115 23 July 1603, *CSP, Venetian, 1603–7*, X, p. 68.

116 Scaramelli, *CSP, Venetian, 1603–7*, X, p. 77.

117 I am grateful to Matthew Voight for this suggestion, made at the Ninth International Conference of Medieval and Renaissance Scottish Literature and Language, St Andrews 1999.

118 Scaramelli, 13 August 1603; *CSP, Venetian, 1603–7*, X, p. 81.

119 Anne Clifford, *The Diaries of Lady Anne Clifford*, ed by D. J. H. Clifford (Stroud: Alan Sutton Publishing Ltd, 1992), p. 29.

CHAPTER THREE

1 Middaugh, 'The Golden Tree', p. 158.
2 Carleton to Chamberlain, 22 December 1603; cited in E. K. Chambers, *The Elizabethan Stage* (Oxford: Clarendon Press, 1923), III, p. 279.
3 Daniel, *The Vision*, pp. 17–42, p. 30, ll. 191–3. The editorial assignment to the masquers of the speeches describing the goddesses is inaccurate.
4 Chambers, III, pp. 272, 278–9.
5 Michael Shapiro, *The Children of the Revels: The Boy Companies of Shakespeare's Time and Their Plays* (New York: Columbia University Press, 1977), pp. 193–6, 230–1.
6 Chambers, III, pp. 273–7.
7 Carleton to Chamberlain, 15 January 1604, in Lee Jr, pp. 53–9.
8 Herford and Simpson, X, p. 450.
9 James is recorded as remarking to the Venetian ambassador at the performance of *The Masque of Beauty* that 'he intended this function to consecrate the birth of the Great Hall which his predecessors had left him built merely in wood, but which he had converted into stone'; *CSP, Venetian, 1607–10*, XI, p. 86.
10 Howard Colvin (gen. ed.), *The History of the King's Works* (London: Her Majesty's Stationery Office, 1982), IV, Part II, p. 144. See also Simon Thurley, *The Royal Palaces of Tudor England: Architecture and Court Life, 1460–1547* (New Haven and London: Yale University Press for the Paul Mellon Centre for Studies in British Art, 1993), pp. 112–20.
11 Daniel, *The Vision*, p. 32, l. 259.
12 Thurley, pp. 120, 129; Per Palme, *The Triumph of Peace: A Study of the Whitehall Banqueting House* (London: Thames and Hudson, 1957), pp. 130–1.
13 Palme, pp. 113–14. Ernst Law, *The History of Hampton Court Palace in Tudor Times* (London: George Bell & Sons, 1885), p. 165.
14 Thurley, p. 210.
15 Ibid., p. 120.
16 For a description of the galleries of the second Whitehall Banqueting House, see Orazio Busino's description of *Pleasure Reconciled to Virtue* in 1618: Orgel and Strong, I, p. 282. For the third Whitehall Banqueting House, see John Charlton, *The Banqueting House Whitehall* (London: Her Majesty's Stationery Office, 1964), p. 18.
17 Daniel, *The Vision*, p. 29, ll. 144–5.
18 Daniel, *The Vision*, p. 32, ll. 262–5.
19 Barroll, 'The Court of the First Stuart Queen', p. 191.
20 Arbella Stuart to her uncle, Gilbert Taylor, Earl of Shrewsbury, 18 December 1603, in Sara Jayne Steen (ed.), *The Letters of Lady Arbella Stuart* (New York and London: Oxford University Press, 1994), p. 197. Steen identifies the named women as Catherine Howard, Countess of Suffolk and Lady Audrey

Walsingham, Keeper of Queen Anna's wardrobe. Barroll identifies Lady
Walsingham as a member of Anna's 'Drawing-Chamber': Barroll, 'The Court
of the First Stuart Queen', p. 204.

21 Thomas Platter (1599), cited in Helen Hackett, 'Shakespeare's Theatre', in
Kiernan Ryan (ed.), *Shakespeare: Texts and Contexts* (Basingstoke: Macmillan,
2000), pp. 31–48, p. 41.

22 Arnold notes Elizabeth's practice of gifting her women, and the rumours that
surrounded Anna's inheritance, alteration and wearing of Elizabeth's clothes;
Janet Arnold (ed.), *Queen Elizabeth's Wardrobe Unlock'd: The Inventories of the
Wardrobe of Robes Prepared in July 1600 Edited from Stowe MS 557 in the British
Library, MS LR 2/121 in the Public Record Office, London, and MS V.b.72 in
the Folger Shakespeare Library, Washington DC* (Leeds: Maney, 1988), pp. 174–5.
For the value of textiles and embroidery see Roziska Parker, *The Subversive
Stitch: Embroidery and the Making of the Feminine* (London: The Women's
Press, 1984), pp. 68–9.

23 Daniel, *The Vision*, p. 37, ll. 406–12.

24 Ibid., p. 36, ll. 400–1.

25 Ibid., p. 36, ll. 406–7.

26 Ibid., p. 33, l. 305.

27 Carleton to Chamberlain, 15 January 1604, in Lee Jr, p. 55.

28 Ibid., p. 55.

29 Kathryn Schwarz, 'Amazon Reflections in the Jacobean Queen's Masque',
Studies in English Literature 1500–1900, 35 (1995), 293–319, p. 300.

30 Daniel, *The Vision*, p. 36, l. 302.

31 Ibid., p. 32, l. 260.

32 Ibid., pp. 32–3, ll. 281–2.

33 Maurer, 'Reading Ben Jonson's *Queens*'; Lewalski, *Writing Women*, pp. 36–9;
Purkiss, *The Witch in History*, pp. 202–6; Wynne-Davies, 'The Queen's
Masque'; Schwarz, 'Amazon Reflections'.

34 The Venetian ambassador, 22 January 1609; Herford and Simpson, X, p. 494.

35 Jonson, *Queens*, p. 137, l. 647.

36 Ibid., p. 136, l. 484.

37 Ibid., p. 137, ll. 640–2.

38 John Webster, *Monuments of Honour*, in *The Complete Works of John Webster*,
ed. by F. L. Lucas (London: Chatto and Windus, 1966) III, pp. 311–39;
William Drummond, *The Entertainment of the High and Mighty Monarch
Charles ... into ... Edinburgh, the fifteenth of June, 1633* (Edinburgh, 1633);
Elizabeth McGrath, 'Local Heroes: The Scottish Humanist Parnassus for
Charles I', in Edward Chaney and Peter Mack (eds), *England and the
Continental Renaissance: Essays in Honour of J. B. Trapp* (Woodbridge: Boydell
Press, 1990), pp. 257–70.

39 Jonson, *The King's Entertainment, Passing to his Coronation*, cited in Maurer,
'Reading Ben Jonson's *Queens*', p. 245.

40 David Riggs, *Ben Jonson: A Life* (London and Cambridge, MA: Harvard University Press, 1989), p. 164.

41 This analysis is influenced by Suzanne Gossett, '"Man-maid, Begone!": Women in Masques', *English Literary Renaissance*, 18 (1988), 96–113.

42 Vitruvius, *The Ten Books on Architecture*, trans. by Morris Hicky Morgan (New York: Dover, 1960), p. 72.

43 Jonson, *Queens*, p. 135, ll. 377–8.

44 Mary Russo, *The Female Grotesque: Risk, Excess and Modernity* (New York and London: Routledge, 1995), p. 54.

45 The stage was raised four feet from the hall floor; Orgel and Strong, I, p. 131, citing the Declared Accounts of the Audit Office. See also Orgel and Strong, I, pp. 138, fig. 7, 282.

46 Purkiss, p. 203.

47 John R. Spencer (trans.), *Filarete's Treatise on Architecture* (New Haven and London: Yale University Press, 1965), I, p. 119. Eugene R. Cunnar, '(En)gendering Architectural Poetics in Jonson's *Masque of Queens*', *LIT: Literature-Interpretation-Theory*, 4 (1993), 145–60.

48 Jonson, *Queens*, p. 136, l. 524.

49 Jonson, *Queens*, p. 135, l. 403.

50 Wynne-Davies, 'The Queen's Masque', p. 83.

51 The 'age of gold is also perforce an age of machines'; Orgel, *The Jonsonian Masque*, p. 138.

52 Jonson, *Queens*, p. 137, ll. 711–13.

53 Jonson, *Hymenaei*, p. 84, ll. 227–8; Jonson, *Blackness*, p. 49, ll. 46–50; Jonson, *Beauty*, pp. 69–70, ll. 218–23.

54 Jonson, *Oberon*, in *Ben Jonson: The Complete Masques*, ed. by Stephen Orgel (London and New Haven: Yale University Press, 1975), pp. 159–73, pp. 167–8, ll. 213–18.

55 Jonson, *Hymenaei*, p. 79, ll. 99–101.

56 Thomas Campion, *The Lords' Masque*, pp. 95–123.

57 Jonson, *Queens*, pp. 137, ll. 422–3, 134, ll. 331–9.

58 Jonson, *Queens*, p. 134, ll. 242–3.

59 John Peacock, *The Stage Designs of Inigo Jones: The European Context* (Cambridge: Cambridge University Press, 1995), pp. 168–9.

60 John Peacock, 'Inigo Jones as a Figurative Artist', in Lucy Gent and Nigel Llewellyn (eds), *Renaissance Bodies: The Human Figure in English Culture c. 1540–1660* (London: Reaktion Books, 1990), p. 170.

61 Michael Leslie, 'The Dialogue between Bodies and Souls: Pictures and Poesy in the English Renaissance', *Word & Image*, 1 (1985), 16–30. Ellen Chirelstein uses Jones's design for Tethys in *Tethys' Festival* as an example of this movement; Chirelstein, 'Lady Elizabeth Pope: The Heraldic Body', in Gent and Llewellyn, pp. 36–59, p. 59.

62 Chirelstein, 'Lady Elizabeth Pope', p. 39.

63 Carleton to Chamberlain, January 1604, in Lee Jr, p. 54.
64 *CSP, Venetian, 1617–19*, XV, p. 80; Lindley, *Trials*, pp. 7–8.
65 This costume has not been unequivocally identified as used in performance; Orgel and Strong, I, pp. 152–3.
66 Ellen Chirelstein, 'Lady Elizabeth Pope', p. 58.
67 Patrick Hannay, *Second Elegi*, in *The Nightingale, Sheretine and Mariana, a Happy Husband: Elegies on the Death of Queene Anne. Songs and Sonnets* (London: Nathaniel Butter, 1622), p. 201.
68 Criticisms of the aristocratic practice of exposing the breasts typically originated beyond the court, such as the bare-breasted noblewoman epitomising pride in the pamphlet for Anne Turner's execution in 1615. Lindley, *Trials*, reprints but does not date the pamphlet; plate 7.
69 Jonson, *Queens*, p. 136, l. 557.
70 Aileen Ribero cites Taylor's *A Glasse for Gentlewomen to Dresse themselves by* (1624) which attacks women for baring 'their armes beyond that which is fit for everyone to behold'; Ribero, *Dress and Morality* (London: B. T. Batsford, 1986), p. 82, citing Taylor, p. 28.
71 Schwarz, 'Amazon Reflections', p. 299.
72 Sir Walter Ralegh refers to this myth only to dismiss it; 'but that they [Amazons] cut off the right dug of the breast, I doe not find to be true'; *The Discoverie ... of Guiana* (New York: Argonaut Press, 1971), cited in Louis Montrose, 'The Work of Gender in the Discourse of Discovery', in Stephen Greenblatt (ed.), *New World Encounters* (Oxford: University of California Press, 1993), pp. 177–217, p. 202.
73 Schwarz, 'Amazon Reflections'; Stephen Orgel, 'Jonson and the Amazons', in Elizabeth Harvey and Katharine Eisaman Maus (eds), *Soliciting Interpretations: Literary Theory and Seventeenth-Century English Poetry* (Chicago: University of Chicago Press, 1990), pp. 119–39.
74 Jonson, *Queens*, p. 542.
75 Noting that 'Representations of the Amazon are ubiquitous in Elizabethan texts', Montrose identifies the figure of the Amazon as a fantasy trope of Renaissance England; Louis Montrose, '*A Midsummer Night's Dream* and the Shaping Fantasies of Elizabethan Culture: Gender, Power, Form', in Ferguson et al. (eds), *Rewriting the Renaissance*, pp. 65–87.
76 Schwarz, 'Amazon Reflections', p. 300.
77 Orgel, 'Jonson and the Amazons', pp. 125–6. Diane Purkiss provides the most nuanced analysis of James's own interests in the figure of the witch; Purkiss, pp. 199–230.
78 Jonson, *Queens*, p. 132, l. 106.
79 Schwarz, 'Amazon Reflections', p. 294.
80 Ibid., p. 307.
81 Purkiss, pp. 202–6.
82 Sherry Ortner, 'Is Male to Female as Culture is to Nature?', in Michelle

Zimbalist Rosaldo and Louise Lamphère (eds), *Woman, Culture and Society* (Stanford: Stanford University Press, 1974), pp. 67–87, p. 84.
83 Gossett, '"Man-maid, Begone!"'.

CHAPTER FOUR

1 John Fynnet to Mr Trumbull, 23 October 1612, in Edmund Sawyer (ed.), *Memoirs of Affairs of State in the Reigns of Q. Elizabeth and K. James I. Collected (Chiefly) from the Original Papers of the Right Honourable Sir Ralph Winwood* (London: W. B. for T. Ward), p. 403.

2 Chamberlain to Carleton, London, 17 June 1612, in McClure, I, p. 360. Everett Green, p. 27.

3 Chamberlain to Carleton, London, 31 December 1612, in McClure, I, p. 399.

4 Chamberlain to Carleton, 31 December 1612, in McClure, I, p. 399.

5 Chamberlain to Ralph Winwood, in McClure, I, p. 418.

6 Lewalski, *Writing Women*, p. 50.

7 Everett Green, p. 34; citing Roger Coke, *A Detection of the Court and State of England* (London, MDCCXIX), I, p. 73. Lewalski, *Writing Women*, p. 50.

8 Chamberlain to Alice Carleton, 18 February 1613, in McClure, I, p. 423. Jerzy Limon, *The Masque of Stuart Culture* (London and Toronto: Associated University Presses, 1990), pp. 125–6.

9 Roy Strong, *Henry, Prince of Wales and England's Lost Renaissance* (London: Thames & Hudson, 1986), pp. 138–83. Beaumont, *The Masque of the Inner Temple and Gray's Inn*, pp. 125–49.

10 Middaugh, 'The Golden Tree', p. 230.

11 Chamberlain to Carleton, 9 November 1616, in McClure, II, p. 32.

12 Chamberlain to Carleton, 10 June 1613, in McClure, I, pp. 456–7. *A Relation of the Royall, Magnificent, and Sumptuous Entertainment Given to the High and Mighty Princesse Anna, at the Renowned Citie of Bristoll* (London, 1613).

13 Strong, *Henry, Prince of Wales*, pp. 175–83; David Norbrook, '"The Masque of Truth": Court Entertainments and International Protestant Politics in the Early Stuart Period', *The Seventeenth Century*, 1 (1986), 81–110.

14 Norbrook, '"The Masque of Truth"', pp. 81–2, 89.

15 Meliadus means 'Miles a Deo' or 'soldier of God': Jonson, *Prince Henry's Barriers*, in *Ben Jonson: The Complete Masques*, ed. by Stephen Orgel (London and New Haven: Yale University Press, 1975), pp. 142–58; Strong, *Henry, Prince of Wales*, pp. 141–2; Frances Yates, *Shakespeare's Last Plays: A New Approach* (London: Routledge and Kegan Paul, 1975), pp. 17–37.

16 Antonio Foscarini, Venetian Ambassador in England, to the Doge and Senate: 9 November 1612, in *Calendar of State Papers and Manuscripts relating to English Affairs, Existing in the Archives and Collections of Venice, and in other Libraries of Northern Italy*, XII, 1610–13, ed. by Horatio F. Brown (London: His Majesty's Stationery Office, 1905), p. 444. Foscarini to the Doge and Senate, 11 January 1613, in ibid., p. 474.

17 Norbrook, '"The Masque of Truth"', p. 89.
18 Lewalski, *Writing Women*, pp. 52–3.
19 Everett Green, p. 354.
20 D. Jocquet, *Les Triomphes, Entrees, Cartels, Tournois, Ceremonies, et aultres Magnificences, Faites en Angleterre, & au Palatinat, pour le Mariage & Reception, de Monsiegneur le Prince Frideric V Comte Palatin du Rhin, Electeur du Sainct Empire, Duc de Baviere &c. Et de Madame Elisabeth, Fille Unique et Princesse de la Grande Bretagne, Electrice Palatine du Rhin &c. Son Espouse* (Heidelberg: Gotard Vogvelein, 1613), F–Fv. Chamberlain to Alice Carleton, 18 February 1613, in McClure, I, p. 424.
21 Fradenburg, pp. 212.
22 Norbrook, '"The Masque of Truth"', p. 83.
23 Walter R. Davies (ed.), *The Works of Thomas Campion* (London: Faber & Faber, 1969), p. 260, note 38, his translation. Campion, *The Lords' Masque*, pp. 115–16, ll. 364–7.
24 Ibid., Davies, p. 260, note 38, his translation.
25 Jocquet, H3v. My translation.
26 Lewalski, *Writing Women*, p. 53.
27 George Chapman, *The Memorable Masque*, in David Lindley (ed.), *Court Masques: Jacobean and Caroline Entertainments 1605–1640* (Oxford: Oxford University Press, 1995), pp. 74–91, p. 75, ll. 47–55.
28 David Norbrook, 'The Reformation of the Masque', p. 98.
29 Jocquet, H2, H3v.
30 Jocquet, H3v. My translation.
31 Jocquet, Cv, B3v.
32 On the ongoing associations between Princess Elizabeth and Elizabeth I see Lewalski, *Writing Women*, p. 48.
33 Campion, *The Lords' Masque*, pp. 105, l. 7; 111, ll. 211–14.
34 Ibid., p. 112, ll. 243–45.
35 Beaujoyeulx, *Le Balet Comique*, pp. 22–3.
36 *Ballet de Vandosme*, pp. 237–69.
37 Ovid, *The Metamorphoses*, in *Ovid's Selected Works*, ed. by J. C. and M. J. Thornton, Everyman's Library: Classical (London: J. M. Dent, 1955), pp. 307–11.
38 Philip Edwards, 'Introduction' to *The Masque of the Inner Temple and Gray's Inn*, in Spencer and Wells, p. 128.
39 Hesiod, *Works and Days*, in *The Poems of Hesiod*, trans. by R. M. Frazer (Norman: University of Oklahoma Press, 1983), pp. 97–8, ll. 47–63.
40 Ibid., p. 98, ll. 63–6.
41 I Timothy 2.12–15.
42 Campion, *The Lords' Masque*, p. 109, ll. 132–3.
43 Ibid., p. 112, l. 255.

44 Leonard Barkan, '"Living Sculptures": Ovid, Michelangelo and *The Winter's Tale*', *English Literary History*, 48 (1981), 639–67, pp. 650–1.

45 Bruce R. Smith, 'Sermons in Stones: Shakespeare and Renaissance Sculpture', *Shakespeare Studies*, 17 (1985), 1–23, pp. 2, 3.

46 John Weever, *Ancient Funerall Monuments Within the United Monarchie of Great Britaine, Ireland, and the Ilands Adjacent* (London: Thomas Harper, 1631), p. 11; cited in Smith, p. 3.

47 Norbrook, 'The Reformation of the Masque', p. 97.

48 Limon, pp. 52–91.

49 Jonson, *Blackness*, pp. 56–7, ll. 236–42.

50 Shapiro, pp. 37, 68.

51 John Fletcher and William Shakespeare, *The Two Noble Kinsmen*, ed. by Walter Cohen, in *The Norton Shakespeare*, ed. by Stephen Greenblatt (London and New York: W. W. Norton, 1997), pp. 3195–280, 3.5.139–48.

CHAPTER FIVE

1 Strong, *Henry, Prince of Wales*, p. 106; Lewalski, *Writing Women*, p. 98.

2 J. D. Alsop, 'William Welwood, Anne of Denmark and the Sovereignty of the Sea', *Scottish Historical Review*, 59 (1980), 171–4, p. 172. Ronald M. Meldrum (ed.), *Translations and Facsimiles of the Original Latin Letters of King James I of England (VI of Scotland), to his Royal Brother-in-Law, King Christian IV of Denmark* (Hassocks: Harvester Press, 1977), pp. 175–9, 181–3, 186–7.

3 Lewalski, *Writing Women*, p. 98.

4 James Knowles, 'The "Running Masque" Recovered: A Masque for the Marquess of Buckingham (c. 1619–20)', *English Manuscript Studies*, 9 (2000), 79–135, p. 79.

5 David Lindley, *Thomas Campion* (Leiden: E. J. Brill, 1986); Lindley, *Trials*; Purkiss, pp. 214–25; David Lindley, 'Embarrassing Ben: The Masques for Frances Howard', *English Literary Renaissance*, 16 (1986), 343–59; Martin Butler and David Lindley, 'Restoring Astraea: Jonson's Masque for the Fall of Somerset', *English Literary History*, 61 (1994), 807–27.

6 Chamberlain to Carleton, 25 November 1614, in Chambers, III, p. 246.

7 Chambers, III, p. 277.

8 Chamberlain to Carleton, 10 February 1614, in McClure, I, p. 507.

9 *Ballet de Vandosme*, pp. 237–69; *Le Ballet de Renaud*, pp. 97–136.

10 Lindley, *Thomas Campion*, p. 229.

11 This masque was sponsored by Thomas Howard, Robert Cecil and his brother Thomas, Earl of Exeter; David Lindley, 'Who Paid for Campion's *Lord Hay's Masque*?', *Notes and Queries* (1979), pp. 144–5. Campion was sponsored by Sir Thomas Monson, who was under the protection of the Howards; Lindley, *Thomas Campion*, p. 129.

12 Davies lists the Somerset masquers and their allegiances; pp. 212–13, 246. Chamberlain in McClure, I, p. 496.

13 Lindley, *Thomas Campion*, p. 226.

14 Campion, *The Somerset Masque*, in *The Works of Thomas Campion*, ed. by Walter R. Davies, London, Faber & Faber, 1969, pp. 263–84, p. 273.

15 Ibid., pp. 274–5.

16 Lindley, *Thomas Campion*, pp. 220–1, 216.

17 Campion, *Somerset*, p. 273.

18 Ibid., pp. 272–3.

19 Ibid., p. 272.

20 Beaumont, *The Masque of the Inner Temple and Gray's Inn*, p. 139; Jonson, *Beauty*, pp. 61–74.

21 Campion, *Somerset*, p. 269.

22 John Peacock, 'Inigo Jones and the Florentine Court Theater', *John Donne Journal*, 5 (1986), 200–34, pp. 224–6.

23 Samuel Daniel, *Tethys' Festival*, in *Inigo Jones and the Theatre of the Stuart Court*, ed. by Stephen Orgel and Roy Strong (London: Sotheby Parke Bernet, 1973), I, pp. 191–201, p. 193, ll. 7–21.

24 John Orrell, 'The Agent of Savoy at *The Somerset Masque*', *Review of English Studies*, n. s. 28 (1977), 301–4.

25 Henry Peacham, *Minerva Britanna or a Garden of Heroical Devises, Furnished, and Adorned with Emblemes* (London: Wa: Dight, 1612), emblem 13.

26 Romans, 11.20; Peter Davidson, *The Vocal Forest: A Study of the Context of Three Low Countries Printers' Devices of the Seventeenth Century* (Leiden: Academic Press, 1996), pp. 52–3.

27 Bath, p. 17; Davidson, *The Vocal Forest*, p. 38.

28 Gordon, 'The Imagery of Ben Jonson's *The Masque of Blacknesse* and *The Masque of Beautie*'.

29 Davidson, *The Vocal Forest*, p. 32.

30 Campion, *Somerset*, p. 272.

31 Ibid., p. 269.

32 Ibid., pp. 265, 26. Enid Welsford, *The Court Masque: A Study in the Relationship between Poetry and the Revels* (Cambridge: Cambridge University Press, 1927), p. 197.

33 Ibid., p. 271; Jonson, *Beauty*, p. 61, ll. 10–13.

34 Campion, *Somerset*, p. 271.

35 Jocquet, H3r. My translation.

36 Campion, *Somerset*, p. 269.

37 Lindley, *Thomas Campion*, p. 233.

38 Jonson, *Queens*, p. 126, ll. 105–19. Purkiss, pp. 202–3.

39 Campion, *Somerset*, p. 271.

40 Ibid., p. 272.

41 Fradenburg, p. 79.

42 Purkiss, pp. 215–16.

43 Campion, *Somerset*, p. 268.

44 McGowan, *L'Art du Ballet de Cour en France, 1581–1643* (Paris: CNRS, 1963), p. 104.

45 Catherine de Parthenay, Madame de Rohan, *Le Balet de Madame, Le Balet de Madame de Rohan, Autre Balet Representé Devant Madame à Pau le 23 Jour d'Aoust 1592*, in Marcel Pacquot, 'Comédies-ballets Représentées en l'Honnneur de Madame, Soeur du Roi Henri IV', *Revue Belge de Philologie et d'Histoire*, 10 (1931), 969–95.

46 Orgel, *Complete Masques*, pp. 4–5.

47 Anne Burley, 'Courtly Personages: The Lady Masquers in Ben Jonson's *Masque of Blackness*', *Shakespeare and Renaissance Association of West Virginia Selected Papers*, 10 (1985), 49–61.

48 The manuscript of *Cupid's Banishment* is in the Pierpont Morgan Library, New York: MS. MA 1296. The text is published by Cerasano and Wynne-Davies (eds), *Renaissance Drama by Women*, pp. 76–90.

49 Chamberlain to Carleton, 4 January 1617: '[The Queen] is said to aim at the regency if the King goes to Scotland', *CSP, Domestic, 1611–18*, IX, p. 422. Bacon's appointment was recorded by Giovanni Battista Lionello, Venetian Secretary in England, in a letter to the Doge and Senate; *CSP, Venetian, 1615–17*, XIV, p. 412.

50 Chamberlain to Carleton, McClure, II, p. 76.

51 Gerrard to Carleton; *CSP, Domestic, 1611–18*, p. 464.

52 Simon Thurley, former Curator of Historic Royal Palaces (personal correspondence, April 1996). For Gasparo Spinelli's description of the 1527 entertainments, see Sidney Anglo, *Spectacle, Pageantry, and Early Tudor Policy* (Oxford: Clarendon Press, 1969), p. 214.

53 John Orrell, *The Human Stage: English Theatre Design, 1567–1640* (Cambridge: Cambridge University Press, 1988), pp. 38–9, 62. Thurley, p. 183; Colvin, IV, part II, p. 103; IV, part II, p. 111.

54 John Summerson, *Inigo Jones* (Harmondsworth: Penguin, 1966), pp. 44, 47–8. Colvin, IV, part II, p. 122.

55 Prince Charles to James; *Letters to James the Sixth from the Queen, Prince Henry, Prince Charles* (Edinburgh: Maitland Club, 1835), pp. 51–2. The Venetian secretary's comment on 27 April 1617 that 'The prince is going [to Greenwich] tomorrow to stay some weeks' makes Charles's presence at *Cupid's Banishment* a distinct possibility; *CSP, Venetian, 1615–17*, p. 495.

56 Beaumont, *The Masque of the Inner Temple and Gray's Inn*, p. 132. Lewalski, *Writing Women*, pp. 95–9; Pearl Hogrefe, *Tudor Women: Commoners and Queens* (Ames: Iowa State University Press, 1975), p. 136.

57 Chamberlain to Carleton, 10 May 1617; *CSP, Domestic, 1611–18*, p. 465.

58 Sir Anthony Weldon, *The Court and Character of King James* (London, 1650), pp. 130–1.

59 Nichols, *James I*, III, pp. 255–82, 310–25; Mill, *Medieval Plays*, p. 55.

60 For the identities of the masquers see C. E. McGee, '*Cupid's Banishment: A*

Masque Presented to Her Majesty by Young Gentlewomen of the Ladies Hall, Deptford, May 4, 1617', *Renaissance Drama*, n.s. 19 (1988), 226–64, pp. 259–60.

61 White, p. 83.

62 Ibid., p. 85, ll. 139–46.

63 Jonson, *A Challenge at Tilt*, in *Ben Jonson: The Complete Masques*, ed. by Stephen Orgel (London: Yale University Press, 1975), pp. 198–205, p. 200, ll. 76–8.

64 Ibid., p. 203, ll. 140–2.

65 Ibid., p. 85, l. 100.

66 White, p. 84, ll. 2–3, and l. 34.

67 Cerasano and Wynne-Davies, *Renaissance Drama*, p. 196, note 6.

68 *Speeches to the Queen at Bisham, 1592*, in John Nichols (ed.), *The Progresses and Public Processions of Queen Elizabeth* (London: John Nichols and Son, 1823), III, pp. 130–6, p. 134.

69 Townshend, *Tempe Restored*, pp. 478–503. Sabol, pp. 23–4.

70 John Milton, *A Maske Presented at Ludlow Castle*, in *Milton: Poetical Works*, ed. by Douglas Bush (Oxford: Oxford University Press, 1988), pp. 109–39.

71 White, p. 87.

72 In a discussion at *The Queen's Court* conference at the University of Warwick (18–19 April 1998), Sophie Tomlinson commented that Watkins's speech was 'not histrionic'.

73 *Balet de la Reuanche du Mespris d'Amour: Dancé deuant la Royne de la Grande Bretaigne* (London, 1617); I am very grateful to James Knowles for bringing this to my attention.

74 White, p. 83.

75 Ibid., p. 83; G. E. Bentley, *The Jacobean and Caroline Stage* (Oxford: Clarendon Press, 1956), V, p. 1258.

76 White, p. 87.

77 Ibid., p. 88, l. 283.

78 Ibid., p. 88.

79 Ibid., p. 88.

80 Nichols, *James I*, III, p. 295. McGee, '*Cupid's Banishment*', p. 264.

81 See Parker. In the wake of such a re-evaluation, further work has been done on the cultural and gendered status of needlework; see, for example, Dympna Callaghan, 'Looking Well to Linens: Women and Cultural Production in *Othello* and Shakespeare's England', in Jean E. Howard and Scott Cutler Shershow (eds), *Marxist Shakespeares* (London and New York: Routledge, 2001), pp. 53–81.

82 White, p. 88, l. 298.

83 Parker, p. 63.

84 Ibid., p. 96.

85 Ibid., p. 64.

86 Ben Jonson wrote to William Drummond in 1619 describing the bed and about forty of its images and mottoes; Parker, p. 78. Bath, p. 17.

87 Nichols (ed.), *Queen Elizabeth*, II, pp. 65–91.

88 Parker, p. 96.

89 Parker, p. 77; Bath, p. 17.

90 J. Max Patrick (ed.), *The Complete Poetry of Robert Herrick* (New York: New York University Press, 1963), p. 307.

91 Emblems from Whitney's *A Choice of Emblemes* (1586) were embroidered on the Lord Falkland bodice; John L. Nevinson, 'English Domestic Embroidery Patterns of the Sixteenth and Seventeenth Centuries', *Walpole Society*, 28 (1939–40), part I. Geoffrey Whitney, *A Choice of Emblemes* (Leyden, 1586), pp. 220, 230. Huston Diehl, *Index of Icons in English Emblem Books, 1500–1700* (London: University of Oklahoma Press, 1986).

92 John Parkinson, *Paradisi in Sole Paradisus Terrestris* (London: Humfrey Lownes and Robert Young, 1629); *Theatrum Botanicum: The Theater of Plants. Or, an Herball of a Large Extent* (London: Thomas Cotes, 1640).

93 Russell is credited with the design of the gardens at Moor Park in 1617; Strong, *Henry Prince of Wales*, p. 106; Lewalski, *Writing Women*, p. 98. Evidence of intertextuality between herbals and elite embroidery is found in the grape motif of the 'Pear Tree' long cushion at Hardwick Hall, inspired by the botanical work of Jacques le Moyne de Morgues (*La Clef des Champs*, 1586); Thomasina Beck, *The Embroiderer's Garden* (Newton Abbot, Devon: David and Charles, 1988), p. 124.

94 Cerasano and Wynne-Davies, *Renaissance Drama*, p. 77. Boethius, *The Consolation of Philosophy*, trans. by V. E. Watts (Harmondsworth: Penguin, 1969), Book II, V, pp. 68–9.

95 Beryl Rowland (ed. and trans.), *Medieval Woman's Guide to Health: The First Gynaecological Handbook* (London: Croom Helm, 1981), pp. 67–147.

96 John Gerard, *The Herbal, or General History of Plants*, ed. by Thomas Johnson (New York: Dover Publications, 1975), p. 1294.

97 Elissa Weaver, 'Spiritual Fun: A Study of Sixteenth-century Tuscan Convent Theater', in Mary Beth Rose (ed.), *Women in the Middle Ages and the Renaissance: Literary and Historical Perspectives* (Syracuse: Syracuse University Press, 1986), pp. 173–205. A. C. F. Beales, *Education Under Penalty: English Catholic Education from the Reformation to the Fall of James II 1547–1689* (London: Athlone Press, 1963), pp. 203–4.

98 Limon, p. 50.

99 Francis Bacon, 'Of Masques and Triumphs', p. 99.

100 I am grateful to Stephen Orgel for this suggestion.

101 *Ballet de Vandosme*, pp. 247, 265–9.

102 Cerasano and Wynne-Davies, *Renaissance Drama*, p. 78.

103 Jonson, *Hymenaei* in Orgel and Strong, I, p. 105; Jonson, *Queens*, p. 140, l. 510. Cerasano and Wynne-Davies, *Renaissance Drama*, p. 78.

CONCLUSION

1 Antonio Donato to the Venetian Doge and Senate, 14 March 1619; *CSP, Venetian, 1617–19*, XV, pp. 494–5.

2 19 April 1619, *CSP, Domestic, 1619–23*, X, p. 37; Jennifer Woodward, *The Theatre of Death: The Ritual Management of Royal Funerals in Renaissance England 1570–1625* (Woodbridge: The Boydell Press, 1997), p. 167.

3 Nicolo Molin to the Doge and Senate, 13 January 1605; *CSP, Venetian, 1603–7*, X, pp. 208–9.

4 Sir Edward Harwood to Dudley Carleton, 6 March 1619; *CSP, Domestic, 1619–23*, X, p. 21.

5 McClure, II, p. 219. David Mathew, *Catholicism in England 1535–1935 Portrait of a Minority: Its Cultures and Tradition* (London: Catholic Book Club, 1938), p. 60; Harwood, *CSP, Domestic, 1619–23*, X, p. 21.

6 Chamberlain to Carleton, 6 March 1619, *CSP, Domestic, 1619–23*, X, p. 20; Sir Edward Harwood to Carleton, 6 March 1619, *CSP, Domestic, 1619–23*, X, p. 21.

7 Harwood, 6 March 1619, *CSP, Domestic, 1619–23*, X, p. 21; cf. Chamberlain to Carleton, 6 March 1619; Sir Thomas Edmondes to Carleton, 17 March 1619; Chamberlain to Carleton, 27 March 1619, who says 'The will proves to be nothing'; *CSP, Domestic, 1619–23*, X, pp. 20, 25, 27. Harwood himself later retracted the existence of a will, stating that Anna signed only 'a suit for payment of her debts'; Harwood to Carleton, 19 March 1619; *CSP, Domestic, 1619–23*, X, p. 25.

8 *CSP, Venetian, 1617–19*, XV, pp. 494–5.

9 *CSP, Domestic, 1619–23*, X, p. 25.

10 *CSP, Venetian, 1617–19*, XV, pp. 557–8; *CSP, Domestic, 1619–23*, X, p. 25; Chamberlain, in Nichols, *James I*, III, p. 556.

11 Woodward, p. 168.

12 Nichols, *James I*, III, p. 539.

13 Chamberlain, in Nichols, *James I*, III, p. 546. Woodward, p. 168.

14 Chamberlain, in McClure, II, p. 237.

15 Woodward, p. 168; Nichols, *James I*, III, p. 545.

16 Chamberlain, in McClure, II, p. 233; Woodward, p. 169.

17 Cf. Woodward, pp. 172–4.

18 Nikolaus Pevsner and Priscilla Metcalf, *The Cathedrals of England: Southern England* (Harmondsworth: Penguin, 1985), p. 233; Hugh Ross Williamson, *George Villiers First Duke of Buckingham: Study for a Biography* (London: Duckworth, 1940), p. 230.

19 Colvin lists Jones as the hearse's designer, which was constructed by the King's Works; there is no specified commissioner; Colvin, III, Part I, p. 138; IV, Part IV, p. 261.

20 Woodward suggests Maximillian Colt, who made Anna's effigy, as the designer whose commission was eventually used; Woodward, pp. 170–1.

21 Smith, 'Sermons in Stone', p. 3.
22 Woodward, p. 171.
23 Jonson, *Blackness*, p. 47, l. 7.
24 Chamberlain, in Nichols, *James I*, III, pp. 545–6.
25 Middaugh, 'The Golden Tree', pp. 31–6.
26 John Peacock, 'The French Element in Inigo Jones' Masque Designs' in Lindley, *The Court Masque*, pp. 149–68.
27 For documents and scenic designs for *Artenice* see Honorat de Bueil, Sieur de Racan, *Artenice*, in *Inigo Jones and the Theatre of the Stuart Court*, ed. by Stephen Orgel and Roy Strong (London: Sotheby Parke Bernet, 1973), I, pp. 383–8. Sophie Tomlinson, 'She that Plays the King: Henrietta Maria and the Threat of the Actress in Caroline Culture', in Gordon McMullan and Jonathan Hope (eds), *The Politics of Tragicomedy: Shakespeare and After* (London and New York: Routledge, 1992), pp. 189–207, p. 189.
28 William Prynne, *Histrio-Mastix: The Player's Scourge or, Actor's Tragedy (1633)*, ed. by Peter Davison (London and New York: Johnson Reprint Corporation, 1972), vol. 2, index.
29 Tomlinson, 'She that Plays the King'; '"My Brain the Stage": Margaret Cavendish and the Fantasy of Female Performance', in Clare Brant and Diane Purkiss (eds), *Women, Texts and Histories, 1575–1760* (London and New York: Routledge, 1992), pp. 134–63; Gossett, '"Man-maid, Begone!"'; Julie Sanders, '"Twill fit the Players yet": Women and Theatre in Jonson's Late Plays', in Richard Cave, Elizabeth Schafer and Brian Woolland (eds), *Ben Jonson and Theatre: Performance, Practice, Theory* (London and New York: Routledge, 1999), pp. 179–90; '"The Day's Sports Devised in the Inn": Jonson's *The New Inn* and Theatrical Politics', *The Modern Language Review*, 91 (1996), 545–60; Erica Veevers, *Images of Love and Religion: Queen Henrietta Maria and Court Entertainments* (Cambridge: Cambridge University Press, 1989).
30 Martin Butler, *Theatre and Crisis 1632–1642* (Cambridge: Cambridge University Press, 1984), p. 26.
31 See William Davenant, *Salmacida Spolia* (1640), in *Inigo Jones and the Theatre of the Stuart Court*, ed. by Stephen Orgel and Roy Strong (London: Sotheby Parke Bernet, 1973), II, pp. 729–86.
32 Tomlinson, 'She that Plays the King', p. 190. Katherine Eisaman Maus, '"Playhouse Flesh and Blood": Sexual Ideology and the Restoration Actress', *English Literary History*, 46 (1979), 595–617.
33 Thomas Brand, cited by Sandra Richards, *The Rise of the English Actress* (Basingstoke: Macmillan, 1993), p. 1. Townshend, *Tempe Restored*, pp. 478–503; Gossett, '"Man-maid, Begone!"', p. 108.
34 Tomlinson, 'She that Plays the King', p. 192.
35 Richards, p. 2.
36 See Lady Jane Cavendish and Lady Elizabeth Brackley's, *The Concealed Fancies*

(c. 1645), in *Renaissance Drama by Women: Texts and Documents*, ed. by S. P. Cerasano and Marion Wynne-Davies (New York and London: Routledge, 1996), pp. 127–54; Susan Wiseman, *Drama and Politics in the Civil War* (Cambridge: Cambridge University Press, 1998); 'Gender and Status in Dramatic Discourse: Margaret Cavendish, Duchess of Newcastle', in Isobel Grundy and Susan Wiseman (eds), *Women, Writing, History 1640–1740* (London: B. T. Batsford, 1992), pp. 159–77, pp. 160–3. Davenant, *Siege of Rhodes*, ed. by Hedback.

Bibliography

Masque, entertainment and ceremonial texts

Balet de la Reuanche du Mespris d'Amour: Dancé Deuant la Royne de la Grande Bretaigne, London, 1617.

Ballet de Monseigneur le Duc de Vandosme, in *Ballets et Mascarades de Cour de Henri II à Louis XIV*, ed. by Paul Lacroix, Genève, Chez J. Gay et fils, 1868, I, pp. 237–69.

Le Ballet de Renaud, or Discours au Vray du Ballet Dansé par le Roy 1617 in *Ballets et Mascarades de Cour de Henri II à Louis XIV*, ed. by Paul Lacroix, Genève, Chez J. Gay et fils, 1868, II, pp. 97–136.

Beaujoyeulx, Balthasar, *Le Ballet Comique de la Reine (1581)*, ed. by Margaret McGowan, Binghamton, New York, Medieval and Renaissance Texts and Studies, 1985.

Beaumont, Francis, *The Masque of the Inner Temple and Gray's Inn*, ed. by Philip Edwards, in *A Book of Masques in Honour of Allardyce Nicoll*, ed. by T. J. B. Spencer and Stanley Wells, Cambridge, Cambridge University Press, 1967, pp. 125–47.

Brackley, Elizabeth and Jane Cavendish, *The Concealed Fancies*, in *Renaissance Drama by Women: Texts and Documents*, ed. by S. P. Cerasano and Marion Wynne-Davies, New York and London, Routledge, 1996, pp. 127–54.

Burel, John, *The Discription of the Qveenis Maiesties Maist Honorable Entry into the Tovn of Edinbuvrgh, vpon the 19 Day of Maii, 1590*, in *To the Richt High, Lodowick Duke of Lenox, Earl Darnlie, Lord Tarbolton, Methuen and Aubigné, &c. gret Chamberlaine of Scotland, Iohn Bvrel, Wisheth Lang Life, with Happy Succes in all your Attempts, and efter Daith, the Ioyes Euerlasting*, Edinburgh, R. Waldegrave, 1595.

Campion, Thomas, *The Lord Hay's Masque* in *Inigo Jones and the Theatre of the Stuart Court*, ed. by Stephen Orgel and Roy Strong, London, Sotheby Parke Bernet, 1973, I, pp. 115–21.

Campion, Thomas, *The Lords' Masque*, ed. by I. A. Shapiro, in *A Book of Masques in Honour of Allardyce Nicoll*, ed. by T. J. B. Spencer and Stanley Wells, Cambridge, Cambridge University Press, 1967, pp. 95–123.

Campion, Thomas, *The Somerset Masque*, in *The Works of Thomas Campion*, ed. by Walter R. Davies, London, Faber & Faber, 1969, pp. 263–84.

The Ceremonies, Form of Prayer and Service used in Westminster Abbey at the Coronation of King James I and Queen Ann his Consort. With the Coronation of King Charles I in Scotland, London, Randal Taylor, 1685.

Chapman, George, *The Memorable Masque*, in David Lindley (ed.), *Court Masques: Jacobean and Caroline Entertainments 1605–1640*, Oxford, Oxford University Press, 1995, pp. 74–91.

Daniel, Samuel, *Tethys' Festival*, in *Inigo Jones and the Theatre of the Stuart Court*, ed. by Stephen Orgel and Roy Strong, London, Sotheby Parke Bernet, 1973, I, pp. 191–201.

Daniel, Samuel, *The Vision of the Twelve Goddesses*, ed. by Joan Rees, in *A Book of Masques in Honour of Allardyce Nicoll*, ed. by T. J. B. Spencer and Stanley Wells, Cambridge, Cambridge University Press, 1967, pp. 17–42.

Davenant, William, *Salmacida Spolia* in *Inigo Jones and the Theatre of the Stuart Court*, ed. by Stephen Orgel and Roy Strong, London, Sotheby Parke Bernet, 1973, II, pp. 729–86.

Davenant, William, *The Siege of Rhodes*, ed. by Ann-Mari Hedback, Uppsala, Almqvist & Wiksell, 1973.

Fowler, William, *A True Reportarie of the Baptisme of the Prince of Scotland*, in *The Works of William Fowler Secretary to Queen Anne, wife of James VI*, ed. by Henry W. Meikle, Edinburgh, William Blackwood and Sons for the Scottish Text Society, 1936, II, pp. 165–95.

Jocquet, D., *Les Triomphes, Entrees, Cartels, Tournois, Ceremonies, et aultres Magnificences, Faites en Angleterre, & au Palatinat, pour le Mariage & Reception, de Monsiegneur le Prince Frideric V Comte Palatin du Rhin, Electeur du Sainct Empire, Duc de Baviere &c. Et de Madame Elisabeth, Fille Unique et Princesse de la Grande Bretagne, Electrice Palatine du Rhin &c. Son Espouse*, Heidelberg, Gotard Vogvelein, 1613.

Jonson, Ben, *A Challenge at Tilt*, in *Ben Jonson: The Complete Masques*, ed. by Stephen Orgel, London, Yale University Press, 1975, pp. 198–205.

Jonson, Ben, *Haddington Masque*, in *Ben Jonson: The Complete Masques*, ed. by Stephen Orgel, London, Yale University Press, 1975, pp. 107–21.

Jonson, Ben, *Hymenaei*, in *Ben Jonson: The Complete Masques*, ed. by Stephen Orgel, London, Yale University Press, 1975, pp. 75–106.

Jonson, Ben, *Love Restored*, in *Ben Jonson: The Complete Masques*, ed. by Stephen Orgel, London, Yale University Press, 1975, pp. 186–97.

Jonson, Ben, *The Masque of Beauty*, in *Ben Jonson: The Complete Masques*, ed. by Stephen Orgel, London and New Haven, Yale University Press, 1975, pp. 61–74.

Jonson, Ben, *The Masque of Blackness*, in *Ben Jonson: The Complete Masques*, ed. by Stephen Orgel, London and New Haven, Yale University Press, 1975, pp. 47–60.

Jonson, Ben, *The Masque of Queens*, in *Ben Jonson: The Complete Masques*, ed. by Stephen Orgel, London and New Haven, Yale University Press, 1975, pp. 122–41.

Jonson, Ben, *Oberon*, in *Ben Jonson: The Complete Masques*, ed. by Stephen Orgel, London and New Haven, Yale University Press, 1975, pp. 159–73.

Jonson, Ben, *Pleasure Reconciled to Virtue*, in *Ben Jonson: The Complete Masques*, ed. by Stephen Orgel, London and New Haven, Yale University Press, 1975, pp. 263–76.

Jonson, Ben, *Prince Henry's Barriers*, in *Ben Jonson: The Complete Masques*, ed. by Stephen Orgel, London and New Haven, Yale University Press, 1975, pp. 142–58.

Milton, John, *A Maske Presented at Ludlow Castle*, in *Milton: Poetical Works*, ed. by Douglas Bush, Oxford, Oxford University Press, 1988, pp. 109–39.

Montagu, Walter, *The Shepherds' Paradise*, ed. by Sarah Poynting, Malone Society Reprint, Oxford University Press, 1998, vol. 159.

Parthenay, Catherine De, Madame de Rohan, *Le Balet de Madame, Le Balet de Madame de Rohan, Autre Balet Representé Devant Madame à Pau le 23 Jour D'Aoust 1592*, in Marcel Pacquot, 'Comédies-Ballets Représentées en l'Honnneur de Madame, Soeur du Roi Henri IV', in *Revue Belge de Philologie et d'Histoire*, 10 (1931), 969–95.

Racan, Honorat de Bueil, Sieur de, *Artenice*, in *Inigo Jones and the Theatre of the Stuart Court*, ed. by Stephen Orgel and Roy Strong, London, Sotheby Parke Bernet, 1973, I, pp. 383–8.

A Relation of the Royall, Magnificent, and Sumptuous Entertainment Given to the High and Mighty Princesse Anna, at the Renowned Citie of Bristoll, London, 1613.

Speeches to the Queen at Bisham 1592, in *The Progresses and Public Processions of Queen Elizabeth*, ed. by John Nichols, London, John Nichols and Son, 1823; New York, AMS Reprint, 1963, III, pp. 130–6.

Stevenson, David with Peter Graves, *Scotland's Last Royal Wedding: The Marriage of King James VI and Anne of Denmark with a Danish Account of the Marriage Translated by Peter Graves*, Edinburgh, John Donald, 1996.

Townshend, Aurelian, *Tempe Restored*, in *Inigo Jones and the Theatre of the Stuart Court*, ed. by Stephen Orgel and Roy Strong, London, Sotheby Parke Bernet, 1973, II, pp. 479–504.

White, Robert, *Cupid's Banishment: A Maske Presented to Her Majesty by the Young Gentlewomen of the Ladies Hall In Deptford at Greenwich the 4th of May 1617*, in *Renaissance Drama by Women: Texts and Documents* ed. by S. P. Cerasano, and Marion Wynne-Davies, London and New York, Routledge, 1996, pp. 76–90.

Primary sources

MANUSCRIPTS

Anna of Denmark to Cardinal Borghese (31 July, 1601), Add. MS 37021, fol. 25, British Library.

Ashmole MS 1504, Bodleian Library.

Ashmole, Elias, MS Rawl. d.864. fol. 199, *c.* 1630, Bodleian Library.

Denmilne Papers, XXVIII, 33.1.11, no. 8, National Library of Scotland.

Fowler, William, *Description of Emblems*, Hawthornden Papers, XII, fols 36–9, National Library of Scotland.

Johnston, *Mss History of Scotland*, National Library of Scotland, Adv. MSS 35.4.2.

Ramsay, John, MS Douce 280, Bodleian Library.

MS Rawl. Poet. 108, fols 10–11, Bodleian Library.

White, Robert, *Cupid's Banishment: A Maske Presented to Her Majesty By the Young Gentlewomen of the Ladies Hall in Deptford at Greenwich the 4th of May 1617*, Pierpont Morgan Library, New York, MS MA 1296.

PRINTED TEXTS

Akrigg, G. P. V. (ed.), *Letters of King James VI and I*, London, University of California Press, 1984.

Alberti, Leon Battista, *The Ten Books of Architecture: The 1755 Leoni Edition*, New York, Dover Publications, 1986.

Arbeau, Thoinot, *Orchesography*, trans. by Mary Stewart Evans, New York, Dover, 1967.

Arnold, Janet (ed.), *Queen Elizabeth's Wardrobe Unlock'd: The Inventories of the Wardrobe of Robes Prepared in July 1600 Edited from Stowe MS 557 in the British Library, MS LR 2/121 in the Public Record Office, London, and MS V.b.72 in the Folger Shakespeare Library, Washington DC*, Leeds, Maney, 1988.

Bacon, Francis, 'Of Masques and Triumphs', in *Essays*, London, Everyman, J. M. Dent, 1994, pp. 99–100.

Bentley, G. E., *The Jacobean and Caroline Stage*, Oxford, Clarendon Press, 1956.

Boethius, *The Consolation of Philosophy*, trans. by V. E. Watts, Harmondsworth, Penguin, 1969.

Bower, Walter, *Scotichronicon*, in *Scotichronicon by Walter Bower, in Latin and English*, ed. by John and Winifred MacQueen, Aberdeen, Aberdeen University Press, 1993.

Calendar of State Papers, Domestic, 1611–18, ed. by Mary Anne Everett Green, London, Her Majesty's Stationery Office, 1858 – Nendlen, Liechtenstein, Kraus Reprint, 1967, IX.

Calendar of State Papers, Domestic, 1619–23, ed. by Mary Anne Everett Green, London, Her Majesty's Stationery Office, 1858 – Nendlen, Liechtenstein, Kraus Reprint, 1967, X.

Calendar of State Papers, Domestic, Addenda, 1580–1625, ed. by Mary Anne Everett Green, London, Her Majesty's Stationery Office, 1872 – Nendlen, Liechtenstein, Kraus Reprint, 1967, XII.

Calendar of State Papers, Domestic, 1581–90, ed. by Robert Lemon, London, Longman, Green, Longman, Roberts, and Green, 1865 – Nendeln, Liechtenstein, Kraus Reprint, 1967.

Calendar of State Papers Relating to Scotland and Mary, Queen of Scots, 1547–1603, ed. by Annie I. Cameron, Edinburgh, His Majesty's General Register House, 1936, XI.

Calendar of State Papers, Venetian, 1603–7, ed. by Horatio F. Brown, London, His Majesty's Stationery Office, 1900, X.

Calendar of State Papers, Venetian, 1607–10, ed. by Horatio F. Brown, London, His Majesty's Stationery Office, 1904 – Nendlen, Liechtenstein, Kraus Reprint, 1970, XI.

Calendar of State Papers, Venetian, 1610–13, ed. by Horatio F. Brown, London, His Majesty's Stationery Office, 1905, XII.

Calendar of State Papers, Venetian, 1615–17, ed. by Allen B. Hinds, London, His Majesty's Stationery Office, 1908 – Nendlen, Liechtenstein, Kraus Reprint, 1970, XIV.

Calendar of State Papers, Venetian, 1617–19, ed. by Allen B. Hinds, London, His Majesty's Stationery Office, 1909 – Nendlen, Liechtenstein, Kraus Reprint, 1970, XV.

Caroso, Fabritio, *Noblità di Dame*, trans. and ed. by Julia Sutton, Oxford, Oxford University Press, 1986.

Castiglione, Baldesar, *The Book of the Courtier*, trans. by George Bull, Baltimore, MD, Penguin Books, 1967.

Chambers, E. K., *The Elizabethan Stage*, Oxford, Clarendon Press, 1923.

Christian IV, *The King of Denmarkes Welcome*, London, E. Allde, 1606.

Clifford, Anne, *The Diaries of Lady Anne Clifford*, ed. by D. J. H. Clifford, Stroud, Alan Sutton Publishing Ltd, 1992.

Coke, Roger, *A Detection of the Court and State of England*, London, MDCCXIX.

Coplande, Robert, *The Maner of Bace Daunsing*, in *Materials for the Study of the Basse Dance*, ed. by Frederick Crane, New York, Institute of Medieval Music, 1968.

Culpeper, Nicolas, *The English Physician Enlarged*, London, W. Churchill, 1718.

Dallington, Robert, *Method for Travel*, in W. B. Rye (ed.), *England as Seen by Foreigners in the Days of Elizabeth and James the First*, London, John Russell Smith, 1865.

Daly, Peter and Simon Cutter (eds), *Andreas Alciati 2: Emblems in Translation*, London, University of Toronto Press, 1985.

Davenant, William, *The Siege of Rhodes*, ed. by Ann-Mari Hedback, Uppsala, Almqvist & Wiksell, 1973.

Davies, Sir John, *Orchestra or a Poem of Dancing*, ed. by E. M. W. Tillyard, London, Chatto & Windus, 1947.

Drummond, William, *The Entertainment of the High and Mighty Monarch Charles . . . into . . . Edinburgh, the Fifteenth of Iune, 1633*, Edinburgh, 1633.

Elyot, Sir Thomas, *The Book Named the Govenor*, ed. by S. E. Lehmberg, London, Everyman, 1962.

Erasmus, *De civilitate morum puerilium (On Good Manners for Boys)*, trans. by Brian McGregor in *The Collected Works of Erasmus*, ed. by J. K. Sowards, Toronto, University of Toronto Press, 1985, pp. 269–89.

Feuillerat, Albert, *Documents Relating to the Office of the Revels in the Time of Queen Elizabeth*, London, David Nutt, 1908.

The First Printed Catalogue of the Bodleian Library 1605: A Facsimile, Oxford, Clarendon Press, 1986.

Fletcher, John, and William Shakespeare, *The Two Noble Kinsmen*, ed. by Walter Cohen, in *The Norton Shakespeare*, ed. by Stephen Greenblatt, London and New York, W. W. Norton, 1997, pp. 3195–280.

Gerard, John, *The Herbal, or General History of Plants*, ed. by Thomas Johnson, New York, Dover Publications, 1975.

Gibson Craig, J. T. (ed.), *Papers Relative to the Marriage of James the Sixth of Scotland, with the Princess Anna of Denmark; A.D. M.D.LXXXIX. and the Form and Manner of her Majesty's Coronation at Holyrood House*, Edinburgh, The Bannatyne Club, 1823.

Giuseppi, M. S. (ed.), *Great British Historical Manuscripts Commission. Salisbury XVI, Ser. 9*, London, HMSO, 1933.

Giuseppi, M. S. (ed.), *Salisbury (Cecil) Manuscripts (1606), Calendar of the MSS of the Most Honourable the Marquess of Salisbury*, London, Her Majesty's Stationery Office, 1940, XVIII.

Golding, Arthur, *Shakespeare's Ovid Being Arthur Golding's Translation of the Metamorphoses*, ed. by W. H. D. Rouse, London, De la More Press, 1904.

Hailes, Sir David Dalrymple, Lord (ed.), *The Secret Correspondence of Sir Robert Cecil with James VI King of Scotland*, Edinburgh, A. Millar, 1766.

Hall, Edward, *Hall's Chronicle*, London, J. Johnson, F. C. & J. Rivington [etc.], 1809.

Hannay, Patrick, *The Nightingale, Sheretine and Mariana, a Happy Husband: Elegies on the Death of Queene Anne. Songs and Sonnets*, London, Nathaniel Butter, 1622.

Harris, John, *Catalogue of the Drawings Collection of the Royal Institute of British Architects: Inigo Jones and John Webb*, Farnborough, Gregg International, 1972.

Herford, C. H. and Percy and Evelyn Simpson (eds), *Ben Jonson*, Oxford, Clarendon Press, 1925–52, 11 vols.

Hesiod, *Theogony*, in *The Poems of Hesiod*, trans. by R. M. Frazer, Norman, University of Oklahoma Press, 1983.

Hill, R. F. (ed.), *Dramatic Records in the Declared Accounts of the Office of Works 1560–1640*, Oxford, Malone Society Collections, 1977, X.

Hill, Thomas, *The Gardener's Labyrinth*, ed. by Richard Mabey, Oxford, Oxford University Press, 1987.

The History and Life of King James the Sext, Edinburgh, James Ballantyne, 1804.

James VI and I, *Basilikon Doron*, Menston, Scolar Press, 1969.

James VI and I, *The Poems of James VI of Scotland*, ed. by James Craigie, Edinburgh and London, William Blackwood and Sons for the Scottish Text Society, 1958, 2 vols.

The Ioyfull Receiuing of Iames the Sixt of that Name King of Scotland, and Queen Anne his Wife, unto the Townes of Lyeth and Edenborough the First Daie of May Last Past, 1590. Together with the Triumphs Shewed before the Coronation of the said Scottish Queene, London, Henrie Carrie, 1590.

Kinsley, James (ed.), *The Poems of William Dunbar*, Oxford, Clarendon Press, 1979.

Lang, David (ed.), *Original Letters Relating to the Ecclesiastical Affairs of Scotland (1603–25)*, Edinburgh, Bannatyne Club, 1851.

Lauze, F. de, *Apologie de la Danse et de la Parfaicte Methode de l'Enseigner tant aux Cavaliers quax Dames (1623)*, trans. by Joan Wildeblood, London, Frederick Muller Ltd., 1952.

Lee Jr, Maurice (ed.), *Dudley Carleton to John Chamberlain 1603–1624: Jacobean Letters*, New Brunswick, NJ, Rutgers University Press, 1972.

Leith, William Forbes, SJ (ed.), *Narratives of Scottish Catholics under Mary Stuart and James VI*, Edinburgh, William Paterson, 1885.

Leslie, John (Bishop), *The Historie of Scotland*, trans. by James Dalrymple (1596), ed. by E. G. Cody, Edinburgh, Scottish Text Society, 1830.

Letters to James the Sixth from the Queen, Prince Henry, Prince Charles, the Princess Elizabeth and her Husband Frederick King of Bohemia, and from their Son Prince Frederick Henry, Edinburgh, Maitland Club, 1835.

Lindsay, Robert of Pitscottie, *The Historie and Chronicles of Scotland from the Slauchter of King James the First to the Ane Thousande Fyve Hundreith Thrie Scoir Fyftein Zeir*, ed. by Æ. J. G. Mackay, Edinburgh, Scottish Text Society, 1899, 1911.

McClure, Norman Egbert (ed.), *The Letters of John Chamberlain*, Philadelphia, American Philosophical Society, 1939, 2 vols.

McClure Thomson, Elizabeth (ed.), *The Chamberlain Letters*, New York, G. P. Putnam's Sons, 1965.

Macrobius, *Commentary on the Dream of Scipio*, trans. by William Harris Stahl, New York, Columbia University Press, 1952.

Meikle, Henry W., James Craigie, John Purves (eds), *The Works of William Fowler Secretary to Queen Anne, Wife of James VI*, Edinburgh, Scottish Text Society, 1914–40, 3 vols.

Meldrum, Ronald M. (ed.), *Translations and Facsimiles of the Original Latin Letters of King James I of England (VI of Scotland), to his Royal Brother-in-law, King Christian IV of Denmark*, Hassocks, Harvester Press, 1977.

Meyer, Arnold Oskar, *Clemens VIII und Jakob I von England*, Rome, Loestler & Co., 1904.

Middleton, Thomas and Cyril Tourneur, *The Revenger's Tragedy*, ed. by Reginald A. Foakes, Manchester, Manchester University Press, Revels student edition, 1996.

Mignerak, Matthias, *La Practique de l'Aiguille Industrieuse*, Paris, Jean le Clerc, 1605.

Mill, Anna Jean, *Medieval Plays in Scotland*, Edinburgh and London, William Blackwood and Sons, 1927.

Montaigne, Michel de, *Apology for Raymond Sebond*, in *The Complete Essays of Montaigne*, trans. by Donald M. Frame, Stanford, Stanford University Press, 1986, pp. 318–457.

Montaigne, Michel de, 'Of Cannibals', in *The Complete Essays of Montaigne*, trans. by Donald M. Frame, Stanford, Stanford University Press, 1986, pp. 150–58.

Moysie, David, *Memoirs of the Affairs of Scotland*, ed. by J. Dennistoun, Edinburgh, Bannatyne Club, 1830.

Negri, Cesare, *Le Gratie d'Amore: A Facsimile of the Milan 1602 Edition*, New York, Broude Brothers Ltd, 1969.

Nichols, John (ed.), *The Progresses and Public Processions of Queen Elizabeth*, London, John Nicols and Son, 1823; New York, AMS Reprint, 1963, 3 vols.

Nichols, John (ed.), *The Progresses of James I*, New York, AMS Press, undated, 3 vols.

Ovid, *Ovid's Selected Works*, ed. by J. C. and M. J. Thornton, Everyman's Library: Classical, London, J. M. Dent, 1955.

Parkinson, John, *Paradisi in Sole Paradisus Terrestris*, London, Humfrey Lownes and Robert Young, 1629.

Parkinson, John, *Theatrum Botanicum: The Theater of Plants, or, an Herball of a Large Extent*, London, Thomas Cotes, 1640.

Patrick, J. Max (ed.), *The Complete Poetry of Robert Herrick*, Stuart Editions, New York, New York University Press, 1963.

Peacham, Henry, *Minerva Britanna, or a Garden of Heroical Devises, Furnished, and Adorned with Emblemes*, London, Wa: Dight, 1612.

Prynne, William, *Histrio-Mastix: The Player's Scourge or, Actor's Tragedy (1633)*, ed. by Peter Davison, London and New York, Johnson Reprint Corporation, 1972.

Ralegh, Sir Walter, *The Discoverie ... of Guiana*, New York, Argonaut Press, 1971.

Roberts, Henry, *Englands Farewell to Christian the Fourth, Famous King of Denmarke*, London, William Welby, 1606.

Roberts, Henry, *The Most Royall and Honourable Entertainments of the Famous and Renowned King, Christian the Fourth, King of Denmarke, etc*, London, William Barley, 1606.

Rollins, Hyder E. (ed.), *A Handful of Pleasant Delights (1584) by Clement Robinson and Divers Others*, New York, Dover Publications, 1965.

Ronsard, *Oeuvres*, ed. by Isidore Silver, Chicago, University of Chicago Press, 1966.

Rye, W. B. (ed.), *England as Seen by Foreigners in the Days of Elizabeth and James the First*, London, John Russell Smith, 1865.

Sabol, Andrew J., *Four Hundred Songs and Dances from the Stuart Court Masque*, London, University Press of New England for Brown University Press, 1982.

Sawyer, Edmund (ed.), *Memoirs of Affairs of State in the Reigns of Q. Elizabeth and K. James I. Collected (Chiefly) from the Original Papers Of the Right Honourable Sir Ralph Winwood*, London, W.B. for T. Ward, 1725.

Serlio, Sebastiano, *The Five Books of Architecture: An Unabridged Reprint of the English Edition of 1611*, New York, Dover Publications, 1982.

Shorleyker, Richard, [*A Schole-house for the Needle*], London, R. Shorleyker, 1632.

Spencer, John R. (trans.), *Filarete's Treatise on Architecture*, New Haven and London, Yale University Press, 1965, 2 vols.

Spenser, Edmund, *The Faerie Queene*, ed. by A. C. Hamilton, New York, Longman, 1977.

Spottiswoode, John, *The History of the Church of Scotland*, Menston, Scolar Press, 1972.

Steen, Sara Jayne (ed.), *The Letters of Lady Arbella Stuart*, New York and London, Oxford University Press, 1994.

Streitberger, W. R., H. R. Woudhuysen and John Pitcher (eds), 'Jacobean and Caroline Revels Accounts, 1603–42', *Malone Society Collections*, Oxford, Oxford University Press, 1986, XIII.

Stubbs, Philip, *The Anatomy of Abuses (1583)*, ed. by Peter Davison, New York, Johnson Reprint Company, 1972.

Tasso, Torquato, *Jerusalem Delivered*, trans. by Edward Fairfax with an introduction by Roberto Weiss, London, Centaur Press, 1962.

Taylor, John, *The Needle's Excellency*, London, James Boler, 1636.

Thomson, T. (ed.), *The Memoirs of Sir James Melville*, Edinburgh, Bannatyne Club, 1827.

Velasco, Juan Fernandez de, *Relacion de la Iornada del Excmo Condestable de Castilla*, Antwerp, 1604, trans. in W. B. Rye (ed.), *England as Seen by Foreigners in the Days of Elizabeth and James I*, London, John Russell Smith, 1865, pp. 117–24.

Vitruvius, *The Ten Books on Architecture*, trans. by Morris Hicky Morgan, New York, Dover, 1960.

Webster, John, *Monuments of Honour*, in *The Complete Works of John Webster*, ed. by F. L. Lucas, London, Chatto and Windus, 1966, III, pp. 311–39.

Weldon, Anthony, *The Court and Character of King James*, London, 1650.

Whitney, Geoffrey, *A Choice of Emblemes*, Leyden, 1586.

Whitney, Geoffrey, *A Choice of Emblems*, intro. by John Manning, Aldershot, Scolar Press, 1989.

SECONDARY SOURCES

Aasand, Hardin, '"To Blanch an Ethiop, and Revive a Corse": Queen Anne and the *Masque of Blackness*', *Studies in English Literature, 1500–1900*, 32 (1992), 271–85.

Adair, Christy, *Women and Dance: Sylphs and Sirens*, London, Macmillan, 1992.

Alpers, Svetlana, 'Style is What You Make it: The Visual Arts Again', in Berel Lang (ed.), *The Concept of Style*, Philadelphia, University of Pennsylvania Press, 1979, pp. 95–117.

Alsop, J. D., 'William Welwood, Anne of Denmark and the Sovereignty of the Sea', *Scottish Historical Review*, 59 (1980), 171–4.

Anglin, Jay Pascal, 'Frustrated Ideals: The Case of Elizabethan Grammar School Foundations', *History of Education*, 11 (1982), 267–79.

Anglin, Jay Pascal, *The Third University: A survey of Schools and Schoolmasters in the Elizabethan Diocese of London*, Norwood, PA, Norwood Editions, 1985.

Anglo, Sidney, *Spectacle, Pageantry, and Early Tudor Policy*, Oxford, Clarendon Press, 1969.

Apted, Michael, *The Painted Ceilings of Scotland 1550–1650*, Edinburgh, Her Majesty's Stationery Office, 1966.

Apted, Michael and Susan Hannabuss, *Painters in Scotland 1301–1700: A Biographical Dictionary*, Edinburgh, Scottish Record Society, 1978.

Arber, Agnes, *Herbals: Their Origins and Evolution – A Chapter in the History of Botany, 1470–1670*, Cambridge, Cambridge University Press, 1912.

Ashdown, Dulcie M., *Ladies-in-waiting*, London, Arthur Baker, 1976.

Ashton, Robert (ed.), *James I by his Contemporaries*, London, Hutchinson, 1969.

Axton, Marie, *The Queen's Two Bodies: Drama and the Elizabethan Succession*, London, Royal Historical Society, 1977.

Bainton, Ronald H., 'Learned Women in the Europe of the Sixteenth Century', in Patricia H. Labalme (ed.), *Beyond Their Sex: Learned Women of the European Past*, New York, New York University Press, 1980, pp. 117–28.

Bald, R. C., *John Donne: A Life*, Oxford, Clarendon Press, 1986.

Barber, C. L., *Shakespeare's Festive Comedy: A Study of Dramatic Form and its Relation to Social Custom*, Princeton, NJ, Princeton University Press, 1972.

Barkan, Leonard, '"Living Sculptures": Ovid, Michelangelo and *The Winter's Tale*', *English Literary History*, 48 (1981), 639–67.

Barkan, Leonard, *Nature's Work of Art: The Human Body as Image of the World*, London, Yale University Press, 1975.

Barroll, J. Leeds, *Anna of Denmark, Queen of England: A Cultural Biography*, Philadelphia, University of Pennsylvania Press, 2001.

Barroll, J. Leeds, 'The Court of the First Stuart Queen', in Linda Levy Peck (ed.), *The Mental World of the Jacobean Court*, Cambridge, Cambridge University Press, 1991, pp. 191–208.

Bartley, Mary Margaret, 'A Preliminary Study of the Scottish Royal Entries of Mary Stuart, James VI, and Anne of Denmark, 1558–1603', unpublished doctoral dissertation, University of Michigan, 1981.

Bath, Michael, *Speaking Pictures: English Emblem Books and Renaissance Culture*, London, Longman, 1994.

Beales, A. C. F., *Education Under Penalty: English Catholic Education from the Reformation to the Fall of James II 1547–1689*, London, Athlone Press, 1963.

Beck, Thomasina, *The Embroiderer's Garden*, Newton Abbot, Devon, David & Charles, 1988.

Beilin, Elaine V., *Redeeming Eve: Women Writers of the English Renaissance*, Princeton, NJ, Princeton University Press, 1987.

Bellesheim, Alphons, *History of the Catholic Church of Scotland*, Edinburgh, William Blackwood, 1889.

Bentley, G. E., 'The Theatres and the Actors', in Philip Edwards, G. E. Bentley, Kathleen McLuskie and Lois Potter (eds), *The Revels History of Drama in English, vol. IV, 1613–1660*, London and New York, Methuen, 1981, pp. 69–126.

Bergeron, David, *English Civic Pageantry 1558–1642*, London, Edward Arnold, 1971.

Bergeron, David, 'Masculine Interpretation of Queen Anne, Wife of James I', *Biography*, 18 (1995), 42–54.

Bergeron, David M. (ed.), *Pageantry in the Shakespearean Theater*, Athens, GA, University of Georgia Press, 1985.

Bergeron, David M., *Shakespeare's Romances and the Royal Family*, Kansas, University of Kansas Press, 1985.

Bergeron, David M., 'Women as Patrons of English Renaissance Drama', in Guy Fitch Lytle and Stephen Orgel (eds), *Patronage in the Renaissance*, Princeton, NJ, Princeton University Press, 1981, pp. 274–92.

Bevington, David, *Action is Eloquence: Shakespeare's Language of Gesture*, Cambridge, MA, Harvard University Press, 1984.

Bliss, William, 'The Religious Belief of Anne of Denmark', *English Historical Review*, 4 (1889), 110.

Blunt, Wilfred and Sandra Raphael, *The Illustrated Herbal*, London, Frances Lincoln, 1994.

Borum, Poul, *Danish Literature: A Short Critical Survey*, Copenhagen, The Danish Institute, 1979.

Boucher, Francois, *Twenty Thousand Years of Fashion: The History of Costume and Personal Adornment*, New York, Harry N. Abrams Inc., 1969.

Bowle, John, *Charles I: A Biography*, London, Weidenfeld & Nicolson, 1975.

Brady, Jennifer and W. H. Herendeen (eds), *Ben Jonson's 1616 Folio*, London and Toronto, Associated University Presses, 1991.

Brainard, Ingrid, 'The Role of the Dancing Master in Fifteenth-Century Society', *Fifteenth Century Studies*, 2 (1979), 21–44.

Bray, Alan, *Homosexuality in Renaissance England*, London, Gay Men's Press, 1982.

Bray, Alan, 'Homosexuality and the Signs of Male Friendship in Elizabethan England', *History Workshop*, 29 (1990), 1–19.

Brink, Jean R., 'Bathsua Reinolds Makin: "Most Learned Matron"', *Harvard Language Quarterly*, 54 (1991), 313–26.

Brink, Jean R., *Female Scholars: A Tradition of Learned Women Before 1800*, Montreal, Eden Press, 1980.

Brissenden, Alan, *Shakespeare and the Dance*, London, Macmillan, 1981.

Bristol, Michael D., *Carnival and Theater: Plebian Culture and the Structure of Authority in Renaissance England*, New York, Methuen, 1985.

Burley, Anne, 'Courtly Personages: The Lady Masquers in Ben Jonson's *Masque of Blackness*', *Shakespeare and Renaissance Association of West Virginia Selected Papers*, 10 (1985), 49–61.

Burt, Ramsay, *The Male Dancer: Bodies, Spectacle, Sexuality*, London and New York, Routledge, 1995.

Butler, Martin, 'Reform or Reverence? The Politics of the Caroline masque', in J. R. Mulryne and Margaret Shewring (eds), *Theatre and Government Under the Early Stuarts*, Cambridge, Cambridge University Press, 1993, pp. 118–56.

Butler, Martin, *Theatre and Crisis 1632–1642*, Cambridge, Cambridge University Press, 1984.

Butler, Martin and David Lindley, 'Restoring Astraea: Jonson's Masque for the Fall of Somerset', *English Literary History*, 61 (1994), 807–27.

Byard, Margaret M., 'The Trade of Courtiership: The Countess of Bedford and the Bedford Memorials; a Family History from 1585 to 1607', *History Today*, 29 (1979), 20–8.

Callaghan, Dympna, 'Looking Well to Linens: Women and Cultural Production in *Othello* and Shakespeare's England', in Jean E. Howard and Scott Cutler Shershow (eds), *Marxist Shakespeares*, London and New York, Routledge, 2001, pp. 53–81.

Callaghan, Dympna, *Shakespeare Without Women: Representing Gender and Race on the Renaissance Stage*, London and New York, Routledge, 2000.

Carlisle, Nicholas, *A Concise Description of the Endowed Grammar Schools in England and Wales*, London, Baldwin, Craddock and Joy, 1818.

Carlton, Charles, *Charles I: The Personal Monarch*, London, Routledge & Kegan Paul, 1983.

Carpenter, Sarah, 'Early Scottish Drama', in R. D. S. Jack (ed.), *History of Scottish Literature, Volume I: Origins to 1660 (Medieval and Renaissance)*, Aberdeen, Aberdeen University Press, 1988, pp. 199–212.

Cast, David, 'Speaking of Architecture: The Evolution of a Vocabulary in Vasari, Jones, and Sir John Vanbrugh', *Journal of the Society of Architectural Historians*, 52 (1993), 179–88.

Cerasano, S. P. and Marion Wynne-Davies (eds), *Gloriana's Face: Women, Public and Private, in the English Renaissance*, New York and London, Harvester Wheatsheaf, 1992.

Cerasano, S. P. and Marion Wynne-Davies (eds), *Renaissance Drama by Women: Texts and Documents*, London and New York, Routledge, 1996.

Charlton, John, *The Banqueting House Whitehall*, London, Her Majesty's Stationery Office, 1964.

Chedgzoy, Kate, Melanie Hansen and Suzanne Trill (eds), *Voicing Women: Gender and Sexuality in Early Modern Writing*, Keele, Keele University Press, 1996.

Cheney, Patrick and P. J. Klemp, 'Spenser's Dance of the Graces and the Ptolomaic Universe', *Studia Neophilologica: A Journal of Germanic and Romance Languages and Literature*, 56 (1984), 27–33.

Chibnall, Jennifer, '"To that Secure Fix'd State": The Function of the Caroline Masque Form', in David Lindley (ed.), *The Court Masque*, Manchester, Manchester University Press, 1984, pp. 78–93.

Chirelstein, Ellen, 'Lady Elizabeth Pope: The Heraldic Body', in Gent, Lucy and Nigel Llewellyn (eds), *Renaissance Bodies: The Human Figure in English Culture c. 1540–1660*, London, Reaktion Books, 1990, pp. 36–59.

Christensen, Thorkild Lyby, 'Scoto-Danish Relations in the Sixteenth Century: The Historiography and some Questions', *Scottish Historical Review*, 48 (1969), 80–97.

Colvin, Howard (gen. ed.), *The History of the King's Works*, London, Her Majesty's Stationery Office, 1982.

Cooper, James, *Four Scottish Coronations*, Aberdeen, Aberdeen Ecclesiological Society and Glasgow Ecclesiological Society, 1902.

Cooper Allbright, Ann, 'Incalculable Choreographies', in Goellner, Ellen W. and Jacqueline Shea Murphy (eds), *Bodies of the Text: Dance as Theory, Literature as Dance*, New Jersey, Rutgers University Press, 1995, pp. 157–81.

Cowan, Edward J., 'The Darker Version of the Scottish Renaissance: The Devil and Francis Stewart', in Ian B. Cowan and Duncan Shaw (eds), *The Renaissance and Reformation in Scotland: Essays in Honour of Gordon Donaldson*, Edinburgh, Scottish Academic Press, 1983, pp. 125–40.

Creaser, John, '"The Present Aid of this Occasion": The Setting of *Comus*', in David Lindley (ed.), *The Court Masque*, Manchester, Manchester University Press, 1984, pp. 111–34.

Cunnar, Eugene R., '(En)gendering Architectural Poetics in Jonson's *Masque of Queens*', *LIT: Literature-Interpretation-Theory*, 4 (1993), 145–60.

Daly, Peter M., *Literature in the Light of the Emblem: Structural Parallels between the Emblem and Literature in the Sixteenth and Seventeenth Centuries*, Toronto and London, University of Toronto Press, 1979.

Davidson, Peter, 'The Entry of Mary Stewart into Edinburgh, 1561, and other Ambiguities', *Renaissance Studies*, 9 (1995), 416–29.

Davidson, Peter, *The Vocal Forest: A Study of the Context of Three Low Countries Printers' Devices of the Seventeenth Century*, Leiden, Academic Press, 1996.

Davidson, Peter and Thomas M. McCoog SJ, 'Father Robert's Convert: The Private Catholicism of Anne of Denmark', *Times Literary Supplement*, 24 November 2000, pp. 16–17.

Davidson, Peter, Dominic Montserrat and Jane Stevenson, 'Three Entertainments for the Wedding of Mary Queen of Scots written by George Buchanan: Latin Text and Translation', *Scotlands* (1995), 1–10.

Davies, H. Neville, 'The Limitations of Festival: Christian IV's State Visit to England in 1606', in J. R. Mulryne and Margaret Shewring (eds), *Italian Renaissance Festivals and their European Influence*, Lampeter, Edwin Mellen Press, 1992, pp. 311–36.

Davies, Walter R. (ed.), *The Works of Thomas Campion*, London, Faber & Faber, 1969.

de Lafontaine, Henry Cart (ed.), *The King's Musick: A Transcript of Records Relating to Music and Musicians, 1460–1700*, New York, Da Capo Press, 1973.

Diehl, Huston, *Index of Icons in English Emblem Books, 1500–1700*, London, University of Oklahoma Press, 1986.

Digby, George Wingfield, *Elizabethan Embroidery*, New York, Thomas Yoseloff, 1964.

Dolmetsch, Mabel, *Dances of England and France 1450–1600*, London, Routledge and Kegan Paul, 1959.

Donaldson, Gordon, 'Introduction', *Scottish Historical Review*, 48 (1969), 1–5.

Donnelly, Marian C., 'Theaters in the Courts of Denmark and Sweden from Frederik II to Gustav III', *Journal of the Society of Architectural Historians*, 43 (1984), 328–40.

Dow, James, 'Scottish Trade with Sweden 1512–80', *Scottish Historical Review*, 48 (1969), 64–79.

Dow, James, 'Scottish Trade with Sweden 1580–1622', *Scottish Historical Review*, 48 (1969), 124–150.

Dundas, Judith, '"Those Beautiful Characters of Sense": Classical Deities and the Court Masque', *Comparative Drama*, 16 (1982), 166–79.

Dunnigan, Sarah M., 'The Creation and Self-creation of Mary Queen of Scots: Literature, Politics and Female Controversies in Sixteenth-century Scottish Poetry', *Scotlands*, 5 (1998), 65–88.

Dunnigan, Sarah M., 'Scottish Women Writers *c.* 1560–1650', in Douglas Gifford and Dorothy McMillan (eds), *A History of Scottish Women's Writing*, Edinburgh, Edinburgh University Press, 1997, pp. 15–43.

Dusinberre, Juliet, *Shakespeare and the Nature of Women*, London, Macmillan, 1975.

Edwards, Philip, G. E. Bentley, Kathleen McLuskie and Lois Potter (eds), *The Revels History of Drama in English, vol. IV, 1613–1660*, London and New York, Methuen, 1981.

Ellacombe, Henry N., *The Plant-lore and Garden-craft of Shakespeare*, Exeter, William Pollard, 1878.

Enright, Michael J., 'King James and his Island: An Archaic Kingship Belief?', *Scottish Historical Review*, 55 (1976), 29–40.

Evans, D. Wyn, 'A Short Survey of Scandinavian Libraries in Great Britain, together with a List of the Sixteenth-Century Danish and Icelandic Books in the National Library of Scotland', *Nordisk Tidskrift för Bok- och Biblioteksväsen* (1967), Uppsala.

Evans, Robert C., '"Other Men's Provision": Ben Jonson's Parody of Robert White in *Pleasure Reconciled to Virtue*', *Comparative Drama*, 24 (1990), 55–77.

Everett Green, Mary Anne, *Elizabeth, Electress Palatine and Queen of Bohemia*, London, Methuen, 1909, revised by S. C. Lomas.

Ezell, Margaret J. M., *The Patriarch's Wife: Literary Evidence and the History of the Family*, Chapel Hill, University of North Carolina Press, 1987.

Ferrante, Joan M., 'The Education of Women in the Middle Ages in Theory, Fact, and Fantasy', in Patricia H. Labalme (ed.), *Beyond Their Sex: Learned Women of the European Past*, New York, New York University Press, 1980, pp. 9–42.

Fisher, N. R. R., 'The Queenes Courtes in her Councell Chamber at Westminster', *English Historical Review*, 108 (1993), 314–37.

Fitch Lytle, Guy and Stephen Orgel (eds), *Patronage in the Renaissance*, Princeton, NJ, Princeton University Press, 1981.

Foster, Susan Leigh, *Reading Dancing: Bodies and Subjects in Contemporary American Dance*, Berkeley, University of California Press, 1986.

Foster, Susan Leigh, 'Textual Evidences', in Ellen W. Goellner and Jacqueline Shea Murphy (eds), *Bodies of the Text: Dance as Theory, Literature as Dance*, New Brunswick NJ, Rutgers University Press, 1995, pp. 231–46.

Fradenburg, Louise Olga, *City, Marriage, Tournament: Arts of Rule in Late Medieval Scotland*, Madison, WI, University of Wisconsin Press, 1991.

Franko, Mark, *Dance as Text: Ideologies of the Baroque Body*, Cambridge, Cambridge University Press, 1993.

Franko, Mark, *The Dancing Body in Renaissance Choreography (c. 1416–1589)*, Birmingham, AL, Summa Publications, 1986.

Franko, Mark, 'Mimique', in Goellner, Ellen W. and Jacqueline Shea Murphy (eds), *Bodies of the Text: Dance as Theory, Literature as Dance*, New Jersey, Rutgers University Press, 1995, pp. 205–16.

Franko, Mark, 'Renaissance Conduct Literature and the Basse Danse: The Kinesis of *Bonne Grace*', in Richard C. Trexler (ed.), *Persons in Groups: Social Behaviour as Identity Formation in Medieval and Renaissance Europe*, Binghamton, NY, Medieval and Renaissance Texts and Studies, 1985, pp. 55–66.

Franko, Mark, 'La Théâtralité du Corps Dansant', in Jean Cèard, Marie Madeleine Fontaine and Jean-Claude Margolin (eds), *Le Corps à la Renaissance*, Paris, Amateurs de Livres, 1987, pp. 243–52.

Freeman, Margaret, *Herbs for the Medieval Household*, New York, Metropolitan Museum of Art, 1943.

Fryer, Peter, *Staying Power: The History of Black People in Britain*, London, Pluto Press, 1984.

Fumerton, Patricia, *Cultural Aesthetics: Renaissance Literature and the Practice of Social Ornament*, Chicago and London, University of Chicago Press, 1991.

Gade, J. A., *Christian IV: King of Denmark and Norway*, London, George Allen & Unwin, 1927.

Gardiner, Dorothy, *English Girlhood at School: A Study of Women's Education through Twelve Centuries*, London, Oxford University Press, 1929.

Gent, Lucy and Nigel Llewellyn (eds), *Renaissance Bodies: The Human Figure in English Culture c. 1540–1660*, London, Reaktion Books, 1990.

Gibb, M. A., *Buckingham: 1592–1628*, London, Jonathan Cape, 1939.

Godshalk, W. L., 'Recent Studies in Samuel Daniel (1975–1990)', *English Literary Renaissance*, 24 (1994), 489–502.

Goellner, Ellen W. and Jacqueline Shea Murphy (eds), *Bodies of the Text: Dance as Theory, Literature as Dance*, New Brunswick NJ, Rutgers University Press, 1995.

Goldberg, Jonathan, *James I and the Politics of Literature: Jonson, Shakespeare, Donne, and Their Contemporaries*, London, Johns Hopkins University Press, 1983.

Gordon, D. J., 'Hymenaei: Ben Jonson's Masque of Union', *Journal of the Warburg and Courtauld Institutes*, 8 (1945), 107–45.

Gordon, D. J., 'The Imagery of Ben Jonson's *The Masque of Blacknesse* and *The Masque of Beautie*', *Journal of the Warburg and Courtauld Institutes*, 6 (1943), 122–41.

Gossett, Suzanne, '"Man-maid, Begone!": Women in Masques', *English Literary Renaissance*, 18 (1988), 96–113.

Greenblatt, Stephen (ed.), *Marvellous Possessions: The Wonder of the New World*, Oxford, Clarendon Press, 1991.

Greenblatt, Stephen (ed.), *Representing the English Renaissance*, London, University of California Press, 1988.

Gregg, Pauline, *King Charles I*, London, J. M. Dent & Sons, 1981.

Gurr, Andrew, *The Shakespearean Stage 1574–1642*, Cambridge, Cambridge University Press, 1980, second edition.

Gurr, Andrew, *The Shakespearian Playing Companies*, Oxford, Clarendon Press, 1996.

Hackett, Helen, 'Shakespeare's Theatre', in Kiernan Ryan (ed.), *Shakespeare: Texts and Contexts*, Basingstoke, Macmillan, 2000, pp. 31–48.

Hall, Kim F., 'Sexual Politics and Cultural Identity in *The Masque of Blackness*', in Sue-Ellen Case and Janelle Reinelt (eds), *The Performance of Power: Theatrical Discourse and Politics*, Iowa City, University of Iowa Press, 1991, pp. 3–18.

Hall, Kim F., *Things of Darkness: Economies of Race and Gender in Early Modern England*, Ithaca and London, Cornell University Press, 1995.

Hanna, Judith Lynne, *To Dance is Human: A Theory of Nonverbal Communication*, Chicago, University of Chicago Press, 1987.

Hanna, Judith Lynne, *The Performer – Audience Connection: Emotion to Metaphor in Dance and Society*, Austin, TX, University of Texas Press, 1983.

Harben, Henry A., *A Dictionary of London*, London, Herbert Jenkins Ltd, 1918.

Harris, John, Stephen Orgel and Roy Strong, *The King's Arcadia: Inigo Jones and the Stuart Court*, London, Arts Council of Great Britain, 1973.

Hicks, Leo, SJ, 'The Embassy of Sir Anthony Standen in 1603' (parts I–IV), *Recusant History*, Part I, 5 (1959–60), 91–128; Part II, 5 (1959–60), 184–222; Part III, 6 (1961–62), 163–94; Part IV, 7 (1963–64), 50–81.

Hogrefe, Pearl, *Tudor Women: Commoners and Queens*, Ames, Iowa State University Press, 1975.

Howard, Skiles, *The Politics of Courtly Dancing in Early Modern England*, Amherst, MA, University of Massachusetts Press, 1998.

Howarth, David (ed.), *Art and Patronage in the Caroline Courts: Essays in Honour of Sir Oliver Millar*, Cambridge, Cambridge University Press, 1993.

Howe, Elizabeth, *The First English Actresses: Women and Drama 1660–1700*, Cambridge, Cambridge University Press, 1992.

Jack, R. D. S. (ed.), *A Choice of Scottish Verse 1560–1660*, London, Hodder and Stoughton, 1978.

Jack, R. D. S., *The Italian Influence on Scottish Literature*, Edinburgh, Edinburgh University Press, 1972.

Jack, R. D. S., 'Poetry under King James VI', in R. D. S. Jack (ed.), *History of Scottish Literature, Volume I: Origins to 1660 (Medieval and Renaissance)*, Aberdeen, Aberdeen University Press, 1988, pp. 125–40.

Jacobsen, Grethe, 'Women's Work and Women's Role: Ideology and Reality in Danish Urban Society, 1300–1500', *Scandinavian Economic History Review*, 31 (1983), 3–20.

Jansen, F., J. Billeskov and P. M. Mitchell (eds), *Anthology of Danish Literature: Middle Ages to Romanticism*, Carbondale, IL, Southern University Press, 1972.

Jensen, Frede P., 'Peder Vinstrup's Tale ved Christian 4.s Kroning: et Teokratisk Indlaeg', *Historisk Tidsskrift*, 12 (1966–67), 375–94.

Jensen, Minna Skafte (ed.), *A History of Nordic Neo-Latin Literature*, Odense, Odense University Press, 1995.

Jexlev, Thelma, 'Scottish History in the Light of Records in the Danish National Archives', *Scottish Historical Review*, 48 (1969), 98–106.

Johnson, Anthony W., *Ben Jonson: Poetry and Architecture*, Oxford, Clarendon Press, 1994.

Johnson, Paul, *Elizabeth I: A Study in Power and Intellect*, London, Weidenfeld & Nicolson, 1974.

Jones, Pamela, 'Spectacle in Milan: Cesare Negri's Torch Dances', *Early Music*, 14 (1986), 182–96.

Jordan, Elizabeth T., 'Inigo Jones and the Architecture of Poetry', *Renaissance Quarterly*, 44 (1991), 280–319.

Joseph Benson, Pamela, *The Invention of the Renaissance Woman: The Challenge of Female Independence in the Literature and Thought of Italy and England*, University Park, PA, Pennsylvania State University Press, 1992.

Kamm, Josephine, *Hope Deferred: Girls' Education in English History*, London, Methuen, 1965.

Kantorowicz, Ernst, *The King's Two Bodies: A Study in Medieval Political Theology*, Princeton, Princeton University Press, 1957.

Kehler, Dorothea, 'Shakespeare's Emilias and the Politics of Celibacy', in Dorothea Kehler and Susan Baker (eds), *In Another Country: Feminist Perspectives on Renaissance Drama*, London, The Scarecrow Press, 1991, pp. 157–78.

King, Margaret L., *Women of the Renaissance*, Chicago, University of Chicago Press, 1991.

Kirstein, Lincoln, *Movement and Metaphor: Four Centuries of Ballet*, London, Pitman Publishing, 1971.

Knowles, James, 'The "Running Masque" Recovered: A Masque for the Marquess of Buckingham (c. 1619–20)', *English Manuscript Studies*, 9 (2000), 79–135.

Knowles, James, 'Toys and Boys: The (Homo)erotics of the Jacobean Masque', conference paper, *Disputing Manliness in Early Modern Britain*, Birkbeck College, University of London, 10 July 1997.

Kogan, Stephen, *The Hieroglyphic King: Wisdom and Idolatry in the Seventeenth-century Masque*, London and Toronto, Associated University Presses, 1986.

Krontiris, Tina, *Oppositional Voices: Women as Writers and Translators of Literature in the English Renaissance*, London, Routledge, 1992.

Labalme, Patricia H. (ed.), *Beyond Their Sex: Learned Women of the European Past*, New York, New York University Press, 1980.

Laroque, François, *Shakespeare's Festive World: Elizabethan Seasonal Entertainment and the Professional Stage*, trans. by Janet Lloyd, Cambridge, Cambridge University Press, 1991.

Lausund, Olav, 'Splendour at the Danish Court: The Coronation of Christian IV', in J. R. Mulryne and Margaret Shewring (eds), *Italian Renaissance Festivals and their European Influence*, Lampeter, Edwin Mellen Press, 1992, pp. 289–310.

Law, Ernst, *The History of Hampton Court Palace in Tudor Times*, London, George Bell & Sons, 1885.

Lazard, Madeleine, 'Le Corps Vêtu: Signification du Costume à la Renaissance', in Jean Cèard, Marie Madeleine Fontaine and Jean-Claude Margolin (eds), *Le Corps à la Renaissance* Paris, Amateurs de Livres, 1987, pp. 77–94.

Le Roy Ladurie, Emmanuel, *Carnival: A People's Uprising at Romans 1579–80*, trans. by Mary Feeny, London, Scolar Press, 1980.

Leach, Maria and Jerome Fried (eds), *Standard Dictionary of Folklore, Mythology and Legend*, New York, Funk & Wagnalls, 1950.

Lee, Maurice Jr, 'King James' Popish Chancellor', in Ian B. Cowan and Duncan Shaw (eds), *The Renaissance and Reformation in Scotland: Essays in honour of Gordon Donaldson*, Edinburgh, Scottish Academic Press, 1983, pp. 170–82.

Leslie, Michael, 'The Dialogue between Bodies and Souls: Pictures and Poesy in the English Renaissance', *Word & Image*, 1 (1985), 16–30.

Lewalski, Barbara Kiefer, 'Lucy, Countess of Bedford: Images of a Jacobean Courtier and Patroness', in Kevin Sharpe and Steven N. Zwicker (eds), *Politics of Discourse*, London, University of California Press, 1987, pp. 52–77.

Lewalski, Barbara Kiefer, *Writing Women in Jacobean England*, London and Cambridge, MA, Harvard University Press, 1993.

Limon, Jerzy, *The Masque of Stuart Culture*, London and Toronto, Associated University Presses, 1990.

Lindley, David (ed.), *The Court Masque*, Manchester, Manchester University Press, 1984.

Lindley, David, 'Embarrassing Ben: The Masques for Frances Howard', *English Literary Renaissance*, 16 (1986), 343–59.

Lindley, David, *Thomas Campion*, Leiden, E. J. Brill, 1986.

Lindley, David, *The Trials of Frances Howard: Fact and Fiction at the Court of King James*, London and New York, Routledge, 1993.

Lindley, David, 'Who Paid for Campion's *Lord Hay's Masque*?', *Notes and Queries* (1979), 144–5.

Llewellyn, Nigel, 'The Royal Body: Monuments to the Dead, for the Living', in Lucy Gent and Nigel Llewellyn (eds), *Renaissance Bodies: The Human Figure in English Culture c. 1540–1660*, London, Reaktion Books, 1990, pp. 218–40.

Lloyd, Christopher and Simon Thurley (eds), *Henry VIII: Images of a Tudor King*, Oxford, Phaidon Press, 1990.

Lockyer, Roger, *Buckingham: The Life and Political Career of George Villiers, First Duke of Buckingham 1592–1628*, London and New York, Longman, 1984.

Loewenstein, Joseph, 'Printing and "the Multitudinous Presse": The Contentious Texts of Jonson's Masques', in Jennifer Brady and W. H. Herendeen (eds), *Ben Jonson's 1616 Folio*, London and Toronto, Associated Universities Presses, 1991, pp. 168–91.

Loomie, Albert J., SJ, 'A Jacobean Crypto-Catholic: Lord Wotton', *The Catholic Historical Review*, LIII (1968), 328–45.

Loomie, Albert J., SJ, 'King James' I's Catholic Consort', *Huntington Library Quarterly*, 34 (1971), 303–16.

Lutte, Meredith, 'Recent Research in European Dance, 1400–1800', *Early Music*, 14 (1986), 4–14.

Lynch, Michael, 'Queen Mary's Triumph: The Baptismal Celebrations at Stirling in December 1556', *Scottish Historical Review*, LXIX (1990), 1–21.

Lythe, S. G. E., *The Economy of Scotland in its European Setting 1550–1625*, Westport, CT, Greenwood Press, 1969.

McClelland, John, 'Le Corps et ses Signes: Aspects de la Semiotique Géstuelle à la Renaissance', in Jean Cèard, Marie Madeleine Fontaine and Jean-Claude

Margolin (eds), *Le Corps à la Renaissance*, Paris, Amateurs de Livres, 1987, pp. 267–77.

Macfarlane, Alan, *Marriage and Love in England 1300–1840*, Oxford, Basil Blackwell, 1986.

McGee, C. E., '*Cupid's Banishment: A Masque Presented to Her Majesty by Young Gentlewomen of the Ladies Hall, Deptford, May 4, 1617*', *Renaissance Drama*, n.s. 19 (1988), 226–64.

McGowan, Margaret, *L'Art du Ballet de Cour en France, 1581–1643*, Paris, CNRS, 1963.

McGowan, Margaret, 'Le Corps Dansant: Source d'Inspiration Ésthétique', in Jean Cèard, Marie Madeleine Fontaine and Jean-Claude Margolin (eds), *Le Corps à la Renaissance*, Paris, Amateurs de Livres, 1987, pp. 229–41.

McGowan, Margaret, *Ideal Forms in the Age of Ronsard*, Berkeley, University of California Press, 1985.

McGrath, Elizabeth, 'Local Heroes: The Scottish Humanist Parnassus for Charles I', in Edward Chaney and Peter Mack (eds), *England and the Continental Renaissance: Essays in Honour of J. B. Trapp*, Woodbridge, Boydell Press, 1990, pp. 257–70.

Mackie, J. D. (ed.), *Negotiations between King James VI and I and Ferdinand I Grand Duke of Tuscany*, London, Oxford University Press, 1927.

Mackie, J. D., 'A Secret Agent of James VI', *Scottish Historical Review*, 9 (1926), 376–86.

Mackie, J. D., 'The Secret Diplomacy of King James VI in Italy prior to his Accession to the English throne', *Scottish Historical Review*, 21 (1924), 267–82.

Mclean, Ian, *The Renaissance Notion of Woman: A Study in the Fortunes of Scholasticism and Medical Science in European Intellectual Life*, Cambridge, Cambridge University Press, 1980.

Major, John M., 'The Moralization of the Dance in Elyot's *Governour*', *Studies in the Renaissance*, 5 (1958), 27–36.

Manning, R. J., 'Rule and Order Strange: A Reading of Sir John Davies' *Orchestra*', *English Literary Renaissance*, 15 (1985), 175–94.

Marcus, Leah Sinanoglou, 'Masquing Occasions and Masque Structure', *Research Opportunities in Renaissance Drama*, 24 (1981), 7–16.

Marshall, Rosalind K., *Virgins and Viragos: A History of Women in Scotland from 1080–1980*, London, Collins, 1983.

Martinet, Marie Madeleine, 'Le Corps Observé et l'Espace de l'Observateur dans l'Iconographie de la Renaissance Anglaise', in Jean Cèard, Marie Madeleine Fontaine and Jean-Claude Margolin (eds), *Le Corps à la Renaissance*, Paris, Amateurs de Livres, 1987, pp. 213–16.

Mathew, David, *Catholicism in England 1535–1935 Portrait of a Minority: Its Cultures and Tradition*, London, Catholic Book Club, 1938.

Maurer, Margaret, 'Reading Ben Jonson's *Queens*', in Sheila Fisher and Janet E. Halley (eds), *Seeking the Woman in Late Medieval and Renaissance Writings*, Knoxville, University of Tennessee Press, 1989, pp. 233–64.

Maus, Katherine Eisaman, '"Playhouse Flesh and Blood": Sexual Ideology and the Restoration Actress', *English Literary History*, 46 (1979), 595–617.

Meagher, John C., 'The Dance and the Masques of Ben Jonson', *Journal of the Warburg and Courtauld Institutes*, 25 (1962), 258–77.

Mendelson, Sara Heller, *The Mental World of Stuart Women: Three Studies*, Brighton, Harvester Press, 1987.

Middaugh, Karen Lee, 'The Golden Tree: The Court Masques of Queen Anna of Denmark', unpublished doctoral dissertation, Case Western Reserve University, 1994.

Mill, Anna Jean, 'The Records of Scots Medieval Plays: Interpretations and Misinterpretations', in Adam J. Aitken, Matthew P. McDiarmid and Derrick S. Thomson (eds), *Bards & Makars: Scottish Language and Literature: Medieval and Renaissance*, Glasgow, University of Glasgow Press, 1977, pp. 136–42.

Miller, A. H., 'The Wedding-tour of James VI in Norway', *Scottish Review*, 21 (1893), 142–61.

Mitchell, P. M., *A History of Danish Literature*, Copenhagen, Gyldendal, 1957.

Montgomerie, A., 'King James VI's Tocher Gude and a Local Authority Loan of 1590', *Scottish Historical Review*, 37 (1958), 11–16.

Montrose, Louis Adrian, '*A Midsummer Night's Dream* and the Shaping Fantasies of Elizabethan Culture: Gender, Power, Form', in Margaret W. Ferguson, Maureen Quilligan and Nancy J. Vickers (eds), *Rewriting the Renaissance: The Discourses of Sexual Difference in Early Modern Europe*, Chicago and London, University of Chicago Press, 1986, pp. 65–87.

Montrose, Louis Adrian, '"Shaping Fantasies": Figurations of Gender and Power in Elizabethan Culture', in Stephen Greenblatt (ed.), *Representing the Renaissance*, London, University of California Press, 1988, pp. 31–64.

Montrose, Louis, 'The Work of Gender in the Discourse of Discovery', in Stephen Greenblatt (ed.), *New World Encounters*, Oxford, University of California Press, 1993, pp. 177–217.

Mullaney, Steven, *The Place of the Stage: License, Play and Power in Renaissance England*, Ann Arbor, MI, Michigan University Press, 1995.

Mulryne, J. R. and Margaret Shewring (eds), *Italian Renaissance Festivals and their European Influence*, Lampeter, Edwin Mellen Press, 1992.

Mulryne, J. R. and Margaret Shewring (eds), *Theatre and Government under the Early Stuarts*, Cambridge, Cambridge University Press, 1993.

Murray, John Tucker, *English Dramatic Companies 1558–1642*, London, Constable & Co. Ltd, 1910.

Myers, A. R., 'The Book of the Disguisings for the Coming of the Ambassadors of Flanders, December 1508', *Bulletin of the Institute of Historical Research*, 54 (1981), 120–8; n.s. 19 (1988), 227–64.

Nagler, A. M., *Theatre Festivals of the Medici 1539–1637*, New Haven and London, Yale University Press, 1964.

Nevinson, J. L., 'English Domestic Embroidery Patterns of the Sixteenth and Seventeenth Centuries', *Walpole Society*, 28 (1939–40), part I.

Norbrook, David, '"The Masque of Truth": Court Entertainments and International Protestant Politics in the Early Stuart Period', *The Seventeenth Century*, 1 (1986), 81–110.

Norbrook, David, 'The Reformation of the Masque', in David Lindley (ed.), *The Court Masque*, Manchester, Manchester University Press, 1984, pp. 94–110.

Oakley, Stewart, *The Story of Denmark*, London, Faber & Faber, 1972.

Orgel, Stephen, and Roy Strong (eds), *Inigo Jones and the Theatre of the Stuart Court*, London, Sotheby Parke Bernet, 1973, 2 vols.

Orgel, Stephen, *Ben Jonson: The Complete Masques*, London and New Haven, Yale University Press, 1975.

Orgel, Stephen, *Impersonations: The Performance of Gender in Shakespeare's England*, Cambridge, Cambridge University Press, 1996.

Orgel, Stephen, 'Jonson and the Amazons', in Elizabeth Harvey and Katharine Eisaman Maus (eds), *Soliciting Interpretations: Literary Theory and Seventeenth-Century English Poetry*, Chicago, University of Chicago Press, 1990, pp. 119–39.

Orgel, Stephen, *The Jonsonian Masque*, New York, Columbia University Press, 1967.

Orgel, Stephen, 'Making Greatness Familiar', *Genre*, 15 (1982), 41–8.

Orgel, Stephen, 'Plato, the Magi, and Caroline Politics: A Reading of *The Temple of Love*', *Word & Image*, 4 (1988), 663–77.

Orgel, Stephen, 'To Please the King: A Review of Mark Franko, *Dance as Text*', *Times Literary Supplement*, 4 February, 1994, p. 24.

Orgel, Stephen, 'Review of *Four Hundred Songs and Dances from the Stuart Court Masque*, ed. by Andrew Sabol', *Criticism, a Quarterly for Literature and the Arts*, 21 (1979), 362–5.

Orrell, John, 'The Agent of Savoy at *The Somerset Masque*', *Review of English Studies*, ns 28 (1977), 301–4.

Orrell, John, *The Human Stage: English Theatre Design, 1567–1640*, Cambridge, Cambridge University Press, 1988.

Ortner, Sherry, 'Is Female to Male as Nature Is to Culture?', in Michelle Zimbalist Rosaldo and Louise Lamphère (eds), *Woman, Culture and Society*, Stanford, Stanford University Press, 1974, pp. 67–87.

Osborne, June, *Hampton Court Palace*, London, Her Majesty's Stationary Office, 1990.

Palme, Per, *The Triumph of Peace: A Study of the Whitehall Banqueting House*, London, Thames & Hudson, 1957.

Panofsky, Erwin, *Studies in Iconology: Humanistic Themes in the Art of the Renaissance*, New York, Harper Torchbooks, 1962.

Parker, Rozsika, *The Subversive Stitch: Embroidery and the Making of the Feminine*, London, The Women's Press, 1984.

Parry, Graham, *The Golden Age Restor'd: The Culture of the Stuart Court, 1603–42*, Manchester, Manchester University Press, 1981.

Parry, Graham, 'The Politics of the Jacobean Masque', in J. R. Mulryne and

Margaret Shewring (eds), *Theatre and Government under the Early Stuarts*, Cambridge, Cambridge University Press, 1993, pp. 87–117.

Paster, Gail Kern, 'The Idea of London in Masque and Pageant', in David M. Bergeron (ed.), *Pageantry in the Shakespearean Theater*, Athens, GA, University of Georgia Press, 1985, pp. 48–64.

Peacock, John, *Chronicle of Western Fashion from Ancient Times to the Present Day*, New York, Harry N. Abrams Inc., 1991.

Peacock, John, 'The French Element in Inigo Jones' Masque Designs', in David Lindley (ed.), *The Court Masque*, Manchester, Manchester University Press, 1984, pp. 149–68.

Peacock, John, 'Inigo Jones as a Figurative Artist', in Lucy Gent and Nigel Llewellyn (eds), *Renaissance Bodies: The Human Figure in English Culture c. 1540–1660*, London, Reaktion Books, 1990, pp. 154–79.

Peacock, John, 'Inigo Jones and the Florentine Court Theater', *John Donne Journal*, 5 (1986), 200–34.

Peacock, John, 'Inigo Jones' Catafalque for James I', *Architectural History*, 25 (1982), 1–5.

Peacock, John, *The Stage Designs of Inigo Jones: The European Context*, Cambridge, Cambridge University Press, 1995.

Pearl, Sara, 'Sounding to Present Occasions: Jonson's Masques of 1620–5', in David Lindley (ed.), *The Court Masque*, Manchester, Manchester University Press, 1984, pp. 60–77.

Pearson, Jacqueline 'Women Writer and Women Readers: The Case of Aemilia Lanier', in Kate Chedgzoy, Melanie Hansen and Suzanne Trill (eds), *Voicing Women: Gender and Sexuality in Early Modern Writing*, Keele, Keele University Press, 1996, pp. 45–54.

Pevsner, Nikolaus and Priscilla Metcalf, *The Cathedrals of England: Southern England*, Harmondsworth, Penguin, 1985.

Polhemus, Ted, 'Dance, Gender and Culture', in Helen Thomas (ed.), *Dance, Gender and Culture*, London, Macmillan, 1993, pp. 3–15.

Purkiss, Diane, 'Producing the Voice, Consuming the Body: Women Prophets of the Seventeenth Century', in Isobel Grundy and Susan Wiseman (eds), *Women, Writing, History, 1640–1740*, London, B. T. Batsford, 1992, pp. 139–58.

Purkiss, Diane, *The Witch in History: Early Modern and Twentieth-century Representations*, London and New York, Routledge, 1996.

Putnam, Clare, *Flowers and Trees of Tudor England*, London, Hugh Evelyn, 1972.

Ravelhofer, Barbara, '"Virgin Wax" and "Hairy Men-Monsters": Unstable Movement Codes in the Stuart Masque', in David Bevington and Peter Holbrook (eds), *The Politics of the Stuart Court Masque*, Cambridge, Cambridge University Press, 1998, pp. 244–72.

Read Baskerville, Charles, 'Dramatic Aspects of Medieval Folk Festivals in England', *Studies in Philology*, 17 (1920), 19–87.

Reyher, Paul, *Les Masques Anglais: Étude sur les Ballets et la Vie de Cour en Angleterre (1512–1640)*, Paris, Libraririe Hachette, 1909.

Ribero, Aileen, *Dress and Morality*, London, B. T. Batsford, 1986.

Richards, Sandra, *The Rise of the English Actress*, Basingstoke, Macmillan, 1993.

Richer, Jean, 'Le Corps Microcosme comme Systeme de Marquage Zodiacal', in M. T. Jones-Davies (ed.), *Shakespeare et le Corps à la Renaissance*, Paris: Les Belles Lettres, 1991, pp. 9–16.

Riggs, David, *Ben Jonson: A Life*, Cambridge, MA and London, Harvard University Press, 1989.

Riis, Thomas, *Should Auld Acquaintance Be Forgot . . .: Scottish–Danish Relations c. 1450–1707*, Odense, Odense University Press, 1988, 2 vols.

Roberts, Alisdair F. B., 'The Role of Women in Scottish Catholic Survival', *Scottish Historical Review*, LXX (1991), 129–50.

Rose, Mary Beth, *The Expense of Spirit: Love and Sexuality in English Renaissance Drama*, Ithaca and London, Cornell University Press, 1988.

Rose, Tessa, *The Coronation Ceremony of the Kings and Queens of England and the Crown Jewels*, London, Her Majesty's Stationery Office, 1992.

Rowland, Beryl (ed. and trans.), *Medieval Woman's Guide to Health: The First Gynecological Handbook*, London, Croom Helm, 1981.

Russo, Mary, 'Female Grotesques: Carnival and Theory', in Teresa de Lauretis (ed.), *Feminist Studies / Critical Studies*, Basingstoke, Macmillan, 1988, pp. 213–29.

Russo, Mary, *The Female Grotesque: Risk, Excess and Modernity*, New York and London, Routledge, 1995.

Sachs, Curt, *World History of the Dance*, trans. by Bessie Schonberg, New York, Norton, 1937.

Salomon, Nanette, 'Positioning Women in Visual Convention: The Case of Elizabeth I', in Betty S. Travitsky and Adele F. Seoff (eds), *Attending to Women in Early Modern England*, Newark, University of Delaware Press, 1994, pp. 64–95.

Sanders, Julie, '"The Day's Sports Devised in the Inn": Jonson's *The New Inn* and Theatrical Politics', *The Modern Language Review*, 91 (1996), 545–60.

Sanders, Julie, '"Twill Fit the Players Yet": Women and Theatre in Jonson's Late Plays', in Richard Cave, Elizabeth Schafer and Brian Woolland (eds), *Ben Jonson and Theatre: Performance, Practice and Theory*, London and New York, Routledge, 1999, pp. 179–90.

Sanderson, James L., *Sir John Davies*, Boston, Twayne Publishers, 1975.

Saslow, James, *Florentine Festivals as* Theatrum Mundi: *The Medici Wedding of 1589*, London and New Haven, Yale University Press, 1996.

Saunders, Alison, '"La Beauté que Femme Doibt Avoir": La Vision du Corps dans les Blasons Anatomiques', in Jean Cèard, Marie Madeleine Fontaine and Jean-Claude Margolin (eds), *Le Corps à la Renaissance*, Paris, Amateurs de Livres, 1987, pp. 39–59.

Sawday, Jonathan, *The Body Emblazoned: Dissection and the Human Body in Renaissance Culture*, London and New York, Routledge, 1995.

Schwarz, Kathryn, 'Amazon Reflections in the Jacobean Queen's Masque', *Studies in English Literature 1500–1900*, 35 (1995), 293–319.

Scotland, James, *The History of Scottish Education: Volume One – From the Beginning to 1872*, London, University of London Press, 1969.

Shapiro, Michael, *The Children of the Revels: The Boy Companies of Shakespeare's Time and Their Plays*, New York, Columbia University Press, 1977.

Sharpe, Kevin, *Criticism and Compliment: The Politics of Literature in the England of Charles I*, Cambridge, Cambridge University Press, 1987.

Shell, Alison, *Catholicism, Controversy and the English Literary Imagination, 1558–1660*, Cambridge, Cambridge University Press, 1999.

Shire, Helena Mennie, *Song, Dance and Poetry of the Court of Scotland under James VI*, Cambridge, Cambridge University Press, 1969.

Shorter, Edward, *The Making of the Modern Family*, London, Collins, 1976.

Siddiqi, Yumna, 'Dark Incontinents: The Discourses of Race and Gender in Three Renaissance Masques', *Renaissance Drama*, 23 (1992), 139–63.

Smith, Bruce R., 'Sermons in Stones: Shakespeare and Renaissance Sculpture', *Shakespeare Studies*, 17 (1985), 1–23.

Smith, Judy and Ian Gatiss, 'What Did Prince Henry Do with his Feet on Sunday 19 August 1604?', *Early Music*, 14 (1986), 198–207.

Smuts, R. Malcolm, *Court Culture and the Origins of a Royalist Tradition in Early Stuart England*, Philadelphia, University of Pennsylvania Press, 1987.

Spencer, T. J. B. and Stanley Wells (eds), *A Book of Masques in Honour of Allardyce Nicoll*, Cambridge, Cambridge University Press, 1967.

Stafford, Helen G., *James VI of Scotland and the Throne of England*, New York, D. Appleton-Century, 1940.

Stallybrass, Peter, 'Patriarchal Territories: The Body Enclosed', in Margaret W. Ferguson, Maureen Quilligan and Nancy J. Vickers (eds), *Rewriting the Renaissance: The Discourses of Sexual Difference in Early Modern Europe*, Chicago and London, University of Chicago Press, 1986, pp. 123–42.

Stallybrass, Peter, '"Wee Feaste in our Defense": Patrician Carnival in Early Modern England and Robert Herrick's *Hesperides*', *English Literary Renaissance*, 16 (1986), 234–52.

Staniland, Kay, *Embroiderers: Medieval Craftsmen*, London, British Museum Press, 1991.

Starkey, David (ed.), *Henry VIII: A European Court in England*, London, Collins & Brown in association with the National Maritime Museum, Greenwich, 1991.

Steen, Sara Jayne, 'Fashioning an Acceptable Self: Arbella Stuart', *English Literary Renaissance*, 18 (1988), 78–95.

Stock, Phyllis, *Better than Rubies: A History of Women's Education*, New York, Capricorn Books, 1978.

Stone, Lawrence, *The Family, Sex and Marriage in England 1500–1800*, Harmondsworth, Penguin, 1988.

Strickland, Agnes, *Lives of the Queens of England*, London, Henry Colburn, 1844.

Strong, Roy, *Art and Power: Renaissance Festivals 1450–1650*, London, Boydell Press, 1984.

Strong, Roy, *The Cult of Elizabeth: Elizabethan Portraiture and Pageantry*, London, Thames & Hudson, 1977.

Strong, Roy, 'Festivals for the Garter Embassy at the Court of Henri III', *Journal of the Warburg and Courtauld Institutes*, 22 (1959), 60–70.

Strong, Roy, *Henry, Prince of Wales and England's Lost Renaissance*, London, Thames & Hudson, 1986.

Strong, Roy, *Splendour at Court: Renaissance Spectacle and Illusion*, London, Weidenfeld and Nicolson, 1973.

Suleiman, Susan Rubin (ed.), *The Female Body in Western Culture: Contemporary Perspectives*, Cambridge MA and London, Harvard University Press, 1986.

Summerson, John, *Inigo Jones*, Harmondsworth, Penguin, 1966.

Swain, Margaret H., *Historical Needlework: A Study of Influences in Scotland and Northern England*, London, Barrie and Jenkins, 1970.

Teague, Frances, 'The Identity of Bathsua Makin', *Biography*, 16 (1993), 1–17.

Thesiger, Sarah, 'The *Orchestra* of Sir John Davies and the Image of the Dance', *Journal of the Warburg and Courtauld Institutes*, 36 (1973), 277–304.

Thomas, Helen (ed.), *Dance, Gender and Culture*, London, Macmillan, 1993.

Thomson, David, *Renaissance Architecture: Critics, Patrons, Luxury*, Manchester and New York, Manchester University Press, 1993.

Thoren, Victor E. (with contributions by John R. Christianson), *The Lord of Uraniborg: A Biography of Tycho Brahe*, Cambridge, Cambridge University Press, 1990.

Thurley, Simon, 'The Banqueting and Disguising Houses of 1527', in David Starkey (ed.), *Henry VIII: A European Court in England*, London, Collins & Brown, 1991, pp. 64–9.

Thurley, Simon, *The Royal Palaces of Tudor England: Architecture and Court Life 1460–1547*, New Haven and London, Yale University Press for the Paul Mellon Centre for Studies in British Art, 1993.

Tomlinson, Sophie, '"My Brain the Stage": Margaret Cavendish and the Fantasy of Female Performance', in Clare Brant and Diane Purkiss (eds), *Women, Texts and Histories 1575–1760*, London and New York, Routledge, 1992, pp. 134–63.

Tomlinson, Sophie, 'She that Plays the King: Henrietta Maria and the Threat of the Actress in Caroline Culture', in Gordon McMullan and Jonathan Hope (eds), *The Politics of Tragicomedy: Shakespeare and After*, London and New York, Routledge, 1992, pp. 189–207.

Travitsky, Betty and Adele F. Seoff (eds), *Attending to Women in Early Modern England*, Newark, University of Delaware Press, 1994.

Usher Henderson, Katherine, and Barbara F. McManus (eds), *Half Humankind: Contexts and Texts of the Controversy about Women in England, 1540–1640*, Chicago, University of Illinois Press, 1985.

Veevers, Erica, *Images of Love and Religion: Queen Henrietta Maria and Court Entertainments*, Cambridge, Cambridge University Press, 1989.

Venet, Gisele, 'Le Corps, la Musique et les Mots à la Fin de la Renaissance', in Jean Cèard, Marie Madeleine Fontaine and Jean-Claude Margolin (eds), *Le Corps à la Renaissance*, Paris, Amateurs de Livres, 1987, pp. 217–28.

Wade, Mara R., 'Festival Books as Literature: The Reign of Christian IV of Denmark (1596–1648)', *The Seventeenth Century*, 7 (1992), 1–14.

Wade, Mara R., 'Heinrich Schütz and "det Store Bilager" in Copenhagen (1634)', *Schütz-Jahrbuch: Im Auftrage der Internationalen Heinrich-Schütz-Gesellschaft*, 11 (1989), 32–52.

Wade, Mara R., *Triumphus Nuptialis Danicus: German Court Culture and Denmark, the 'Great Wedding' of 1634*, Wiesbaden, Harrassowitz Verlag, 1996.

Ward, Adolphus, 'James VI and the Papacy', *Scottish Historical Review*, 2 (1905), 249–52.

Ward, Adolphus, 'Review of *Was Frederick II's Daughter, Anne, Queen of Great Britain, a Convert to Catholicism?*, by W. Plenkers, Copenhagen, 1888', *English Historical Review*, 3 (1888), 795–8.

Ward, John M., 'The English Measure', *Early Music*, 14 (1986), 15–20.

Ward, John M., 'The Maner of Dauncing', *Early Music*, 4 (1976), 127–42.

Warner, George F., 'James VI and Rome', *English Historical Review*, 20 (1905), 124–7.

Warner, Marina, *Monuments and Maidens: The Allegory of the Female Form*, London, Weidenfeld and Nicolson, 1985.

Watanabe-O'Kelly, Helen, 'Festival Books in Europe from Renaissance to Rococo', *The Seventeenth Century*, 3 (1988), 181–201.

Weaver, Elissa, 'Spiritual Fun: A Study of Sixteenth-century Tuscan Convent Theater', in Mary Beth Rose (ed.), *Women in the Middle Ages and the Renaissance: Literary and Historical Perspectives*, Syracuse, Syracuse University Press, 1986, pp. 173–205.

Welsford, Enid, *The Court Masque: A Study in the Relationship between Poetry and the Revels*, Cambridge, Cambridge University Press, 1927.

Wiesner, Merry E., 'Spinster and Seamstresses: Women in Cloth and Clothing Production', in Margaret W. Ferguson, Maureen Quilligan and Nancy J. Vickers (eds), *Rewriting the Renaissance: The Discourses of Sexual Difference in Early Modern Europe*, Chicago, University of Chicago Press, 1986, pp. 191–205.

Wigley, Mark, 'Untitled: The Housing of Gender', in *Sexuality & Space*, Princeton, Princeton Architectural Press, Princeton Papers on Architecture, 1992, pp. 327–89.

Wilkinson, B., *The Coronation in History*, London, The Historical Association, 1953.

Williams, Ethel Carleton, *Anne of Denmark: Wife of James VI of Scotland: James I of England*, London, Longman, 1970.

Williamson, Hugh Ross, *George Villiers First Duke of Buckingham: Study for a Biography*, London, Duckworth, 1940.

Willson, David Harris, *King James VI and I*, London, Jonathan Cape, 1956.

Wilson, Adrian, 'The Ceremony of Childbirth and its Interpretation', in Valerie Fildes (ed.), *Women as Mothers in Pre-industrial England*, London and New York, Routledge, 1990, pp. 68–107.

Wilson, Jean, *Entertainments for Elizabeth I*, Woodbridge, D. S. Brewer, 1980.

Wiseman, Susan, *Drama and Politics in the Civil War*, Cambridge, Cambridge University Press, 1998.

Wiseman, Susan, 'Gender and Status in Dramatic Discourse: Margaret Cavendish, Duchess of Newcastle', in Isobel Grundy and Susan Wiseman (eds), *Women, Writing, History 1640–1740*, London, B. T. Batsford, 1992, pp. 159–77.

Wittkower, Rudolf, *Architectural Principles in the Age of Humanism*, London, Academy Editions, 1973.

Woodward, Jennifer, *The Theatre of Death: The Ritual Management of Royal Funerals in Renaissance England 1570–1625*, Woodbridge, The Boydell Press, 1997.

Wormald, Jenny, *Mary Queen of Scots: A Study in Failure*, London, George Philips, 1988.

Wynne-Davies, Marion, 'The Queen's Masque: Renaissance Women and the Seventeenth-Century Court Masque', in S. P. Cerasano and Marion Wynne-Davies (eds), *Gloriana's Face: Women, Public and Private, in the English Renaissance*, New York and London, Harvester Wheatsheaf, 1992, pp. 79–104.

Yates, Frances A., *Astraea: The Imperial Theme in the Sixteenth Century*, London and Boston, Routledge & Kegan Paul, 1975.

Yates, Frances A., *French Academies of the Sixteenth Century*, London and New York, Routledge, 1988.

Yates, Frances A., *Shakespeare's Last Plays: A New Approach*, London, Routledge and Kegan Paul, 1975.

Zeeburg, Peter, 'The Inscriptions at Tycho Brahe's Uraniborg', in Minna Skafte Jensen (ed.), *A History of Nordic Neo-Latin Literature*, Odense, Odense University Press, 1995, pp. 251–66.

Index

Note: literary works can be found under authors' names.